D0909401

GASTONIA
1929

THE STORY OF THE

GASTONIA
1929

LORAY MILL STRIKE

JOHN A. SALMOND

The University of North Carolina Press *Chapel Hill & London*

© 1995
The University of
North Carolina Press
Frontispiece:
Ella May Wiggins,
September 1929
(Courtesy Australian Picture
Library/Bettman)
Manufactured in the
United States of America

The paper in this book meets the
guidelines for permanence and durability
of the Committee on Production Guidelines
for Book Longevity of the Council on
Library Resources.

Library of Congress
Cataloging-in-Publication Data
Salmond, John A.
Gastonia 1929 : the story of the Loray Mill
strike / by John A. Salmond.
p.   cm.
Includes bibliographical references and
index.
ISBN 0-8078-2237-X (cloth : alk. paper)
1. Textile Workers' Strike, Gastonia, N.C.,
1929.   I. Title.
HD5325.T42   1929.G377   1995
331.89'2877'009756773—dc20   95-8517
                                        CIP

99 98 97 96 95   5 4 3 2 1

To Robert John Ralph Henningham

CONTENTS

ILLUSTRATIONS

PREFACE

f one thinks of the southern Piedmont as a rough arc stretching from Danville, Virginia, to Birmingham, Alabama, then Gastonia, North Carolina, is located at its center. Gaston County, of which Gastonia is the county seat, had by 1929 come to contain more textile plants than any other county in the world, and some Gastonians proudly claimed that there were more looms and spindles within its hundred-mile radius than in that of any other southern city. Few doubted the boast, for since 1880 both the county and the city had undergone a profound industrial and economic transformation. Originally dotted with small and not particularly profitable farms, Gaston County had both the natural and the human resources, in its abundance of water and its large potential labor force, to make the transition to a textile center with extraordinary rapidity. Working the land had always been hard there, and thousands of unsuccessful farmers were only too ready to furnish the manpower for the mills. Though in 1929 there were still some forests to be found in Gaston County's gently rolling landscape, and its most fertile land was still being farmed, the dominant features of its flattish topography were "cotton mills and industrial villages."[1]

In 1929, Gastonia had a population of 17,000. The 1920s had been a time of substantial construction in the city, resulting in a downtown area of solid business enterprises, including both stores and office blocks, as well as an impressive array of public buildings, all brand spanking new. The radical journalist Mary Heaton Vorse commented after her first visit that the town gave the impression of "having sprung from the earth fully equipped." Gastonia had "a new city hall, a new courthouse, a new county jail," and "a splendid new high school," each of them fine, solid structures. This decade had seen a boom in residential construction as well, mainly due to the conspicuous consumption of the town's elite. The mill owners and managers increasingly moved away from their mills and built themselves huge, beautiful, lavishly furnished homes in the city's uptown area. These houses were removed both physically and conceptually from the mill villages where the bulk of Gastonians lived, and the town's leading professional people—the lawyers, the doctors, the real estate agents, and the clergy—generally followed the mill owners' example. Gastonia, then, was a town clearly divided by class, as aerial photographs of the time show. In the uptown area of these photographs one sees the large, elegant houses with their commodious gardens, divided by the business center and the railroad tracks from the drab, identical mill villages. Dominating the mill-district landscape is the huge, ugly Loray Mill, the largest in the whole South, located in West Gastonia. The mile of road separating town and suburb amply illustrated the community's class division. This road began at the large houses with their pleasant gardens and ended at the gates of the huge brick mill. Behind the mill lay its village, "a flock of little houses all alike, perched each one on brick stilts." Night and day, wrote Vorse, "men women and children from the little houses go into the mill. It is their whole life."[2]

Gaston County's smaller centers—Bessemer City, Belmont, and Mount Holly—presented much the same aspect. They were all divided communities: the owners and those whom they did business with lived on one side of the tracks, the mill workers on the other, and they met increasingly rarely. They would meet in 1929 as a wave of violent strikes swept through the Piedmont's textile communities. This book is the story of the most famous of these.[3]

The violence that accompanied the strike at the Loray Mill; the fatal shooting of Gastonia's police chief, Orville Aderholt, and the strike's balladeer, Ella May Wiggins; the international outcry at May's death and at how the state failed to punish her killers yet imposed savage sentences on those strikers accused of the police chief's murder; and the determination of the militant Communist Party of the United States to use these events to further world revolution have together given them a particular resonance that has resolutely refused to fade away over the years. Even today, the town of Gastonia is deeply divided over what to do with the now-abandoned Loray Mill. For some it is a symbol of a violent past best forgotten; for others it is the site of the most significant event in the town's history and should therefore be preserved.

The purpose of this book is simply to tell the story of the events of 1929. I have no overarching thesis to present, though some perspectives will, I hope, arise from the narrative that follows. If anything, I think this work reinforces those historians who still insist on the power of class as an explanatory factor in the historical process, but in the hope that a well-told story has a justification of its own, I have tried to minimize my intrusions into the tale.

The study had its genesis in the Empress of China restaurant, in Melbourne's Chinatown. After a splendid meal, Professor Robert Allen of the University of North Carolina, Dr. Lucy Frost of La Trobe University, and I began to talk about the South. Bobby and Lucy are both southerners and grew up in smallish cities—Lucy in Maryville, Tennessee, and Bobby across the mountains in Gastonia. As they talked about shared experiences, and particularly as Bobby recalled his growing childhood awareness that he lived in a town in which something terrible had occurred, something never to be talked about openly, we all decided that one of us had to try and unravel the Gastonia story. I got elected to the job. I remember that night with great warmth, and I thank them both for their continuing encouragement as I went about my allotted task. Bobby turned over his own Gastonia files to me, including several taped interviews with strike participants that he had made when he was a student at Davidson College, while Lucy carefully read the completed manuscript, making several important suggestions toward its improvement.

My friends Bill and Christina Baker, of the University of Maine, also encouraged me to begin this work, and they have been greatly supportive throughout its gestation. Tina too grew up in Gastonia and has talked to me often about the way her increasingly frequent inquiries about the town's "secret" were always gently but firmly discouraged. Both of the Bakers had also interviewed strike participants, and they generously made their tapes available to me. It was through them, too, that I met Si and Sophie Gerson—survivors of that tumultuous year, 1929—whose vivid recollections have formed such an important source for this book. My thanks to all these people is profound. Such generosity with time, memory, and resources has turned the business of research into pleasure.

Thanks are also due to the myriad archivists and libraries at Wayne State University, La Trobe University, the Chicago Historical Society, the Perkins Library at Duke University, and especially the Southern Historical and North Carolina Collections at the University of North Carolina at Chapel Hill, for their labors in locating material for me and their patience in answering my many queries. Moreover, the research could not have been done at all without the considerable financial support of the Australian Research Council and the research fund of the La Trobe University School of Humanities. La Trobe's Outside Studies Program Committee generously approved an extended period of leave, during which much of the research and the bulk of the writing was completed.

My friends and fellow scholars Jan Jackson, Bruce Clayton, Bill Breen, Jack Cell, Alan Frost, and Tim Minchin all read the manuscript at various stages during its completion, and the book benefited greatly as a result. During 1993, Alan Johnston, of Deakin University, and Richard L. Watson Jr., my mentor at Duke University, were constant sources of encouragement and advice, as Anthony Wood, of Monash University, has been throughout. Laraine Dumsday unflinchingly went about the task of translating my scribblings into readable sentences, and did so with rare skill, high good humor, and sound comment. At the University of North Carolina Press, Lewis Bateman has been a source of encouragement from the beginning of the project, and Christi Stanforth's skilled editing has greatly improved the manuscript. My colleagues in La Trobe University's history department were, as always, unfailing in their support and keen in their constructive criticism. Few scholars have such a felicitous atmosphere in which to work. My thanks to them all, and to those many friends whose continuing support one can only accept with bemused gratitude.

My greatest debt, as always, is to my family, to my children and grandchildren. Much of the research and writing for this book, to my great good fortune, has been done with my grandchildren close at hand. Bill, Hilary, Jim, and Tom Washington, of Burlington, North Carolina, and Lucy and Robert Henningham, of Melbourne and Cairns, have all shared joyously and irreverently in its making, and in doing so they have taught me much about priorities. The five others will readily understand why the work is dedicated to my youngest grandson, Robert John Ralph Henningham, who is so special to us all.

1 THE SETTING

Ella Ford was raised by her grandparents in the mountains of western North Carolina, and she married while still in her teens. She and her husband tried to farm in the hills, but it was "hard living." They simply could not make do, and that, she said, was "why we went down to the cotton mill one winter." Many mountain people did that at first, working in the mills during the winter and then going back to their farms for the growing season. But as times got harder, fewer and fewer returned to the farms. They had "got into the habit" of being mill workers and town dwellers, according to Ella.[1]

She got work at the Loray Mill in Gastonia, by far the largest mill in Gaston County. There she did various jobs, sometimes making as much as twelve dollars a week. The work was hard, however, and the conditions were increasingly unhealthy. Moreover, things were always changing at the mill. Some people had "to work faster and faster" to make the same money, while others found their jobs reclassified as piecework, which resulted in a serious drop in income. The stretch-out system had come to Loray, and it "wasn't long before two beam boys were doing the work of seven." Machinery replaced workers in many departments, and soon "one man was doing the work of three under the old system. They cut all thru the mill."[2]

The workers resisted the changes as best they could. In 1928 the manager who had introduced the most severe of them was driven from the town amid great public celebration. "But other managers came," Ford said, the stretch-out gathered pace, and the workers remained bewildered and angry. Despite the shortage of jobs, they would often "get talking about a strike." In 1929, the strike came.[3]

There were hundreds of thousands of people like Ella Ford in the southern Piedmont, people who made the always difficult and often painful transition from farm to factory. As historians Jacquelyn Hall,

Robert Korstad, and James Leloudis stated with great definition, "textile mills built the new South," changing the lives of all that they touched. "Beginning in the 1880s," they wrote, "business and professional men tied their hopes for prosperity to the whirring of spindles and the beating of looms." The post–Civil War destruction of the region's independent farmers was the key to this growth. Merchants made money out of the tenant and share-cropping systems that replaced one-owner farms, and with this capital they built mills—hundreds of them. The dispossessed white farmers provided the labor, and soon the southern textile industry was "underselling northern competitors" so successfully that "by the end of the Great Depression, the Southeast replaced New England as the world's leading producer of cotton cloth, and the industrializing Piedmont replaced the rural Coastal Plain as pacesetter for the region."[4]

The twin keys to the spectacular rise of the southern textile industry were cheap labor and the availability of local investment capital. As Gavin Wright has written, "The spread in tenancy and the decline in farm size increased the number of farm families for whom factory work seemed an acceptable alternative. From the 1870s to the end of the century, employment grew at nearly 10 percent per year with no detectable upward pressure on wages." By the turn of the century, southern mill owners were able to pay their workers at rates between 30 and 50 percent below those of their New England counterparts, a decisive competitive advantage. By this time the mill boom had enveloped the region, and every little town wanted its own mill. Textile mills became a matter of such civic pride that the bulk of the capital to finance their building was raised locally: stock was sold in small amounts to small investors to whom local boards of directors were responsible. Wright was one of a long line of commentators on the industry's growth to draw attention to the disadvantages of this mode of development. With their local perspectives and limited experience, these first mill men, as Broadus Mitchell long ago pointed out, were like "a set of blundering children, some a little more apt than others." Yet without this local involvement, this intense civic boosterism, it is doubtful whether the industry could have taken root as completely as it did.[5]

Of course, the workers had much to learn, too: they had to make the conversion from an agricultural to an industrial way of life. Here the key institution was the mill village—management's answer, in industry historian James Hodges's words, to "the practical problem of assembling a workforce in small towns and rural places." As Hall and her colleagues have observed, "nothing better symbolized the new industrial order than the mill villages that dotted the Piedmont landscape." The industrial development of the Piedmont could not have occurred without them. Reflecting "rural expectations as well as practical considerations," these "mill hills" certainly made it easier for management to control their workforce. Because of their unincorporated nature, no taxes needed to be paid on them, and those who lived there played no part in local politics. Yet the villages also "reflected the workers' heritage and served their needs." By the 1930s this village system was in decline, and when most commentators looked on them, they saw misery, oppression, and squalor. These things certainly always existed in mill villages; yet to those who worked and lived there, the village also became home—a neighborhood where friendships were formed and developed and a distinctive and sustaining culture evolved. By 1905, "'one long mill village' ran along the arc of the southern Piedmont."[6]

The family labor system, too, "helped smooth the path from field to factory." Women and children had always been essential to farmwork, and the mill owners understood this fact and adapted it to their own needs. "They promoted factory work as a refuge for impoverished women and children from the countryside, hired family units rather than individuals, and required the labor of at least one worker per room as a condition for residence in a mill-owned house." Yet at the same time, these strategies fit in with the needs of working families, who wanted a place where the members could all work together as they had done on the farm. Moreover, as Hall and her colleagues have pointed out, this ability to move as a family from farm to factory and, indeed, to combine the two, like the people in Ella Ford's story did, gave these first factory workers a sense of freedom, of an "alternative identity" that enabled them to resist, to a degree, the demands of management. Their children, however—again like those in Ford's narrative—"eventually came to the mills to stay."[7]

The mill village was obviously a creation of managerial self-interest, yet it also provided the space within which the distinctive mill workers' culture could develop and "familiar ways of thinking and acting" could be gradually transformed into a "new way of life." Both contemporary observers and later analysts of village society have been far too inclined to describe it as essentially thin, lacking sustenance, and breeding an apathetic, irrational social type that could be easily controlled by mill interests. Now we know better. Hall and her team have described a vital, evolving, cooperative culture, one of considerable variety and strength, and much more than the sum of management's designs. The mill-village culture represented "a compromise between capitalist organization and worker's needs."[8]

Not all of the recent writing on mill-village culture provides such a positive view of its main characteristics or of those who made it. I. A. Newby, David Carlton, and Douglas Flamming, for example, have each stressed the virulent racism of the villagers—something Hall and her colleagues have tended to ignore. In his superb *Plain Folk in the New South*, Newby describes a singularly unattractive world but at the same time remains deeply sympathetic to those who lived in it. Life was often nasty, brutish, and short there; Newby is particularly convincing in his contention that the often shocking living conditions in the villages caused health problems that had immense economic and social consequences, problems whose legacy persists to this day. Moreover, the sustaining qualities of egalitarianism and individualism in the rural culture that mill villagers had left behind were not those best suited to enable them to confront their employers in a disciplined, cohesive way as they sought some means of improving the condition of their lives. Flamming, too, talks of the "darker implications" of mill-village life, in particular of its coercive aspects, especially in the area of accepted behavior. Moreover, social isolation too often led to violence—to workers' venting their hostility not on their employers or on hapless African Americans but rather on their fellow workers. Nevertheless, he argues, though such disputes were both frequent and disruptive, they did not necessarily mean that community feeling did not exist or even that the notion of "family" is hopelessly romantic. Rather, they simply signify that, as in most communities, life in mill villages was at times riven by tension between individuals, families, or competing social groups. Essentially, Carlton, Newby, and Flamming all share the view of Hall and her team that what developed in these mill hills was much more than the sum of the owners' wishes. Rather, the villagers created their own world, their own common culture. "Neither docile nor foolhardy," writes Robert Zieger, "millworkers relied primarily on themselves, regarding the plans of union organizers and the programs of government bureaucrats skeptically, forever weighing these instruments of change against the likelihood of deterioration in their circumstances." To this wariness may be added a similar skepticism toward the blandishments of their employers.[9]

What about the workplace itself? Here the owner obviously had more control. Work in the mill, with its repetitive tasks, closely supervised and governed by rigid notions of time, bore little resemblance to the slower rhythms of agricultural life. It was dirty, and the workday was long (though perhaps not particularly long for farm folk, who were used to working from sunup to sundown), but the pay was better. Furthermore, in the first decades of the industry's growth, the potential harshness was moderated somewhat by fairly relaxed work patterns. There was often time to talk, to eat lunch in a leisurely fashion, even to slip home to check on the younger children—an important consideration, given that women represented a large percentage of the labor force (49.9 percent in 1890, 45 percent as late as 1900). Sometimes, if the occasion warranted it, workers simply walked off the job. Elections were usually celebrated in this manner, as was the advent of a singular attraction, such as a circus. Often these practices resulted from the fact that the workers had direct access to the owner; there was an element of personal involvement which, while doubtless paternalistic, at least afforded workers some chance of directly influencing the conditions under which they labored, either to protest the decisions of a supervisor considered harsh or unjust or even, at times, to influence policy directly. Management, anxious to keep production levels up, would often accede to such limited demands. Moreover, when demand for labor was high, workers always had the opportunity to move elsewhere. Owners and managers came to know the limits of their authority. Nowhere is this more obvious than in the decision, even in times of labor shortage, to restrict black labor in the mills to janitorial tasks. The extreme racism of the white workers would not have permitted otherwise. It may have made good economic sense, as Flamming points out, to have hired African Americans for more advanced work, and many textile leaders were anxious to do so. Those who tried, however, "quickly learned that such efforts were counterproductive." Violence, walkouts, and political action was the inevitable result, as workers successfully fought to keep blacks out of the mills.[10]

The balance between the positive and negative aspects of mill work —a relatively relaxed work pace versus long hours and low wages— was not a stable situation, however. Even in the early years of development, there was unrest from time to time, as some workers turned to either the Knights of Labor or the National Union of Textile Workers to defend their interests. A succession of strikes around the turn of the century, culminating in the Haw River strike in Alamance County, North Carolina, suggests that the secure world desired by the manufacturers was always ripe for the shattering. Yet unionism was scarcely a significant factor in the textile industry prior to World War I. When workers attempted to control their labor conditions, they were much more inclined to do so on their own. Shortage of labor and, hence, the ability to move on gave them a bargaining power that was independent of any organization and much more attuned to the individualism of their cultural roots. When workers protested their conditions of labor, then, it was much more likely to be through spontaneous, often personal action than through concerted, union-directed protest.[11]

In response to such manifestations of unrest, owners answered not by repression or union-bashing, except in quite isolated instances, but by making it more difficult to move. In part, this move forced wage rates upward. Between 1902 and 1907, for example, "the earnings of male weavers in South Carolina rose by 58 percent, those of female weavers by 65 percent, and those of spinners by 138 percent," while the cost of living rose by only 9 percent. There were other means of increased competition for labor as well: inducements of all kinds were offered to entice workers from one mill to another. Finally, manufacturers made real efforts to improve the quality of life in their villages; they built better houses with modern plumbing, beautified the surroundings, and provided a range of social and recreational services for their employees, from holiday camps to company-sponsored "welfare work," all in an attempt to bind their workers to them and thereby bring stability to the industry. To a limited degree, in the decade before World War I, these measures worked. As Wright pointed out, "the mill-village, family labor system"—the expenditure on welfare work in order to promote stability—"did have a certain internal logic," as long as times stayed good.[12]

Times were certainly very good during the First World War. The wartime demand for cotton cloth sparked another boom, so there was

another round of mill construction, while existing mills started to oper-
ate around the clock, further stimulating the demand for labor in a
tight wartime situation. The inevitable result was that wages throughout the Piedmont rose to new heights, often tripling in the years between 1915 and 1920. Any relationship between farm and textile wages
was now well and truly shattered, prompting further movement to
the mills.[13]

The boom continued till 1920, when it broke with dramatic sudden-
ness. Wartime overexpansion was compounded by several other factors. Lucrative foreign markets were lost due to the Harding administration's tariff policies and the development of the industry in other
parts of the world, such as India. Changes in women's fashions added
to the trouble. "Young women in the 1920s hiked their skirts six inches
above the ankle, then all the way to the knee, causing consternation
among their elders and panic in the textile industry." The Great Depression, which for the rest of the country did not begin until much
later in the decade, for textiles started with the armistice and did not
let up.[14]

The response of the managers was to cut costs, which translated
into an attack on the wage gains of the past few years. Somewhat to the
managers' surprise, the mill hands fought back, for heightened wages
had brought heightened expectations; moreover, the war boom had
altered the composition of the mills' labor force. Family labor was on
the decline; more and more of the operatives were adult workers supporting themselves, men and women living independently of families;
and an increasing percentage were male—a trend that accelerated as
the troops returned from overseas. These workers comprised the first
generation to see the mills as providing a permanent vocation and no
longer as simply supplementing farm income, thus the wage cuts im-
pinged directly on their sense of self-worth.[15]

From 1919 to 1921, industrial strife rocked the Piedmont as workers
flocked to join the AFL's United Textile Workers (UTW), which before the war had had no presence in the South at all. Locals grew so
rapidly that as workers fought to preserve their incomes, the central
office could not keep up with the process. Manufacturers were equally
determined not to give an inch to union demands, and the industry
was convulsed by a wave of strikes, sometimes accompanied by violence from both sides. Aided by the business downturn, which soon

transformed labor shortage to labor surplus, management proved to be stronger than labor. In North Carolina managers were always able to call on the state, through the use of the state militia, to keep the plants working. The local unions, inadequately supported by the UTW central organization, soon collapsed, and industrial peace of a sort returned to the Piedmont. Profoundly shaken, the mill manufacturers took two truths from the experience. The first was an abiding hatred of unions and a determination to prevent their future formation, under whatever aegis, in their region. The second was that slashing wages drastically as a means of cutting costs and maintaining profit margins was too disruptive; they would need to find other means to achieve this end.[16]

During the 1920s, this search was successful. Hard times led to bankruptcies, which offered the opportunity for consolidation. More and more mills fell into fewer hands. Men like J. Spencer Love of Burlington Industries became textile giants, taking over mills that had been locally owned. Ownership of other plants, like Gastonia's Loray Mill, passed outside the region and occasionally even outside the country. These powerful mill men set about finding a new solution to the problems of declining profitability, and they found it in the rise of new technology and new productive techniques. Men and women were replaced by machines wherever possible, the number of operatives needed to perform particular tasks was greatly reduced, and employees were made to work, really *work*, around the clock. Gone was the relaxed prewar pace of operation. In its place came fast, labor-saving machinery; massive job reorganization, including much greater resort to piecework; and new, restrictive supervisory practices, all against a backdrop of such a massive labor surplus that the need to hang onto workers was no longer a factor. Consequently, most mills abandoned or greatly restricted their welfare activities during the decade. Others cut the cost of village maintenance to the bone. The result was a steady deterioration in working and living standards.[17]

Gavin Wright has argued that given the labor surplus (especially the numbers of men over thirty for whom no work commensurate with their expectations could be found) and the limited prospects of wage reductions, the introduction of such management practices as those instituted was inevitable. For the workers, however, the whole nature of employment had changed, as Ella Ford pointed out. The workplace was now a situation of tension. Men with more machines to tend now ran where they had once ambled; women found timepieces—"hank-clocks," they called them—installed on each piece of machinery they used; gone was the chance to chat with one's neighbor, let alone to make the occasional trip home to see the children. Even going to the bathroom was likely to come under scrutiny from a new breed of unsympathetic, aggressive supervisors.[18]

Women, especially those over thirty, were particularly hard hit. Besides losing their cherished flexibility, as a result of job reorganization or consolidation they often found themselves transferred from wage rates to piecework rates, with a resultant drop in income. Furthermore, as mills began to be run on a round-the-clock schedule, it was women, increasingly, who worked the night shift, because they had to be home during the day to care for their children. Hanging over male and female workers alike was the dark cloud of job insecurity. It was easy to get yourself laid off, for there was always someone to take your place. It was not so easy to find another job, especially given the owners' network, which was reinforced by company spies.[19]

Manufacturers called these new practices by various names and were extremely proud of them. Workers referred to them collectively as "the stretch-out," and they hated them. And in 1929, despite the labor surplus, the power of management, the intimidation of union members, and the impotence of the UTW and other national labor institutions, thousands of textile workers in the southern Piedmont resisted the stretch-out in the only way they knew how: by walking off the job. On March 12, 1929, in Elizabethton, Tennessee, the entire workforce of the Bemberg and Glantzoff rayon plant struck. Led by young women workers, the strikers closed down the mill, starting the year off in a tumultuous way. Before 1929 was over, thousands of workers had followed their lead. In South Carolina, eighty-one separate strikes involving 79,027 workers were recorded. Almost all of these actions were organized without union leadership, very much in the "personal" or spontaneous tradition of prewar protest. In North Carolina even more workers were involved. In Forest City, in Charlotte, in Pinesville, in Leaksville—all over the Piedmont, in fact—workers protested the "hard rules" of the new industrial order.

Most of the 1929 strikes were short, relatively quickly settled, and soon forgotten, but some of them were violent and prolonged. In Elizabethton, following the pattern established between 1919 and 1921, eight hundred troops were called in to break the strikers' resistance, while AFL official Edward F. McGrady and UTW organizer Albert Hoffman were both roughed up by vigilantes purportedly acting on behalf of the town's businessmen. Their lives were threatened, and they were driven beyond the city limits and warned never to return. More tragic were the events in Marion, North Carolina, where a prolonged strike in the town's three mills resulted in not only the sending of troops to force their reopening but also the death of six strikers. On October 2, 1929, special deputies (who allegedly were drunk at the time) opened first on pickets at the Baldwin Mill, killing six of them and wounding twenty-five more. But of the many strikes of protest that year, none has become better known than the one that occurred in Gastonia, North Carolina, at the huge Loray Mill.[20]

In 1924, Gaston County marked half a century of progress with a pageant. In the preface to the play a prominent manufacturer wrote, "Gaston County, amazed at its own progress, humbly wonders what the next decade may bring forth." The play concluded with a herald delivering a similar message:

> O ye, who watched this pageantry
> Of vision, Old and New,
> Go forth a part of ages past
> And live your part as well.
> Build greater than your fathers built
> For they have built for you.[21]

In truth, Gaston County and its county seat, Gastonia, had much to celebrate. In previous decades, their progress had closely followed the contours of the textile industry's general development. The county was created by an act of the state legislature in 1846, and the development of its cotton textile industry started two years later. It was not for textiles that Gaston County first became known, however: for a time the county was the state's center for whiskey distilling. The economic development of both Gaston County and Gastonia, which was incorporated in 1877 with a population of 236, was at first slow, but this situation changed in 1887, when the combined efforts of R. C. G. Love, George A. Gray, J. D. Moore, and John H. Craig resulted in the building of the Gastonia Cotton Manufacturing Company's first mill. Two more followed in 1893, another in 1896, another in 1899, and another two—one of which was the Loray Mill—in 1900. Seven cotton textile plants were thus constructed in Gastonia alone within twelve years, and by 1900 the town's population had grown to five thousand, while similar development had occurred in nearby Bessemer City, Belmont, and Mount Holly. These first mills were founded by local people and financed by widely subscribed local investment, as Gaston County started down the road of development. By 1935, the county would have the largest number of mills of any American county and would be generally known as the nation's "combed yarn manufacturing center." Gastonia would be called "the city of spindles."[22]

In 1901, at the Arlington Cotton Mills in Gastonia, George W. Ragan produced the South's first "combed" yarns. As the cotton boom accelerated, this was to be the county's special claim to distinction. By 1920, Gaston County's ninety functioning mills were producing 80 percent of all the fine combed yarn made in America. Observers noted that the county had only slightly more churches than mills and that some local businessmen seemed in danger of confusing the two. The wartime boom in the industry was strongly felt in the county. Wages and profits both soared, and even more mills were organized amid an orgy of speculation, when the Gaston County slogan seemed to be "organize a mill a week." By war's end, the county already had more mills than any other in the country.[23]

As in the industry's basic pattern, Gaston County's boom was followed by, if not a crash, then a marked slowing of growth, and the textile industry there never again reached wartime levels of profitability. Yet the community remained optimistic; so much had been achieved in such a comparatively short time that it was difficult to believe that progress would not continue, provided that the textile manufacturers, Gaston's acknowledged leaders, were allowed free rein. The community was a particularly tight-knit one, its business, civic and religious leaders bound together in a web of civic, patriotic, and religious organizations. As one surveys the lists of church membership, Masonic lodge affiliations, membership of the local American Legion post, of the Rotary Club, the Civitans, the Kiwanis, the Lions, even the Daughters of the American Revolution, the same names keep occurring. Some of them were to be key players in the dramatic events of 1929. For example, Major A. L. Bulwinkle and district solicitor John G. Carpenter were both on the Board of Deacons of the Holy Trinity Evangelical Lutheran church. Bulwinkle and Stephen B. Dolley were charter members of both the Lions Club and the American Legion Post, as was R. Gregg Cherry, and Bulwinkle was also a member of the legal team that both prosecuted the Gastonia strikers and defended those accused of shooting Ella May Wiggins. Such interlocking networks of influence were to be expected in small booster communities like Gastonia, and they help explain the ferocity with which the community defended itself against what were perceived to be alien forces.[24]

The new labor-saving devices of the 1920s were eagerly embraced by Gastonia's manufacturers, and by none more enthusiastically than those who managed the Loray Mill. Built in 1900 by its namesakes, John F. Love and George A. Gray, by 1929 it was, according to Liston Pope, "both the pride and despair of Gastonia." Though Gastonia residents could not help but be impressed by the size of the structure, which literally dominated the town, from its very beginning there was something different about the Loray Mill. The fact that at least half of the money needed for its construction was raised in New York automatically gave it a slightly "northern taint," and this situation was exacerbated in 1919, when ownership passed to the Jenckes Spinning Company, of Pawtucket, Rhode Island. It was thus the first mill in the county "to be owned and operated by outside capital."[25]

Little is known about labor relations in the community during Gastonia's early development. The Knights of Labor were reportedly active there for a few years, but in Gastonia as elsewhere, workers much more commonly signaled their restlessness with aspects of the new industrial order through personalized or spontaneous action—the leaving of work early in order to visit a traveling circus, the 1906 violence against the Loray Mill paymaster over a proposal to hire immigrant labor—than through actions of a more organized nature. Moreover, in the climate of expansion which prevailed, there was always plenty of work available. Gastonia's mills had extremely high turnover rates, reflecting the mill workers' determination to maintain some control over the conditions of their lives.[26]

During its first twenty years, the Loray Mill's labor policies generally had differed little from those elsewhere in the industry. There was a large mill village, with the customary paternalistic relations. The very size of the mill, however, meant two things. First, many of the recruits were first-time mill workers, brought directly from the mountains by recruiting agents; and second, relations between Loray's management and workforce could never be as personal as in the smaller structures. This was possibly one of the reasons why the UTW chose the Loray Mill as the place to start its southern drive during the postwar instability. A local was formed in 1919, and in October of that year, 750 employees walked out in Gaston County's first strike of any significance. In a preview of what was to happen ten years later, the workers were objecting to the dismissal of eight operatives for union membership. The strike was lost, and the men returned to work having gained nothing, but according to Pope, "the seeds of unionism" had been "definitely planted in the community." So had the determination of management to resist the unions.[27]

Once the strike was over, the Jenckes Spinning Company both expanded the mill and changed its character. Weaving was discontinued, and the facility was converted to a yarn mill that manufactured nothing but fabric for automobile tires. To deal with the larger workforce, the company expanded and modernized the village; the additions included extensive welfare services. This expansion continued after 1923, when the Jenckes Company merged with another Rhode Island chain, the Manville Company, even though the industry was now deep in depression. By 1927 the number of employees had increased to 3,500, the total village population was over 5,000, and the welfare services included a company doctor, a baseball team, a bank, and Camp Jenckes, a summer camp in the mountains. Also, wage rates were at least equal to those paid in the county's other mills. Nevertheless, there was a downside to work and life at Loray. Manville-Jenckes had fenced the whole area in and had also taken to locking the doors during working hours, so that employees had to have special permission to leave. Moreover, the welfare workers seemed less interested in helping the workers than in monitoring every aspect of their lives. Company police were constantly visible, and the village had an atmosphere of increasing impersonality, exacerbated by absentee ownership. Workers soon came to refer to the mill as "the jail," and even in a time of labor surplus, turnover was high. Huddled on the outskirts of town, the huge red-brick mill and its village—composed of "several hundred stilted frame-cottages" scattered around it, looking for all the world "like a fussy old hen with a brood of bedraggled chicks"—was not a happy place.[28]

Like most of their contemporaries, the Manville-Jenckes plant's managers saw their salvation in the new management techniques and seized on them with enthusiasm. In 1927 the Loray Mill gave the stretch-out its first application in Gaston County. A new superintendent, G. A. Johnstone, was appointed, with orders to reduce production costs drastically. He went about his work with enthusiasm, dramatically raising workloads, replacing skilled with cheaper labor, and redistributing or abolishing tasks, and within fifteen months the Loray labor force had been reduced from 3,500 to 2,200. He slashed wages, imposing two general reductions of 10 percent, and, more important, put much of the work—especially that done by women—on a piecework basis. The general result was a wage reduction of between 25 and 50 percent, a drastic alteration in the mill's work practices, the bitter alienation of its workers, and the collapse of any lingering notions of a community at Loray.[29]

Management, of course, was delighted at what Johnstone had achieved. In a letter of congratulation given wide currency during the strike, F. L. Jenckes admitted that he had been skeptical about Johnstone's prospects of cutting the payroll by $500,000 annually without any loss of production and was delighted to be proved wrong. Now he thought that $1,000,000 could probably go, and he urged Johnstone to keep up the good work. The workers, though, were of a different mind. The year 1928 was one of unrest at the mill, and workers resisted when they could. On March 5, the entire weave room walked out in protest at wage reductions, which they claimed had reduced their incomes by about half. Their statement of explanation encapsulated the scale of their resentments about the stretch-out. "We were making $30 to $35 a week," it ran, "and were running six to eight looms. Now we are running ten to twelve looms and are getting $15 to $18 a week. We can't live on it. All we are asking is simple justice. A weaver cannot run ten or twelve looms at any price. It is more than a man can stand let alone a woman. There used to be women weavers in the mill but when the number of looms was increased the women all had to give up the work." Low wages were one thing, said Loray weaver Henry Totherow, but the stretch-out was something else. "There just ain't no a-bearin' [it]," he told left-wing journalist Margaret Larkin. "It used to be you could git five, ten minutes rest now and then, so's you could bear the mill. But now you got to keep a-runnin' all the time. Never a minute to git your breath all the long day. I used to run six drawing frames and now I got to look after ten. You jist kain't do it. A man's dead beat at night." There was no union to stir these weavers up; again, this was the spontaneous action of men and women driven beyond endurance by the way their working lives had changed. "The mill is asking something that is impossible," a strike representative stated on March 6. "It is a condition that can't continue to exist if we are to make a living. Most of us have been in this mill for years and have accepted cuts, even recently. But last week's went beyond the limit. So we are out. We believe the public will understand our position if they but knew the facts."[30]

Johnstone's response was simply to wait it out, knowing that spontaneous strikes rarely lasted more than a few days. His instinct was right: the weavers were soon forced back to work. Yet their outburst, especially the terms in which they justified their action, revealed the deep tensions the mill's policies had aroused. Moreover, they found other ways to make these obvious. Liston Pope discovered that later in the year a group of Loray workers staged a kind of charivari in Gastonia's main street. They paraded down the thoroughfare "bearing a coffin in which lay an effigy of the Loray superintendent." Every fifty yards or so "the effigy would sit up and shout: How many men are carrying this thing?" "Eight," the marchers would shout back, and the effigy would retort, "Lay off two; six can do the work." Pope concluded perceptively that these workers "hid a frowning face under a boisterous countenance."[31]

The most obvious demonstration of worker alienation, however, occurred in August 1928 when the company, realizing that Johnstone had outlived his usefulness, announced his replacement. That night worker anger boiled over. Let social scientist Benjamin Ratchford, himself from Gastonia, describe the scene:

On this night in August several trucks, loaded with workers from Loray, mostly young people, paraded through the principal streets of Gastonia. The occupants of the trucks were shouting, laughing, singing, blowing horns, beating tin pans, shooting fire crackers, and in general, staging a genuine, spontaneous celebration. They looked very much like one of the picnic parties that are frequently organized for outings into the country, except that they were somewhat more boisterous. They continued through the city and out about two miles eastward into an exclusive residential section. Here they turned into the driveway of the home of a Mr. Johnstone and continued their celebration, with increased volume, in the driveway, on the lawn and around the house. Mr. Johnstone finally was forced to summon the sherrif [*sic*] and deputies to disperse the crowd and stop the demonstration. The crowd then returned through the city, continuing the celebration.

Ratchford went on to explain that Johnstone, having introduced the stretch-out system to the Loray Mill, "had incurred the intense dislike of the workers." The motor vehicle parades, the noisy demonstrations, the involvement of young people, and the presence of the police to defend mill interests: Gastonia was to see much more of these elements in the year ahead.[32]

Johnstone was gone, and the workers celebrated their victory, but nothing much changed, for as Ella Ford said, "other managers came." Johnstone's replacement, J. L. Baugh, moderated a few of the most objectionable aspects of the new policies but left their essentials in place. The workers remained discontented, and the Gastonia community remained divided, fertile ground for the activities of Fred Erwin Beal and the National Textile Workers Union. Soon the history of Gaston County became intertwined with that of the frankly revolutionary, faction-ridden Communist Party of the United States.[33]

Originally born of left-wing disaffection with the Socialist Party in the heady aftermath of the October Revolution, the American Communist Party spent its first years in a furious factional struggle that was initially conducted underground. Even after its emergence aboveground in 1922, internecine warfare continued, the main line of cleavage being between those who, with Jay Lovestone, believed in "American exceptionalism"—a concept based on "the unique status of being the home base of the foremost capitalist power"—and those who advocated immediate worldwide revolution. The Lovestoneites argued that revolutionary change could hardly be expected in the United States, given that its people had largely been corrupted by an "imperialist-laden" prosperity that was shared by large sections of the working class. Rather, change would occur through patient, strategic political effort. "American exceptionalism" had been briefly tolerated by the Comintern, but with Stalin's consolidation of power and, in 1928, the attendant proclamation that the world had entered the "third period" of revolutionary upsurge, the Lovestoneites were swept from the CPUSA, as were the remaining adherents to the views of Leon Trotsky. By 1932, the orthodox Stalinists, led by William Z. Foster and his protégé Earl Browder, were firmly in control.[34]

The Communist Party's industrial policy had gone through a similar metamorphosis. For most of the decade it had operated through the Trade Union Educational League (TUEL). Formed in Chicago in 1920 and led by William Z. Foster, the TUEL was the most radical group operating within the American labor movement. Its aims were many— industrial unionism, the organization of the unorganized, the formation of a labor party, the eventual establishment of a workers' republic— and its method was "boring from within." The TUEL rejected dual unionism; its policy was rather to infiltrate established trade unions and convert them to Marxist militancy. Its leadership of strikes in Passaic, New Jersey, in 1926, and New Bedford, Massachusetts, two years later had given it a strong constituency among textile workers, but the increasing hostility and conservatism of the AFL leadership, together with Moscow's changing perspectives, led to its dissolution in 1928. The "boring from within" policy was jettisoned in favor of the building of a new labor movement through the establishment of dual unions, and the Trade Union Unity League was created as a rival to the AFL. The new league's program called for militant prosecution of the class war, for mass strikes rather than labor-management cooperation, and the ultimate overthrow of capitalism. Its first affiliate union was the National Textile Workers Union (NTWU).[35]

The NTWU was founded in New Bedford, Massachusetts, in September 1928, at a conference called to discuss the conduct of the recent strike there. Organized on an industrial basis, with James P. Reid as its first president, it was democratic in its governance and unremittingly revolutionary in its "class against class" rhetoric, in accordance with third-wave Communist perspectives. Its negotiating demands included higher wages, shorter hours, equal pay for equal work, and the complete abolition of child labor in the industry. Bitterly antagonistic to its AFL rival, the United Textile Workers (UTW), the NTWU planned to stage its first organizational drive in the American South, for no other reason than that the UTW was about to move in there; in those years the region was, in Theodore Draper's phrase, "virtually terra incognita" for both the union and the Party. The first Communist even to include the South in a speaking tour was the Party's 1928 vice presidential candidate, Benjamin Gitlow. There were no Party district offices in the region, which was ignored both in Party literature and on its priority task lists. Nevertheless, Fred E. Beal was sent out as NTWU's southern organizer in late 1928, after he had received NTWU secretary Albert Weisbord's instructions to use the "rolling wave" strike strategy. This was how the South would be broken, Weisbord believed: by starting a strike in a single mill, then extending it to neighboring mills as time, resources, and circumstances permitted. It was Beal's task to find that first mill.[36]

In 1929 Fred Beal was a thirty-three-year-old New Englander, fleshy, red-haired, and "heavy-faced." The radical journalist Mary Heaton Vorse thought him "boyish" and unassuming, with "absolutely no pose, no front whatsoever, . . . seemingly unconscious that he is a big man hereabouts." Sophie Melvin, who worked with him in Gastonia, described him as "sweet and gentle," with a feeling both for his work and the people he dealt with. "Sweetness" was hardly a usual characteristic for a union organizer in the hostile South, but in other ways Beal was well qualified for the task. He had been a textile worker since the age of fourteen, when he started at a mill in Lawrence, Massachusetts. Beal had joined the International Workers of the World (IWW) in his youth, and in the 1920s he had shifted to the Socialists, not the Communists. Politics was never of much importance to him, however; he was first and foremost an organizer, with little patience for theoretical or ideological concerns. His interest in independent unionism was what eventually drew him to the Communists at the time when they were changing their ideas and when his organizing work in the New Bedford strike had gained him a certain national prominence in left-wing circles. Beal probably joined the Party in 1928, shortly before he began his southern odyssey.[37]

He arrived in North Carolina on New Year's Day 1929, having traveled from New York by motorcycle. His only contact was a blind Party member in Charlotte—"the only functioning member" in the entire

Fred Beal, leader of the strike (Originally published in the Labor Defender)

city, he thought—and it was to his house that he went first. His host was enthusiastic about the prospects of organizing a union in the Charlotte area, given the woeful working conditions in the local mills, and it was there that Beal began his activity. He was unable to get a job in one of the mills, so made his contacts after work, visiting mill families in their homes, talking to them about the union, trying to find out what their real feelings were. He found them wary, partly because of their perceived betrayal by the UTW in 1921, but desperate in the face of the general application of the stretch-out. Slowly he began to sign people up.[38]

It was one of these first union members, O. D. Martins, who pointed him toward Gastonia, which until then had been "just another dot on the industrial map" to Beal. Martins had a brother working at the Loray Mill; he would help Beal organize the workers there. If Beal succeeded in doing that, Martins said, "you'll organize the South"— a statement that unconsciously reinforced Weisbord's "rolling strike" policy. In mid-March Beal decided to go to Gastonia to see for himself. There, at the Loray Mill, he found conditions even worse than those he had encountered in Charlotte, plus a disaffected workforce that was itching for action. He launched a secret union then and there, with Will Truett, a local worker, as its secretary-treasurer. Then, afraid that the situation would outrun his ability to control it, Beal made a swift trip to New York to plead for money and reinforcements.[39]

Party and NTWU officials were delighted at the progress he had made and needed little convincing that the Gastonia situation was just what they had been looking for. Here was their third-period opening in the United States, the beginning of the revolution that would bring about capitalism's collapse, and here, at Loray, was Weisbord's "first mill." If a single man could penetrate so quickly the most inaccessible, most hostile region in the United States, a place where "no Communist organizer had ever ventured before," where might it all end? Beal returned to Charlotte, assured that he would receive all possible support.[40]

When Beal returned from New York, there was a telegram waiting for him from Will Truett. He had been fired from the Loray Mill, he said, because of his union work. Moreover, company police were busily ferreting out other members and summarily dismissing them. Beal knew he had to act, ready or not. Events had simply overtaken him. Accordingly, he and Truett held a secret meeting at the house of a fellow unionist to canvas the possibility of a strike. The enthusiasm was infectious, the resolve grim. Even Beal was moved, and he allowed himself to believe that they "might achieve on this backward Southern soil, a great resounding victory for the American working class." An open meeting was to be called for March 30, 1929. The die, said Beal, was cast.[41]

True to its word, the NTWU sent him the first reinforcements, in the doughty personage of its second vice president, Ellen ("Nellie") Dawson. Variously described as "a wee bit of a girl" or "the little orphan of the strikers," the diminutive, seemingly frail Dawson was in reality anything but that. A veteran of the New England strikes, she was a tough, experienced organizer and a superb stump speaker who delivered her messages in the soft brogue of her native Scotland. She made her Gastonia debut on March 30, urging workers to stand resolute; meanwhile, Manville-Jenckes supervisors stood silently by, noting the names of those present. Heckled by the crowd, especially the women, with cries of "What about the stretch-out? . . . How about

Workers at the Loray Mill vote to continue the strike.
(Courtesy Wide World Photos)

God and the bathtubs? [a reference to the recent remark of a mill-sponsored preacher that as the Lord was not an advocate of frequent bathing, bathtubs were not a necessity for mill-village houses]," the supervisors eventually beat a humiliating retreat.[42]

Beal knew then that there would be no turning back, that the bosses would force the issue on the next working day and that, despite the lack of preparation and resources, the union must meet the challenge. And so the dramatic events began to unfold. On the morning of April 1, five workers were dismissed for attending Saturday's "speakin'." They sang hymns together as more discharged workers arrived at the NTWU's newly acquired union headquarters. As he prepared for a strike meeting called for three o'clock that afternoon, Beal sensed that Gastonia would soon be much more than just a dot on the map.[43]

2 THE STRIKE

At 3 P.M. on April 1, 1929, Fred Beal took that final, fateful step. Standing on the bank beside the railroad track just outside the Loray Mill, he spoke to the assembled workers for nearly an hour. Then, his voice harsh with emotion, he called for a strike vote. The decision was unanimous, and Beal therefore declared that a strike existed "in the Manville-Jenckes Mill, in the name of the National Textile Workers Union, local of Gastonia." It was a historic moment. "Obscure Gastonia was leaping into the limelight," he later observed.[1]

The limelight did not come immediately. Though the strikers marched to the mill gate and were successful in persuading most of the night shift to stay out, the mill management did not seem unduly concerned. Baugh claimed that he had no idea what the strike was about, as no demands had yet been served on him. He expected that it would blow over soon, that by tomorrow things would be back to normal. Even the *Gastonia Daily Gazette*, the mouthpiece of the Gaston County mill owners, which would soon become unbridled in the violence of its antistrike invective, greeted the events calmly enough, pointing out that the pickets had gone about their business entirely peacefully.[2]

The relatively low-key climate was soon replaced by a much more confrontational atmosphere. On April 2, Baugh was presented with the union's demands, all of them specifically directed at the conditions of labor in the mill and of the workers' lives in the village beyond. The list included the elimination of all piecework, hank, or clock systems; the substitution of a standard wage scale; a forty-hour, five-day week, with a minimum weekly wage of $20; equal pay for equal work for women and youth; the abolition of the stretch-out; decent and sanitary housing; the reduction of rent and light charges in the village; and, crucially, recognition of the union. Baugh dismissed these demands out of hand. Quite apart from the practical impossibility of meeting them, Manville-Jenckes had no intention of ever negotiating with the union— any union. To comply with these demands, Baugh told the delegation, would be to "virtually give you the plant," and this Manville-Jenckes would never do. Rather, the company would "pay no attention to the strike." Production would continue as normal; striking workers would be replaced and evicted from the mill village. There was nothing else to be said. Incidentally, Baugh knew the details of the strike committee's demands long before Beal presented them. Right from the start, management had a spy in the striker's ranks: Ed Spenser was ostensibly one of Beal's most loyal deputies, but he in fact kept the mill's chief security officer, Bruce Abernathy, fully informed of all developments. He was subsequently rewarded with an executive position.[3]

It was Baugh's uncompromising refusal even to listen to the strike committee that caused the action to escalate. The company decided to stretch cables of rope across the street in front of the mill in order to keep the pickets back, enabling those who wanted to enter the mill gates to do so without undue harassment. The crowd that gathered there simply tore them down. When management ordered that the ropes be replaced with steel cables, the mood of the strikers changed. The "carnival spirit" which had so far animated them vanished and was replaced by anger and determination. "From a happy, laughing, joking crowd," the *Gastonia Daily Gazette* reported, "the demonstration became a belligerent, threatening mob." Sticks and clubs were waved and occasionally used against the outmanned local police force. Not even the arrival of the town's popular chief of police, the imposing Orville Aderholt, complete with the black ten-gallon hat he habitually wore, could quiet the crowd. The area in front of the mill had become a place of disorder.[4]

The defiance of the strikers and the inability of the city police and sheriff's deputies to control them were the excuse for further escalation. Sheriff Eli Lineberger and Mayor Rankin asked Governor O. Max Gardner for assistance. He responded quickly. By the afternoon of April 3, five units of the North Carolina National Guard, under the command of General J. Van B. Metts, had arrived in Gastonia and had quickly surrounded the mill. The strikers now had "grim-faced troopers" to contend with, and they were not happy about it. They taunted the troops with cries of "Boy Scouts" and "Nasty Guardsmen"

Women strikers battle National Guardsmen.
(Originally published in the Labor Defender*)*

and grabbed at their weapons. Mrs. Charles Corley, who attempted "to wrestle a rifle from a guardsman," gained a certain immortality by being the first of a long line of strikers arrested in 1929. Bertha Tompkinson was arrested, too, for breaking through the troop's lines and "pummelling one of the guardsmen with a stout stick." A "little thing like a bayonet would not stop her," she asserted, and it didn't. Tompkinson's arrest was followed almost immediately by the arrest of sixteen-year-old Ruby McMahon—the first of the dozen-plus arrests she was to incur in 1929 during her metamorphosis from teenager to militant strike leader. Nevertheless, the arrests and the very presence of the troops did bring an end to the disorder. On April 4, few strikers came to jeer at the soldiers, the strike leaders having insisted that they keep at least a block away from the guard line. Beal wanted no violence.[5]

It was during these two days that the *Gastonia Daily Gazette* developed the violent, strident voice it was to use throughout the year. This voice would ignore the issues of the strike and concentrate on attacking its leadership by presenting Beal and those who came to work with him as agents of revolution, insidious destroyers of the American way of life. On April 3, the newspaper printed the first of a series of full-page advertisements supposedly paid for by the citizens of Gaston County in order to alert Gaston County residents to the real issues behind the strike. Beal was a Red, it stated—a Bolshevik who stood "against all American traditions and American government." He was also

> against all religion of whatever kind. . . . The very existence, the happiness and the very way of life even, of every citizen of Gaston County is threatened, and is in the balance, if Beal and his Bolshevik associates succeed in having their way. The question in the minds of many people who belong to the Christian church, who belong to the various patriotic and fraternal organizations is: Shall men and women of the type of Beal and associates, with their Bolshevik ideas, with their calls for violence and bloodshed, be permitted to remain in Gaston County.[6]

This heavy emphasis on the alien nature of the strike's leadership and the connection between the NTWU and the Communist Party had little effect on the strikers. Observers believed that even basic distinctions between labor organizations were lost on them. "A curious phase of the situation," wrote a *New York Times* reporter, "is that the textile workers here appear to be entirely ignorant of the difference between the National Textile Workers Union and the UTW. The Communist speeches of Beal make no impression on them, but they warm up to his attacks on the mill owners and the managers." The Socialist journalist Paul Blanshard, whom the *Nation* quickly dispatched to cover the story, made the same point. "The workers in the strike only know that they are fighting for a better life," he wrote sympathetically.

> They do not know the difference between one union and another, and for them "communism" is simply a general epithet. The employers have shouted "Wolf! Wolf!" so often that now their paroxysms have little effect upon the workers. On the red clay banks of the railroad track they sit in their overalls listening to the Communist strike

leader as he stands on a box in the vacant lot. They hear with blank faces phrases about international solidarity and class power. But when one of their own number stands up and shouts: "Every striker git a scab and the strike will soon be over," they howl with delight. They are tired, undernourished, and uneducated, but even the employers admit that they are becoming aware of their own degradation.

"Communism and the stop-watch," thought Blanshard, had brought to the southern mills "the first serious rebellion in eight years." Moreover, the atmosphere had already become "so charged with fear and bitterness" as to resemble "a civil war."[7]

Doubtless the journalists were correct. Few of the strikers could have had much understanding of their leaders' rhetoric. They were certainly not the conscious vanguard of the revolution that Weisbord was desperately hoping for; rather, they were acting much more out of the tradition of spontaneous protest against real grievances that had animated the Loray weavers the previous year, for example, and would be seen throughout the Piedmont during 1929.

Though there is little evidence that this rhetoric of anticommunism had much effect on the Loray strikers, there is no doubt that the constant emphasis on the alien, menacing nature of Beal and his associates, the threat that they posed to basic traditions and values, did contribute to the growing climate of violence in Gaston County and gave sanction to the violent incidents that did occur. Moreover, it became increasingly difficult for the issues of the strike to be confronted on their merits, despite the strike leadership's valiant efforts to present its case to the community through leaflets and broadsheets. These real issues all too quickly became subsumed in the fight against the alien force, a force that in time came to be identified with the strikers themselves, not just with their leadership. In this sense, the contemporary commentators and others who have insisted that the *Gastonia Daily Gazette*'s violent rhetoric bore considerable responsibility for what was to follow were probably right.[8]

Nevertheless, the strike's opponents did not bear sole responsibility for asserting the centrality of the Communist issue. Fred Beal, reflecting on the strike's early days, ruefully commented that the Communist Party's chief aim in such situations was always "to bring out the political nature of the conflict." The Party was insistent that strikes should not simply become "straight, out and out struggles for unionization." This perspective hampered his Gastonia efforts right from the start, particularly when Jack Johnstone, the Party's central committee representative, was in town, always ready to second-guess Beal, to insist that the correct political line be followed, and to sulk if his opinion was questioned. Even if allowances are made for the ferocious anticommunism that consumed Beal in later life, his observations ring true and were confirmed by another ex-Communist, Paul Crouch. The strike was only a day old when Beal was joined by the Party's first activist, George Pershing, who was sent by both the *Daily Worker* and the Young Communist League. The flamboyant, good-looking Pershing— nephew of Edgar J. Pershing, then chairman of the Indiana Republican State Committee, and more distantly related to the famous military commander "Black-Jack" Pershing—immediately left people in no doubt as to his politics or the strike's real purposes. He was a Bolshevist, he told his first Gastonia audience, sent by the Party to spearhead "a gigantic movement in the entire South," aimed at ousting capitalism from the region. Beal counseled him against making such statements, but in vain. When Pershing and the other Party representatives were in full cry, the *Gastonia Daily Gazette* and those who wished to stress the alien nature of the strike's leadership would always find grist for their particular mill.[9]

There were, of course, those who right from the start considered the Communist issue a red herring and believed that to stress it was to ignore the real issues behind the strike. R. E. ("Fleet") Williams, the Raleigh *News and Observer*'s most experienced reporter, whose long dispatches from Gastonia were models of balanced and informed journalism, constantly ridiculed those who raised the "Communistic bugaboo." The Loray Mill had had its troubles long before the arrival of the NTWU, he reminded his readers on April 6. Beal and Pershing had simply "injected themselves" into an already existing situation of discontent. There was no disorder in Gastonia, the strikers had settled down, their leadership was "counselling peace" and nonviolence, and the strike could soon be settled, provided that "this bogie of communism . . . which has created a vast fear" in the minds of textile interests and public officials could be gotten out of the way. The tragedy of the

Gastonia strike was that those same interests and public officials saw their salvation not in removing the "bogie" but in feeding it.[10]

On April 5, 1929, Tom P. Jimison, a Charlotte attorney, went to Gastonia to see for himself what was happening there. Jimison was an odd sort, a native North Carolinian with roots stretching back to pre-Revolutionary times. Intensely proud of his father's service in the Confederate cause, he was also a committed liberal who had left the Methodist ministry in 1924, after sixteen years in the pulpit, "because of constant conflict between me and the authorities of my church on economic and social questions." He enrolled in the University of North Carolina's law school and was admitted to the bar in 1926. Jimison's life was to be altered significantly by the strike at the Loray Mill, though he did not know it at the time of his first visit there. What he found, however, worried him sufficiently that he wrote to Governor Gardner. The violence of the situation, he told the chief executive, "like Mark Twain's death, has been greatly exaggerated." Despite the *Gastonia Daily Gazette*'s "obvious attempts to incite violence," the strikers were remaining orderly, which was scarcely surprising, given that they were overwhelmingly "our kind of people, good-humored and well-behaved." However, they were very young, or so it seemed to him. "To see the soldiers with guns and bayonets," he said, "suggested hunting rabbits with heavy artillery." The strike leaders were similarly disposed to order, he said; he had heard them urging the strikers to keep their heads and to "do no violence." Indeed, "the strike was being conducted by a brace of mild-mannered, mild-spoken kids." The expressions of violence he had encountered had all come from the other side, and this had bothered him profoundly.[11]

In stressing the youth of the strikers and their leaders, Jimison was simply confirming what other commentators had already drawn attention to during the strike's first days. David Clark, publisher of the *Southern Textile Bulletin*, the organ of the textile manufacturers, believed that was a prime reason for not taking the strike too seriously. It has been started by "two boys and a girl," he wrote dismissively, under whose influence "a number of the employees of the Loray Mill, consisting largely of those under twenty years of age, walked out and created disorder," but there was not the "slightest probability" that the strike would be successful. "The Communist leaders here are, for the most part, bold youngsters," wrote Paul Blanshard. They were "utterly devoted to their cause," he said, and, ominously, "blissfully unaware of the depth of prejudice against them" as they passed out the *Daily Worker*, sneered at the local clergy, and tried to subvert the National Guard. A correspondent for the *Labor Defender*, the journal of the Communist-controlled International Labor Defense (ILD), whose representatives were in Gastonia within a week of the strike's beginning, also remarked favorably on the youthfulness and enthusiasm of many of the strikers. "How happy they are, the young folks, to be taking part in the strike," he enthused. "They are thrilled; the young girls laugh; some have on overalls; they flirt." Not every observer was similarly enthusiastic about the involvement of young people. Much later in the year, testifying for the prosecution at the trial of those accused of conspiring to murder police chief Orville Aderholt, Mrs. Walter Grigg admitted that what she disliked most about the strike was the way it seemed to have caused young people to lose all restraint. They were always making noise, she complained, "hugging and kissing" all the time, once "right before my sister and what company we had one night." [12]

In her complaint, Mrs. Grigg did touch on one reason why young people may have participated so prominently in the strike, over and above the poor working conditions that all Loray laborers shared. No less than young New Yorkers (or young Londoners, for that matter), young Gastonians were part of a youth rebellion, the challenge to Victorian moral values and social attitudes that swept through post–World War I Western culture. Participation in the strike, the freedom it allowed, and the license it gave to challenge authority may have been particularly appealing to young mill workers. Jacquelyn Hall and her colleagues made this perceptive comment about young people's involvement in the wave of strikes that swept through the southern textile mills in 1929: "Young people who had led the protests of the 1920s had come of age in a society very different from the one their parents had known . . . They did not see themselves as temporary sojourners, ready to beat a retreat to the land, or as destitute farmers for whom it was heaven to draw a paycheck, however small. Their identities had been formed in the mill village; they had cast their fate with the mills." [13] Moreover, they were at the same time becoming part of a national, even global culture, a world of radio, Ford cars, and fast-changing value systems: "They quickly assimilated the speeded-up rhythms, the fashions, the popular culture of their generation's changing times." Gastonia's young people, no less than those elsewhere, were caught up in this process of change.[14]

It was the presence of substantial numbers of young women among the strikers, and the way these women acted, that most exercised some observers. Cora Harris, writing in the *Charlotte Observer*, first drew attention to this phenomenon. "If Gastonia has never realized that militant women were within its bounds," she noted, not altogether approvingly, "it certainly knows it now." Commenting on the previous day's mass meeting of strikers, she stated that most of those present were women, "dressed in their gay Easter frocks and a few with spring coats. I was particularly attracted by the popularity of silk stockings." The women listened attentively to the speaker, Ellen Dawson, who urged them to take the lead in spreading the strike, "for there are sixty percent women in the textile industry today." When she had finished, "a well dressed but rather fiery young woman jumped up to the platform and screamed 'yes, they put me in jail and I'm proud of it. I never did nothing to go to jail for. They said it was for disorderly conduct. Well I thank God I can stand up for my rights and I'll go again and shed blood if it will help this 'ere Union.'" Her audience went wild. "A profound applause and a big reception for the daring young woman followed," recorded the less-than-impressed Harris.[15]

The same day, Mary Pressley, writing in the *Charlotte News*, also commented on the female strikers' dress—and their behavior. "To the younger girls of the mill village," she asserted, "the strike is a thrilling affair. It gives them an excuse to ramble about at their leisure, chatting with their friends, and hoping for more excitement. Many of them are wearing knickers or overalls, not at all disconcerted by the contrast of these utilitarian garments with long collars or other feminine adornments."[16]

Two correspondents to the *Gastonia Daily Gazette* stated most strongly the unease that such behavior brought to some minds. "It isn't decent for a respectable lady to go on the streets," wrote one. "I have seen young girls, I mean strikers, going up and down the street with old overalls on and men's caps, with the bills turned behind, cursing us, calling the cops all kind of dirty things." A Loray employee wrote, "What disgusts me is women mixing in this strike. A really to goodness woman would not loiter around, and fight and curse like men. In all strikes, I think, the women ought to go home and leave the men to settle it."[17] Unconventional styles of dress and unseemly, even "un-womanly" behavior: the strike in the Loray Mill was clearly having an unsettling effect on the behavior of some of Gastonia's young women or, to be more accurate, on those who observed them. Again Hall has given us a guide to explaining what was happening. In her rich, multifaceted article on the strike in the Glanztoff mill in Elizabethton, Tennessee, which occurred at the same time as that in the Loray Mill and primarily involved women activists, she writes, "The activists of Elizabethton belonged to a venerable tradition of 'disorderly women,' women who, in times of political upheaval, embody tensions that are half-conscious or only dimly understood. Beneath the surface of a conflict that pitted workers and farmers against a new middle class in the town lay an inner world of fantasy, gender ideology and sexual style."[18] In developing her argument, Hall talks convincingly about the "gender-based symbolism" of their protest style, discussing the inner meaning of their dress patterns, their language, and their gestures as well as emphasizing their style's erotic undercurrent. These young women of Elizabethton, she wrote, "combined flirtation with fierceness on the picket line." Their story was not only firmly part of the female protest tradition; it was also clearly part of their particular quest for the liberating trappings of modernity.[19]

Certainly these same elements—protest in language, dress, and gesture—could be identified among the youthful female strikers of Gastonia. The underlying sexual themes were there as well. The male strike leaders knew this and moved to turn it to their advantage. In the first speech he made to the striking workers, Albert Weisbord, national secretary of the NTWU, urged the women to fraternize with the young National Guardsmen in order to distract them from their duty. "You girls and women, go in a body to these soldiers," he urged. "They are not hard-boiled gunmen" but, rather, young, vulnerable local boys. "Ask these boys Do you mean to shoot us down and stab us and our children?" he went on. "Fraternize with them. Urge them to create trouble in their ranks so when the order comes to shoot us down they won't obey." In the face of such an appeal, he predicted, the women would "see these boys throwing down their guns and uniforms." More than one observer commented on the sexual energy the "handsome and well educated" Pershing seemed to excite among Gastonia's girl strikers. Cora Harris, for example, spoke of his "Chesterfield manner" and remarked that he was surrounded by young women wherever he went. Even Vera Buch, who arrived in Gastonia on April 5 to be Beal's deputy and felt contemptuous of Pershing, admitted the power of his sexual appeal. Many of the young women became besotted with him and were heartbroken when, after only a few weeks, he returned (thankfully, from his perspective) to New York. In Buch's opinion, he had abandoned his post.[20]

Yet, to emphasize unduly the role of young women in the Gastonia strike and to classify the prime reasons for their involvement as psychosexual would be to neglect the centrality of economic and class concerns. Cora Harris got it right: after noting the youthful nature of so many of the female strikers and remarking on their hose, she also commented that there were "some pathetic old women in the crowd" as well, "whose backs were bent with life's heavy burdens." She met Mrs. John Faulbright, who had been a mill worker for nine years and was head of the hastily formed strike relief committee. "[W]ith a babe in her arms and two on the floor," Faulbright told Harris "in an infuriated manner" of the indignities of her existence on a weekly wage of $4.00. She and her husband lived on a combined wage of $18.50 a week, which, by the time the mill had deducted its several charges, was simply not enough to feed and clothe a family. She had spent the previous evening in the city jail, said Mrs. Faulbright, and had been given egg and beef sandwiches for her supper. She reported, it was "the best meal that I had in six months." Mrs. Faulbright was mad at the mill and its management, and "I says a plenty when I gets mad." Mary Pressley made essentially the same point. While the young girls may have found the strike's first days "thrilling" and liberating, the older women were much more serious. They wanted shorter hours and higher wages, an end to the demeaning "hank-clock" and the stretchout, and better living conditions for themselves, their husbands, and especially their children. They would not give in lightly, she said, even if it meant going to jail. They were "prepared to undergo discomfort and even suffering for the cause they had espoused," and they were not too bothered by the epithets thrown at the strike's leadership. As Bertha Hendrix, then a young wife expecting her first child, recollected, it was "the first time I'd ever thought things could be better."

These were the women who had felt most acutely the steady decline in working conditions over the past few years—who had lost status due to the stretch-out and the consequent assumption by men of jobs women had previously filled; who had often lost income due to the shift to piecework; and whose living conditions had deteriorated as a result of management's declining interest in welfare work, or even in providing minimal conditions of decency in their villages. In discussing the life of the strike's female martyr, Ella May Wiggins, Hall and her coauthors commented that she "compelled attention in part because she expressed the needs of women who combined bread-winning with child rearing under conditions that just kept getting worse and worse." Wiggins, they said, had no interest in the Communist bogey. She and women like her "needed no larger than life outsider to blame for the injuries of class." Wiggins worked not at the Loray Mill but at the American Mill in nearby Bessemer City; however, she, Ivy Faulbright, Bertha Hendrix, and many others shared very similar experiences and dreamed very similar dreams.[21]

And so the strike continued into its second week, the intensity of its rhetoric increasing as both sides sought reinforcements. The Communist Party, its satellite agencies, and the NTWU all sent representatives, some of whom stayed for the duration and whose lives were altered by the experience, others who just drifted through. The first to arrive was Vera Buch, who arrived, "weary and rumpled," on April 5. A veteran of the Passaic, New Jersey textile strike of 1926, Buch had been a Party member for nearly ten years and was Weisbord's unmarried lover. Thirty-four years old at the time, and described by the radical journalist Mary Heaton Vorse as a dedicated Communist, she was sent by the Party to "stiffen up" Beal, and she stayed throughout the long year to become the strike's most important day-to-day organizer.

Amy Schechter came next. Sent by the Workers International Relief organization, she was the daughter of the "noted educator" Solomon Schechter, once a reader in Talmudic studies at Cambridge University and later president of New York's Jewish Theological Seminary. Amy had grown up in comparative luxury and was a graduate of New York's prestigious Wadleigh High School as well as Barnard College. In 1920, while working in London, she had joined the British Communist Party, and in 1921 she became a member of the CPUSA. She was a veteran of the 1928 miners' strike and, like Buch, of that year's New

Bedford textile strike. Her elder sister Ruth Schechter Alexander, who spent much of her adult life in South Africa, also became a Communist, joining the British Party after her return from the Cape in the early 1930s. Ironically, their brother Frank, a prominent New York attorney, represented some North Carolina mill interests. Amy was a convinced Communist—a "feverish admirer of Earl Browder," said Vorse—and remained in Gastonia with Buch throughout the strike. She and her sailor husband shared an apartment with Browder in Chicago on the rare occasions they were in town. The ILD sent Karl Marx Reeve, editor of its monthly paper, the *Labor Defender*, and son of the legendary Communist Ella Reeve Bloor, known as "Mother Bloor." Reeve stayed for less than two months, but later he would considerably inflate his role in the strike.[22] Those who passed through were many, including Paul Crouch, who soon became the Party's southern organizer and later an FBI informer; Jack Johnstone, a member of the Party's central committee; and various African American comrades who, after sniffing the reactionary southern air, usually beat a hasty retreat back to the safer climes of New York. Indeed, in later years Buch was inclined to comment acidly on the many who came to Gastonia, found the southern atmosphere totally alien, and "left joyfully," never to return. Those who stuck it out were certainly few.[23]

From time to time, the national office of the NTWU sent General Secretary Weisbord to Gastonia to ginger up the local leadership. He could generally be relied on to raise the level of rhetoric and stir up the passions of the local community. Two issues Weisbord stressed caused great concern among the community's middle- and upper-class residents. One was his insistence that the Loray strike was but the first shot in a battle that would be heard throughout the region. The NTWU's aim, in fact, was a series of rolling strikes that would soon engulf the entire South. "Make this a flame that will spread from Charlotte to Atlanta and beyond," he urged strikers at his first mass meeting, "so that we can have at least 200,000 workers on strike." The *Gastonia Daily Gazette* was so excited by Weisbord's visit that the front page of its next issue was given over to the work of a young mill worker turned cartoonist, who had produced a huge drawing of a snake wound around an American flag under the heading "A Viper that Must be Smashed." In case anyone had missed the point, the cartoon was captioned "Communism in the South, Kill it."[24]

The second issue Weisbord raised, somewhat to Beal's concern, and to the delight of the textile interests, was that of race. From its inception, the Communist Party had stood firmly for the principle of racial equality, and this tenet was reflected in the constitution of the NTWU. Though African Americans constituted a negligible proportion of the Loray workforce, Weisbord insisted that the Loray local reach out to them. "Our union has no color line," he told the strikers, "although the bosses wished you did." Blacks were to be included "on a completely equal basis"; there was absolutely no room for compromise. The *Daily Worker* reported that the "several thousand workers" present gave this sentiment "a tremendous ovation," but this account simply showed that the newspaper had already decided to give Moscow what it wanted to hear rather than attempt to reflect the strike's reality. The race issue was always divisive; few strikers, even the most committed, agreed with the union's policy. The "nigguhs" could join the union if they wanted to, Blanshard reported them as conceding, but they could not meet in the same room as whites—and management could thus always keep the fear of race-mixing in their strike-breaking armory. "How our good mill people can be led by these people who are not our kind, who defy God, flout religion, denounce our government and who are working for social equality among white and black is a mystery," fulminated the *Gastonia Daily Gazette* after Weisbord's speech. "Southern people will never for one instance tolerate such a thing." It was a potent and prescient argument.[25]

During this first visit, Weisbord also introduced a policy that was to be repeated in the months ahead. He announced that he was going to take some representative strikers, "one man, one woman and one child from here," back to New York to speak at Madison Square Garden. In this way, the consciousness of good people everywhere would be raised as to the evils of the southern mill system. The speeches would hopefully generate money as well. And that was how Cecil Burger, Ina Faulbright, and Violet Jones found themselves in the big city. Weisbord went with them, conveniently forgetting his pledge to the strikers to remain in Gastonia as long as he was needed.[26]

Violet Jones's departure did not go unheralded. Her husband, Troy Jones, a Loray Mill worker but a nonstriker, brought suit in the Gaston superior court against Beal, the NTWU and the Loray local, and Weisbord, alleging that they had enticed Violet from her home and dispatched her to New York, thus causing him "great inconvenience and great mental anguish." Violet, for her part, was unrepentant. She still loved Troy, she said tearfully from New York, "but if he stays at work and doesn't help us with this strike it will be the end for us. I'll never go back to him." Her whole family worked in the mill, she said, and after five years she earned no more than nine dollars a week. It just was not enough. The incident was of itself unimportant, especially when it became known that Violet and Troy were not even living together at the time of her departure; nevertheless, Troy Jones's warrant enabled the local police to pursue Beal. At first he could not be found, as he was out of the area organizing elsewhere, but he was eventually arrested and was held overnight before a local judge ordered the warrant annulled. This obvious harassment was indicative of what was to come and represents a prime reason why Tom Jimison became a more or less permanent part of the strike's leadership, at the behest of the American Civil Liberties Union (ACLU). The need for competent legal representation was becoming clear.[27]

In addition, there were other signs of a hardening of attitude toward the strikers. The *Gastonia Daily Gazette* continued to wage its inflammatory campaign, issuing increasingly thinly disguised calls to violence, especially against the strike's leadership. If only Beal and Pershing moved on or were kicked out, ran its April 12 editorial, then all would soon be well. "As long as these two stay here," lamented the editor, "there will be trouble at the Loray and elsewhere." It was "high time" they were deported, all the more so as they had "kindled the fires of hatred and jealousy and of class prejudice in the minds of these people of the Loray Mill." Gastonia's "good people" were "getting tired of these wops from the east side of New York telling our folk what to do and how to do it. It is time we are being rid of them."[28]

A number of the city's "good people" were beginning to express the same sentiments, though not necessarily in quite such crude terms. One of these was Major A. L. Bulwinkle, a local lawyer who had represented the district in the United States Congress from 1920 to 1928 and was then swept from office in the Hoover landslide. Shattered by his defeat, he had immediately found employment as legal counsel to the Loray Mill, and he seemed to enjoy his work as president of the Gastonia post of the American Legion, which he had helped organize on his return from active service in 1919. When Governor Gardner de-

cided on April 9 to remove some of the National Guardsmen stationed
at the mill, it was Bulwinkle who successfully argued that they should
be replaced by a "picked body of deputies chosen from the ranks of
the American Legion as former service men." Sheriff Lineberger was
ordered to organize such a force immediately and to station them at the
mill. The *Gastonia Daily Gazette* thoroughly approved of this move,
but it greatly dismayed the strike leaders, who felt that it materi-
ally increased the potential for violence. Pershing thought there was
"more likelihood of trouble with the Legionnaires who have been made
deputy sheriffs and given quarters at the Loray mills than there had
been with the troops." Beal said the move was "another tactic of the
mill owners . . . to stir up a lynching spirit against the union leaders."
Major Bulwinkle was unofficial commander of these special deputies,
and he remained a shadowy but central figure throughout the year,
pivotal to the Loray Mill's legal opposition to the strikers and to its
growing illegal vigilantism.[29]

Other public figures and community leaders began to speak out
against the strike, especially its instigators. Within days of the walkout, Commissioner Charles A. Wood of the Conciliation Service of the
United States Labor Department had ruled out any prospect of federal mediation by denouncing the strike's leaders as Bolsheviks. It
was hardly a strike at all, he thought, but rather "a form of revolution created by those committed to revolution by mass action. There
is not here any existing common ground upon which employees and
employers can stand."[30] Wood's attitude was echoed loudly from Gastonia's many pulpits. As Liston Pope convincingly demonstrated in his
classic study, the town's preachers were always overwhelmingly opposed to the strike; many of them were simply mouthpieces for the
Loray Mill. Certainly James Myers thought so when he visited Gastonia during the strike's first week on a fact-finding mission for the
Federal Council of Churches. Never had he met such a "cold, unre-
sponsive" group as the Gastonia clergy. "Evidently they have not yet
thought of any connection between the mind of Christ and low wages
or night work for women or child labor," Myers commented. The mill-
village pastors were particularly vehement in their defense of the system. These ministers and their followers "had not visioned as yet the
social meanings of religion," he sadly concluded. Certainly, the strikers
could expect very little sympathy from Gastonia's men of God.[31]

Guardsmen await the strike pickets.
(Originally published in the Labor Defender*)*

Nevertheless, the mill workers did have some sources of spiritual support. As Hall and her coauthors have pointed out, though established denominations remained the bastions of the middle classes in the mill villages—the place where management worshiped—and had little to say to the mill workers, "independence and holiness churches . . . sometimes sheltered the disaffected, and evangelicalism remained a resource upon which strikers could draw." This was true in Gastonia in April 1929. Holiness preachers, most of whom did not have organized churches, addressed the first mass meetings and urged the strikers on. Cora Harris reported on such a meeting, held on the strike's first Sunday. She had previously worshiped at a mill-village church, where she had found plenty of management present but "only a few strikers." When she went to the public meeting area, however, things were different. The strikers were listening not to Beal, Pershing, or Dawson, but to "a tall, rather distinguished-looking elderly man with a large flowing

mustache"—"the Billy Sunday of Loray," she called him. He opened
the service with a hymn, and then took as his text Malachi 3:8, "Will
a man rob God." That, he said, was what the mill owners of Gaston
County did every day: they "robbed God." The stridently atheistic
strike leaders were not happy about sharing platforms with preachers, but it was something they quickly came to realize they would have
to do while they were in the pietistic South. Some of them even had
to clean up their act—especially Pershing, who was fond of taking the
Lord's name in vain. The preachers asked him to stop, and he did. The
Rev. B. V. Mull, in particular, greatly bothered by Pershing's previous
declarations that his religion was "a receipted grocery bill," insisted on
praying over him. The young Communist obediently bowed his head.[32]

Nevertheless, it would be a mistake to claim too much spiritual support for the strikers. Not even the holiness preachers stayed with them
for very long. The Rev. Mull, for example, soon went over to the other
side, because he found membership in the NTWU "antagonistic to his
membership in the Ku Klux Klan"; and while some of the mill-village
pastors occasionally admitted that the workers had had real grievances
under Johnstone's management, they maintained that these problems
were now being eradicated and that the strike was therefore pointless.
The strikers had been misled by their Communist leaders and should
return to work and to the care of those who knew them best, their
employers. As the tide of mob violence increased in Gastonia, the failure of the town's clergy to condemn it was often noticed outside the
community and deservedly criticized. But the tone of the ministers'
responses to the strikers had been firmly set in the strike's first week.
They were, as Pope showed, mere adjuncts of the mill owners.[33]

By the end of the strike's second week, sufficient press attention
had been paid to it, within North Carolina at least, to disturb some
liberals as to the developing potential for violence. The views of the
state's leading newspaper, the *News and Observer*, have already been
noted. Some influential citizens were also beginning to express their
concerns. Chapel Hill social scientist Harriet Herring wrote to Beulah
Amidon of the *Survey Graphic* about the potential for violence that the
"terror over the word Communism" excited, and she blamed Commissioner Wood, as much as anyone, for this complication. He usually kept
in the background, she said, but not in this case. It was a "bit amusing," she thought, "to see North Carolina with her violent antipathy to

federal bureaus, lapping up everything its agent says and putting it in streamer headlines across the papers."[34]

Nevertheless, the strike had occasioned little attention outside the state, except in the increasingly frenzied pages of the *Daily Worker*. Nor was it likely to do so, for it was clearly coming to an end. Production at the Loray Mill had slowed but had never ceased. Vera Buch had noted on her arrival in Gastonia that the eighteen hundred strikers she had been told to expect were simply not there. "There were not one thousand," she said. "There were a few hundred at best." The numbers at the mass meetings were always inflated due to the presence of workers from other mills, but after the first flush of enthusiasm, it was not long before many of the Loray strikers started going back to work. By April 16 the day shift was pretty much back to normal, and the night shift workers were also drifting back. Many strikers, too, had left Gastonia to seek work elsewhere, partly because of inadequate relief supplies. They needed to feed their families. Attendances at mass meetings were falling away, and Beal and his associates were spending increasing amounts of time away from Loray at other strikes in the area that were smaller and usually unorganized but that the NTWU hoped to influence. The Loray management seemed to have won. National attention, therefore, was unlikely.[35] But this situation was to change, thanks to the events of the early morning hours of April 18.

On his arrival in Gastonia, Beal had been able to rent a small wooden shack on the main street of West Gastonia, not far from the mill, and this shack had become the strike headquarters. Once the strike got underway, the need for more space became quickly apparent, especially when Amy Schechter arrived to organize the distribution of food relief. Fortunately, the NTWU was able to hire an empty brick building adjacent to the headquarters, and the strikers went there daily to collect their food supplies. In order to protect these supplies, several strikers slept in these buildings each evening. There were ten there on the night of April 17–18.[36]

The details of what happened in the early hours of the morning can never be fully recovered. What can be said with reasonable certainty is that around 1 A.M., a mob of masked men, variously estimated at between fifty and two hundred strong, descended on the strike headquarters, overpowered the guards and, using axes and sledgehammers, literally hacked the structure to pieces. So thorough was their work that within ten minutes there was nothing left but "a mass of kindling wood." When they turned their attention to the relief headquarters, the mob members found the brick structure more resistant to their hammering, so instead they destroyed everything they found there, scattering flour in the street and grinding eggs and vegetables under their feet until nothing useable was left. They destroyed $225 worth of produce in all. They then melted into the darkness, presumably having done their work in such silence that the majority of the National Guardsmen, sleeping less than one hundred yards away, were left undisturbed, although some of them did arrive after it was all over, just in time to arrest the strikers guarding the building. Amy Schechter, too, was arrested the next morning when she came to inspect the damage. Beal and Pershing were not detained, because they were both away from Gastonia at the time. However, none of the perpetrators were ever caught.[37]

There was considerable disagreement as to who was responsible for the outrage, but Tom Jimison was in no doubt at all. In an angry telegram to Governor Gardner, Jimison blamed "the organized Babbittry of Gaston County" and called it the "logical outcome of the campaign of the *Gastonia Gazette* and sympathizers of mill owners wherein American citizens have been branded opponents of God, religion and the flag because they have asked a living wage." The commanders of the troops "have indulged such talk," he noted, and he went on to remind Gardner that "my clients the strikers look to you with confidence to see that thorough investigation is made and to see they are protected." A few days later he was even more specific. His investigations, he told Forrest Bailey of the ACLU, showed that "the acts of the mob were known and condoned by officers of the National Guard and that members of the military actually participated in the destruction." Moreover, a number of them had been identified; he held affidavits to that effect.[38]

The *Gastonia Daily Gazette* was no less certain as to where responsibility lay. Ultimately, the paper argued, "Beal and Pershing and their crowd are responsible for last night's happening, by whomever committed. Their whole program has been one of incendiarism." A day or two later, the paper was even more direct in assigning the blame to the strikers themselves. Pointing out that the guards were supposedly asleep when the raid occurred—in itself a highly suspicious circumstance—the paper came to the astonishing conclusion that Beal and Pershing had staged the whole affair: they had destroyed their own headquarters in a last, desperate attempt to bolster waning interest in the failing strike. This line the paper ran only for a few days, soon realizing that not even the mill managers' friends would swallow such an explanation.[39]

Certainly those sympathetic to the strike did not. The ACLU was outraged and immediately offered a reward of $100 for the arrest of the perpetrators. Governor Gardner, too, was forced into action. He called on the county solicitor, John G. Carpenter, "to discover and prosecute those who destroyed the headquarters of striking textile workers in Gastonia," and he even retained a private detective to work undercover to assist in ferreting out the villains. A grand jury duly met to investigate the violence, listened to more than seventy witnesses, and eventually concluded that it could find insufficient evidence to fix the blame on anyone. Governor Gardner's detective, Robert L. Lumsden, was no more successful. Most people in Gastonia were afraid to talk to him, he reported to the governor's executive assistant. "It is an impossibility it seems, to get anything worth while [*sic*] direct from any of these mill workers; either the ins or the outs. They are simply NOT going to talk to anyone." People knew who had done the job, all right; it was just that everyone, simply everyone, was "keeping quiet."[40]

Lumsden may have been unsuccessful in finding the perpetrators, but he had identified one aspect of the Gastonia experience in 1929: the climate of fear that had enveloped the town and that made the vigilantism and the recurring acts of violence possible. Writing in 1942, Liston Pope had no doubt as to who had organized the destruction of the strike headquarters. It was the first act of the Committee of One Hundred, a citizens' committee formed "under the aegis of employers," which soon "became the focal point of acts of violence against the strikers." The Committee of One Hundred (or the Black Hundred, as it was sometimes called) soon became part of the demonology for those sympathetic to the strike. "The day the soldiers left Gastonia," wrote Tom Tippett, "the Loray Mill organized its own local force into a Committee of 100, most of whom were deputized as sheriffs or special policemen"; this group conducted a "reign of terror" from then on. The Communist Bill Dunne called it "the strong arm squad of the Loray mill, composed of superintendents, foremen, specially privileged employees, professional thugs and special police deputies," and he said its job was to wage systematic violence against the strikers and those who supported them.[41]

Everyone, it seemed, knew of the Committee. Judge Pender A. McElroy, appointed by Governor Gardner much later in the year to probe the circumstances surrounding the murder of Ella May Wiggins, asked several witnesses such matter-of-fact and detailed questions about its activities that denial was simply not possible. Indeed, the Loray managers made no attempt to disavow its existence, though they vigorously protested that it had no violent purpose. It was not a vigilante group, they said, but rather an exercise in participatory democracy. In order to screen strikers seeking reinstatement, the mill announced, "The mill management recently decided to adopt a new policy . . . to be founded on the opinion of those working in the mill. Thus, a committee of one hundred was appointed, this group being made up of workers from all departments of the mill, representative workers from each section being elected to serve. It was the designated duty of this committee to pass upon the acceptability of those strikers who might apply for their former places in the mill."[42]

Few were fooled by this explanation. Moreover, most knew perfectly well who headed the Committee and directed its activities: Major Bulwinkle. However, its real purpose was hard to document in 1929. Few of its members ever talked about it. Lawyers for the strikers were constantly frustrated in their efforts to obtain relevant evidence that would stand up in court. Indeed, only one former member, H. W. Branch, even agreed to detail the Committee's activities from the witness stand, at the trial of those allegedly responsible for Wiggins's death, and his evidence was eventually deemed inadmissible. Nevertheless, what he told the lawyers was a convincing tale about a highly orchestrated campaign of violence, directed by mill management and run through the mill's intelligence officer, Bruce Abernathy. Its efforts were aimed at destroying the NTWU, and its members were willing "to do everything necessary" to accomplish this. Yet despite Branch's statement, lawyers admitted that they had made little headway in "establishing the existence" of the Committee to a court's satisfaction. It was always a shadowy body, but at the same time central to the unfolding tapestry of violence and tragedy in Gastonia.[43]

Whether or not formation of the Committee of One Hundred was linked to the withdrawal of the National Guardsmen, certainly their departure and replacement by forty special deputy sheriffs was the signal for violence to escalate. Not even their supporters defended the character of some of the men chosen for the job. While they admitted that some of the deputies were of "disreputable character," local authorities complained that "no others could be secured" because the rate of pay was so low. Indeed, ominous signs of an increasingly confrontational approach had occurred even before the destruction of the strike headquarters. On April 17, Ellen Dawson had been arrested and jailed on a New Jersey warrant charging that she had violated federal immigration laws. The charge was a trumped-up one, and Jimison secured her release on bond, but the need for her to return north to defend it soon led to her permanent departure from the Gastonia scene. Vera Buch wished Dawson had not left quite so "joyfully," that she had shown some sense of comradeship for those few who remained to face the violence to come.[44]

They did not have to wait very long for its arrival. In order to prevent picketing, the Gastonia city council had rushed through a local ordinance banning parading in the city without a permit. The strikers determined to challenge this ordinance, both in the courts and on the streets. With the troops gone, violence was only to be expected. On April 22, the union called a mass meeting, which was addressed by Pershing, Buch, Schechter, Beal, and Reeve—the full leadership complement, in fact. Each stressed the need to defy the prohibitive ordinance and to march through the Loray village and down to the business section of town. When the meeting was over, a large crowd, about five hundred strong, set off to make the point. Shortly after entering the city limits, they met with a force of about fifty deputies, armed with pistols, rifles, blackjacks, and bayonets, and with orders to stop the march. The deputies went about their business with a will, attacking the unarmed marchers with a ferocity born of the tension of the past three weeks. Marchers were punched, kicked, pricked with bayonets, and bashed with rifle butts. Thirty were arrested, and many more retreated to their meeting place, cut and bleeding.

Of those injured, two in particular ensured heightened attention for the strike outside the area. W. Legette Blythe, a reporter for the *Charlotte Observer* who had come not to demonstrate but to cover the march, was ordered by one of the newly created deputies, W. W.

Bindeman, to move on. When he was a little tardy doing so, Bindeman, who until the previous day had been employed as a guard at one of the county's chain-gang camps and presumably was used to being obeyed with alacrity, used his pistol to club the reporter into unconsciousness. Bindeman was quickly dismissed for his action, which was roundly condemned by both the mayor and Carpenter, the county solicitor, but from Gastonia's point of view, the damage had been done. "The Blythe incident," reported the *News and Observer*, "has stirred Gastonia as have few occurrences during the strike." Incidentally, Bindeman was not long without work. He was immediately hired by the Loray Mill as a security guard.[45]

The second of the many victims of the violence to be singled out for attention was Ada Howell, a fifty-year-old striker. She had not, in fact, been part of the parade that day but had simply been on her way to the relief store when she met deputy G. B. Prather. He set about her with enthusiasm, severely bruising her head and face, blackening both of her eyes, and cutting her with his bayonet. Photographers caught her dazedly wandering the streets, her clothing "spattered with blood." Later, she told Mary Vorse that Jimison had suggested that she keep the dress as evidence, without washing it, but this she simply could not do: "I didn't have enough dresses to lay these clothes away." Her bewildered conclusion was that the policeman "had acted like crazy men." Howell's story, like Blythe's, helped ensure that the violence in Gastonia did not go unnoticed outside the area. The *News and Observer*, for example, called for immediate state action to restore North Carolina's good name. The "misguided, hysterical people of Gaston" had created "a creature infinitely worse than a cotton mill full of communists, thuggery under the guise of law, doing the business of a corporation chartered in Rhode Island. The textile interests of North Carolina must not feel called upon to make common cause with the Loray Mill in this situation," the editors concluded angrily. They called on the governor to put a stop to displays of "lawlessness on the part of the law."[46]

Of the thirty arrested, many were women; most were strikers, but the group also included Schechter and Buch. The women were held together in the county jail, and most of them had to spend the night there before Jimison could arrange bail. Forty years later, Buch remembered that night as, for her, one of the most significant moments of the whole Gastonia experience. They talked through the night, get-

Ada Howell after her beating (Originally published in the Labor Defender)

ting to know each other, comparing lives, sharing experiences, singing songs—Buch and Schechter sang the Red Flag, the local strikers their own ballads. "It was a time, too, for unburdening a lot of grievances," she later wrote. She and Amy became much closer to the striking women as a result of that one night. For Buch, it was an important step in overcoming the self-doubt that had plagued her since arriving in Gastonia. She knew now that she could be a leader and that the local people would follow her. Increasingly, it was Vera Buch who provided the strike effort with backbone.[47]

One of the grievances they aired then, and one that certainly rankled with the female strike leaders, was the question of who would do the picketing. Always an important issue, the matter had now acquired urgency due to the certainty of violent response. Beal simply refused to picket; that was not the job of the strike leader, he argued, and he would not budge from this position, despite the intense and obvious annoyance it gave his fellow organizers. He defended himself by arguing that, much as he wanted to join the rank and file, the responsibility of being leader precluded him from doing so, to his great regret. But it remained a divisive chord in the ranks of the strike's leadership, one that was reflected in the local strikers' responses to picketing. From the beginning, Beal had stressed that there was to be no violence on the strikers' part, no matter what the provocation, and the strikers had largely followed this rule. Given the escalating level of violence from the other side, however, many of the men itched to retaliate. In particular, they could not see the point of putting themselves at risk on the picket line without their guns. They were willing to picket, they said, but only if they marched armed. When Beal refused to allow this, they refused to go. While Vera Buch's later assertions that women did most of the picketing in Gastonia cannot be sustained—the press reported too many instances of men being arrested for that to be true— it is nevertheless clear that from April 21 until picketing stopped altogether, it was the women who did most of the marching, who faced most of the violence, and who went to jail.[48]

Women were also less inclined to return to work than men. In fact, the men's urge to find work was something the northern-born strike leadership had great difficulty with. Imbued with notions of the collective and of union discipline, they were at first inclined to regard those who went back to the mill to get a little "folding money," who left the village to seek work elsewhere, or who, if they had the chance, simply returned to the family farm, as scabs of the worst order. Women, possibly because of their child-rearing responsibilities, were less inclined to take these routes, hence their reputation for greater resolution. Later, some of the leaders revised their views a little, realizing that northern assumptions were often simply not relevant among these "hill people turned mill workers." "Loyalty to the union did not waver," Carl (then Karl) Reeve remembered, "although in some cases it was unorthodox. A flow and ebb developed in the number of strikers. Some re-entered the mill to earn enough for a little food, then rejoined strike activities." He came to realize that these people—almost always men —"were not ordinary scabs." They were, in fact, "heart and soul with the union."

Sophie Melvin said much the same thing. While she agreed with Buch that there had been "some problems" with guns, she believed that the economic necessity of finding money for food took the men away from Gastonia during the day—something the women, with their children to care for, simply could not do. Moreover, Melvin recalled that contrary to stereotype, the men could not stand their enforced idleness; they hated sitting around the tent colony doing nothing. The women, who usually spent the daylight hours at home anyway, did not find the adjustment so difficult. Whatever the case, they were not, as Eleanor Copenhaver Anderson patronizingly called them, "dear old darling mountaineers," without a clue as to the implications of union membership, nor were they Buch's "complete individualists," with "no conception" of union discipline. Doubtless, many of them never did fully understand these essentially modern, urban concepts; the action of some in supporting the strike call owed much more to "the persistence of traditional personalized forms of protest" in an increasingly impersonal industrial milieu. Others, especially the younger workers, had probably begun to make connections with their urban contemporaries, and even with the Marxist rhetoric of the strike leaders. Still others, neither particularly class-conscious nor socially rebellious, nevertheless saw union action as a potential means of changing the deteriorating conditions of their lives. Members of a complex, evolving, regional working-class culture, they interpreted loyalty to the union in their own ways.[49]

Of course, one of the reasons that Buch increasingly found herself working as the strike's de facto leader was that Beal was often away from Gastonia. In fact, he did not even live there. Always concerned for his personal safety, he had taken a room in Charlotte and was driven to Gastonia each day by his bodyguard, K. O. Byers. His room's location was a closely guarded secret; not even Buch knew where it was or how to contact him. The women, on the other hand, had found rooms in the mill village. Initially, Schechter, Ellen Dawson, and Buch shared a room in a mill boardinghouse, all three sleeping in a single bed. Every week or so Ellen would take a hotel room for one night. The other two would then sneak up the stairs, bathe, wash their hair, and do their laundry—or rather Vera would. Amy would simply "keep on buying new bloomers until all the drawers and suitcases were full of the dirty ones," then send the whole lot to the local laundry. Later, after Dawson had gone, they rented rooms with strikers and their families. Buch lived for a time with the chairman of the strike committee, Roy Stroud, once the owner of a small farm in South Carolina and now a mill worker. He was violently prejudiced "against the Negroes" and boasted of having killed one in South Carolina. Eventually he went over to the "other side," she said—presumably over the race issue—but not before Manville-Jenckes had evicted the family from their village home. Buch then moved to another mill boarding-house. Schechter's residential career was similarly peripatetic. It was doubtless rather unsettling, but again, it allowed the women to be part of the strike community in a way that was not possible for Beal.[50]

Trying to implement Weisbord's ambitious plan to bring the whole southern textile industry under the aegis of the NTWU also kept Beal away from Gastonia. The Loray strike was not the only one in Gaston County where the union was active. At one time or another, Beal was involved in directing, or at least trying to influence, strike activity at the Chadwick-Hansen Mill in Pineville, the Florence Mill in Forest City, and the Wenonah Mill in Lexington. At all of these mills the cause of the strikes was the same: the stretch-out. The protests were short, sharp, spontaneous affairs, very much in the "personal response" tra-dition and quickly settled, usually by a modification of work practices. Beal's influence was probably minimal; nevertheless, his involvement took him away from Gastonia, leaving Buch in effective command.[51]

A more important strike—one in which the NTWU was directly in-volved—was the one at the American Mills in nearby Bessemer City, just six miles from Gastonia. This protest was Pershing's bailiwick be-fore his joyful departure northward; Buch then had to pick it up in addition to her Gastonia duties. Though the Bessemer City mill, like that in Gastonia, was briefly crippled and production took some time to return to normal, in terms of its aims the strike was a failure. Never-theless, the protest did result in the creation of a small but militant NTWU local in Bessemer City, and its members provided vital, sus-tained support for the strikers of the Loray Mill.[52]

Most important of all, the strike at the American Mill drew into the Gastonia story its most famous figure—its balladeer and martyr, Ella May Wiggins. Ella May was born on a farm in Sevierville, Tennes-see, in 1900, but her family was soon caught up in the swift rise and fall of the Appalachian logging industry. The Mays lived a transient existence, moving from camp to camp. During the day, Ella and her mother did the loggers' washing; in the evening, already tapping the raw talent she was to display in Gastonia, the teenager sang for the same loggers. Before she was out of her teens, however, she had mar-ried John Wiggins ("a ne'er-do-well," said some), borne the first of her nine children, and left the mountains for the Piedmont and for life in the textile mills.[53]

Ella May's daughter recalled that her mother had "wanted a life where she could be something or do something," and it was this restless questing that drove her from the hills. She did not find this life in the mill villages. Though Wiggins stayed with her until after the birth of their eighth child, he made no contribution to the support of the family. From her early twenties Ella May was the effective breadwinner. She worked in a succession of mills in the Piedmont before settling in Gaston County. Along the way, she had lost four of her children—not all at once, as the legend came to run, but successively, from various ailments. One died from pellagra, which Wiggins's biographer, Lynn Haessly, termed "the classic disease of Southern rural poverty." The death of her children left an "indelible mark" on Wiggins; of that there can be no doubt. The mills had kept her away from her children, and she hated the management for that. The separation of mill mothers from their children was a recurring theme in many of the ballads she wrote during the strike.[54]

Even before the events of 1929, Ella May had displayed strong signs of an unconventional and independent temperament, and she had also acquired a reputation among management as a troublemaker. When Wiggins left her, she reverted to her maiden name and took a lover, Charlie Shope, with whom she had her ninth child, Ella Charlotte, in November 1927; Shope was listed on the birth certificate as the father. A *Southern Textile Bulletin* article published after her death claimed that "her reputation" had been "so bad" that "long before she ever heard of communism," she had been thrown out of "several mill villages." Ella May "was a "hard boiled" type of woman," the writer recalled, "who loved a quarrel and a fight, and her home had been the scene of many disorders." She was emphatically not, in the writer's eyes, "a woman whose character was beyond complaint."[55]

The mill in which she was working when the NTWU came to Gaston County had a reputation for being one of the worst in the area; her past troubles had probably made this mill her last resort. Owned by the Goldberg family, who made a fortune by buying failing mills and "running them tightly," the American Number Two mill in Bessemer City paid wages regarded as low even for Gaston County. As a spinner, Ella May earned only about nine dollars a week for the twelve-hour night shift. It was nowhere near enough to provide for her family, even though the cottage they rented was cheaper than those in the

Children of African American textile workers in Stumptown, the Bessemer City neighborhood where Ella May lived (Originally published in the Labor Defender*)*

mill village. They lived in Stumptown, along with Bessemer City's African Americans. (Partly because of its wage policy, nearly half of the American Mill's workers were black, making it unique in Gaston County.) Because of her independence, the conditions of her life, and her dream of a better one, Ella May Wiggins welcomed the union with open arms. When the American Mill struck, she was one of the first to walk out. She was never to work again.[56]

The escalating violence in Gastonia, particularly the destruction of the strike headquarters and the attack on Legette Blythe, caught the attention of the northern press and news agencies, some of which sent reporters and feature writers to cover the protest. One of the first to come was Mary Heaton Vorse, the radical journalist and labor activist, who had been commissioned to produce an article on the strike for *Harper's*. She arrived in the wake of the first wave of violence and was frankly appalled at what she found. The odds were far from equal, she thought; indeed, it was scarcely a strike at all—more of "a relief

Fred Beal (holding child) with a group of strikers. Clarence Miller is standing at the extreme left. W. McGinnis, who was also eventually charged with murder, is directly behind Beal. (Originally published in the Labor Defender*)*

station." The leadership was inexperienced, frightened, and divided. Beal was so overwhelmed by the situation that he stayed in Charlotte, "leaving the girls in the field alone," and among those girls, his absence created a huge well of resentment in which the picketing issue loomed particularly large. For his part, Beal was highly critical of the New York office's lack of support and was depressed at the way Buch and Schechter criticized him and refused to acknowledge his leadership. The obvious love the strikers had for him, however, helped sustain his commitment. Vorse was sympathetic toward Beal, though she agreed that he had his deficiencies as a leader. "His shoulders, though broad, were not quite broad enough to carry the burden of so much hatred," she later wrote. Nevertheless, one could doubt neither the hold he had on the strikers nor the hope that he gave them. As he walked among them at strike meetings, she said, "the faces of the gaunt, earnest men and the meagerly clad women broke into smiles at the sight of him."

On the other hand, the women, in Vorse's view, did not understand that they were no longer in Passaic, New Jersey—that attitudes formed on the picket lines of northern strikes, or in Party dogma sessions, had no relevance in the South. "You know," Buch once remarked despairingly, "It's strange about these people. They are Americans like we are and yet our foreign workers in the North are much more comprehensible to us." Vorse admired Buch's dedication and courage. "She is faultlessly fearless," she wrote in her diary. Unfortunately, she also considered Buch totally unimaginative, "a pedantic communist," mouthing dogmatic irrelevancies. Moreover, she was convinced that the unkempt Schechter, with her "feverish" admiration of Earl Browder, whom she phoned every evening, was unbalanced. Vorse also found her physically unappealing: her hair was perpetually standing on end, and she always looked as if she needed a wash. "Give her nice new clothes and she would be dirty in a day," was her dismissive comment. The strike had overwhelmed them all, and they wanted desperately to go home, yet duty and idealism kept them at their posts. Vorse, who remained in Gastonia for several weeks, soon came to moderate her views on Buch, with whom she developed a firm friendship. Eventually they shared a room in the town. Her first impressions of the strike, however, were correct. The battle was lost, in part due to deficiencies in leadership, no doubt, but also due to the lack of support from the Party's central office. As Party factionalism intensified, support for its workers in the field decreased proportionally. There was never enough money for even the most basic of union activities. Both Beal and Buch recalled that they put out very few leaflets or information sheets, because they could not afford them.

The relief effort was similarly hampered by inadequate funds. Amy would never know until quite late each afternoon what cash the New York office planned to make available to her. Then, Buch said, "she would have to race to Gastonia to buy food and would give out packages of beans, flour and other staples to the strikers." The organizers, too, had to wait for the daily telegram to learn whether they would eat that night. It was, said Buch, "a hand-to-mouth affair, a wretched situation, beyond our control and also beyond our understanding." Their enthusiasm, she conceded with feeling, "was considerably dampened by our pitiful lack of means," and their anger intensified as they came to realize that funds contributed by sympathizers for their relief were being diverted to purposes the Party considered more pressing. Mean-

while, the *Daily Worker* continued to print wild exaggerations of the
success of the strike—so at variance with reality that Buch and the
others tried to prevent strikers from reading them—but by the end of
April, the mill's management had clearly won.[57]

Mary Vorse came to profoundly admire the collective spirit of the
strike leaders, for they were isolated and obviously out of their depth,
yet extremely committed. "The spectacle of the Northern strikers,
these ardent young people, so remote from home, so surrounded with
the hate of the well-to-do, so surrounded with the affection of the
workers, is a strange one indeed," she remarked in her diary. They
were "very middle class and very refined in their aspect," and though
they had been at strikes before, they had never experienced such isolation, such hostility. There had always been some friendly faces in the
general community. Not in Gastonia. Not even Vorse fully appreciated
the depth of the town's hatred of the strikers until after she suggested
to Tom Jimison that a few of the town's more prominent women be
asked to contribute to a milk fund, so that at least the strikers' infants
would get proper nourishment. This type of gesture had been made
in Passaic and in other strikes with which she had been associated.
His bitter reply—"You don't understand. You think, in the North, of
workers as human beings. The folk here think of them as 'hands'"—
brought home to the journalist the chasm that existed between the
strikers and the good citizens of Gastonia.[58]

Nevertheless, Buch and the others stuck to their tasks. Their days
—"those busy, purposeful, frustrating Loray days," as she later described them—took on a routine of sorts, starting with the meeting
of the strike committee each morning at nine and ending with the
evening's rally or, for variation, educational lecture (usually about
an aspect of life in the Soviet Union) and, finally, a song session.
In between there was much to be done: there were the pickets to
see to, the children to care for, the scabs to visit and attempt to
convert, the meager relief supplies to distribute. When Beal was in
town, he would hold union leadership training classes each morning.
Those who attended regularly included Red Hendricks, Dewey Martin,
Russell Knight, Delmar Hampton, Gladys Wallace, Louis McLoughlin, William McGinnis, Ruby McMahon, Robert Allen, and Ella May.
Keeping themselves busy, as they undoubtedly did, prevented the
leaders from dwelling too directly on the obvious fact of failure.[59]

In the confidence of victory, accompanied by the knowledge that the strikers were running out of food and morale, Baugh and his advisers acted on a threat they had been making since the strike's beginning. With the mill running virtually at full capacity, they decided that there was no need to allow any more strikers to return to work. Consequently, on May 6 the management announced that evictions from the mill village would begin the next day; only those pronounced by the company physician as unfit to be moved would be allowed to remain. The following morning the deputies assigned to the job went about their work with enthusiasm. The first house to be entered was that of J. A. Valentine, a member of the strike committee. He and his family were summarily ejected and their furniture dumped in the yard, although his six-year-old daughter, Sylvia, was recovering from smallpox and "still bore definite signs of the disease" on her face. By nightfall the village had taken on a "disorganized appearance"—it looked like "a gypsy encampment," Mary Vorse thought, with families clustered in small groups around piles of old furniture and household utensils. Some of them were even cooking in front of their homes or sitting on chairs there, watching the new occupants, people who had taken their jobs, moving in under the watchful eyes of the deputies. The management evicted the residents of two hundred homes, or about a thousand people in all.

Though some of those turned out were charged with "affray" or "boisterous cursing," there was in fact remarkably little resistance. When the deputies came to move Mrs. Etta McClure, the mother of five children, she "expressed her opinion to the officers freely . . . in language that could not be termed civil under the greatest stretch of imagination" and threatened "to burn the whole place up." She eventually calmed down, however, and moved out with the rest. Her husband, also a striker, had gone back to the mountains to farm, and "she seemed at a loss as to what to do." However, she refused to let the company store her furniture. "I'll let it rot first," she said. Only John Robinson, of all the evictees, threatened the deputies with firearms, and he was soon overpowered, though Daisy McDonald reportedly put a pistol on the table and threatened to shoot anyone who handled her aged mother roughly or tried to hurry her out of their house. In fact, most of those evicted left of their own accord, dispirited and bewildered, itself a sign of their collapsing morale. The strike leaders could do little

Evicted striker's family (Originally published in the Labor Defender*)*

except promise that they would provide the strikers with tents, which were due soon from New York. Few people believed them.[60]

But the evictions did spark further national attention on events in Gastonia. Both Vorse and Tom Tippett, a freelance labor journalist, filed angry stories that were picked up by northern dailies and liberal magazines, while the ACLU increased its activities on the strikers' behalf, organizing an emergency aid committee headed by Norman Thomas. Such well-known and socially prominent citizens as Corliss Lamont, Frederick Vanderbilt Field, George Dupont Jr., Herbert Croly, Arthur Garfield Hays, and Susan Brandeis were among the seventy-odd who signed an appeal for funds. The evictions and the publicity surrounding them also ensured that when a delegation of strikers came to Washington to take their case to the nation's legisla-

tors—or, more particularly, to lobby the Senate Committee on Manufactures to support Montana senator Burton K. Wheeler's proposal for
an investigation into the southern textile industry—the press would
give them more than passing attention.[61]

Carl Reeve led the delegation of six men and five women, which
included "Red" Hendricks, later to be tried for his life; tiny fourteen-
year-old Binnie Green, described by the *New York World* as a "Textile
Mill Waif"; and Ella May. She had been chosen because of the enthusiasm with which she had thrown herself into strike activity and the
aptitude she had displayed for it. She was a regular attender at Beal's
classes on union issues and became one of Bessemer City's best organizers. This trip to Washington was her first time outside the Piedmont.[62]

The delegation had little luck with the senators, most of whom
had already left Washington, though Senator Wheeler and Robert La
Follette did meet with them individually. They fared no better at
the annual convention of the national Women's Trade Union League
(WTUL), which they had hoped to address. Led by Reeve and carrying an NTWU banner, they attempted to seize the podium, but the
convention adjourned rather than let them have the floor. It was "unfortunate," said Ethel Smith of the WTUL's board of directors, "that
Communist workers got into Gastonia and organized the strikers."
The NTWU was "under Communist leadership," she asserted, and in
her view, the middle-class, AFL-oriented WTUL ladies should thus
have nothing to do with the ragged group. A few individual delegates
listened to the strikers, however, to the obvious discomfort of some of
their fellows.[63]

The delegation had one quite fortuitous moment of triumph. On
May 10, as they drifted rather aimlessly about the Capitol, the strikers
happened to run into Lee Slater Overman, the junior senator from
North Carolina. He was engaged in the pleasurable task of escorting
a delegation of young women from Greensboro's University of North
Carolina Women's College around the hallowed halls when he came
upon the little group. There was a remarkable contrast between the
sleek, well-fed young college women and the shabby, emaciated millhands. Overman tried to look the other way, but he could not. With
obvious reluctance he started to talk to them. Refusing to believe that
Binnie Green was fourteen, he stupidly told her to get back to school.

Binnie Green, a fourteen-year-old striker who toured for the ILD
(Originally published in the Labor Defender*)*

In the awkward silence that followed, it was Ella May who seized the moment. She took the senator on. How could mill children go to school? she demanded. "How can I send my children to school when I can't make enough to clothe them decently? When I go to the mill at night I have to lock them up at night by their lone selves. I can't have anyone to look after them. Last winter when two of them were sick with the flu I had to leave them at home in bed when I went to work. I can't get them enough good clothes to send them to Sunday School." [64]

"Lock them up at night by their lone selves": that was the phrase the press seized on. Though Senator Overman excused himself from the gathering as soon as he could—in pursuit, quipped one newsman, of the "glorious girls" from Greensboro—the damage had been done. Ella May's outburst made national news, and the delegation was sought after by journalists, anxious for similar stories of deprivation. In vain did North Carolina's aging senior senator, Furnifold Simmons, deplore the group's conduct, claiming that they had been "very carefully dressed in their poorest garments." Reeve was right when he called it "a break through in the national coverage of the strike." And it was in large part due to Ella May, whom the *New York World* inaccurately termed a "tiny mother of four children." Her star was on the rise, at least in strike and Party circles. By the end of the month, the *Daily Worker* was calling her the "militant Bessemer City strike speaker."[65]

The publicity the delegation received at least had the effect of galvanizing the Party leadership into action. Tents eventually arrived from New York, and so did some reinforcements for the organizers. Nineteen-year-old Sophie Melvin of the Young Communist League (YCL) came to work with the younger children; Edith Saunders Miller, one year older than Sophie, came with her husband Clarence to help with those a little older. These three young idealists's lives were to change in the weeks ahead.

Sophie Melvin recalled the days spent in the tent colony, as it came to be called, as busy and fulfilling. She had hitchhiked down from New York, responding to a call for volunteers. Born in the Ukraine in 1910, Melvin had come to the United States with her family in 1921, after the death of her father. She had been active in YCL work since 1924, and at the age of sixteen, she had helped organize a children's playground during the Passaic strike, thus freeing their mothers for strike activity. This was her job in Gastonia as well, relieving the women of child care during parts of the day so that they could attend meetings, help develop the colony's site, or just get some sleep. Here she worked closely with Daisy McDonald, a tall, dark, immensely dignified striker, part Cherokee and sole breadwinner for her family of seven children. Her husband, a tubercular man with only one leg, was unable to work. Intensely loyal to the NTWU, she and her family suffered much for her commitment. In some recompense, the Party arranged for her son, Elmer, to attend a Young Pioneer's camp in the Soviet Union. Edith Miller worked with the teenagers, holding regular classes that included discussions of political and economic issues. These classes' content would become notorious during the Aderholt trial.[66]

The tent colony was erected on a vacant lot on North Loray Street, owned by Henry Myers, one of the few local citizens who publicly supported the NTWU. Equally important, he helped finance the purchase of lumber for a new headquarters building there, to be erected by the strikers themselves. In terms of restoring their morale, Beal considered nothing more important than the construction of this simple shed. It bound them together again, he said. The sixteen-by-twenty-six-foot structure was finished on May 18, and the strikers celebrated with a

Tom Jimison (back row with felt hat) and a group of strikers. "Red" Hendricks is directly in front of Jimison. Daisy McDonald is second from the left in the back row. (Originally published in the Labor Defender*)*

"jollification." A crowd of more than a thousand people, obviously not all from the Loray Mill, attended this dedication: there was barbecue, there was fun and a feeling of community, there was a string band for young people to dance to. Beal, Buch and Reeve all spoke, praising the strikers for their loyalty "in sticking to the union," but on the whole, it was simply a night of fun and song.

Though Ella May, "the minstrel of the strike," is not recorded as singing that night, she probably did, for as Beal later recollected, "no evening passed without getting a new song from our Ella May. . . . She would stand somewhere in a corner, chewing tobacco or snuff and fumbling over the notes of a new poem scribbled on the back of a union leaflet. Suddenly someone would call for her to sing and other voices would take up the suggestion. Then in a deep, resonant voice she would give us a simple ballad." Perhaps that night she sang her most famous song, "Mill Mother's Lament," which in its poignant words of deprivation and hope said so much about her own life and dreams.

> We leave our home in the morning
> We kiss our children goodbye
> While we slave for the bosses
> Our children scream and cry.
>
> And when we draw our money
> Our grocers' bills to pay
> Not a cent to keep for clothing
> Not a cent to lay away.
>
> And on that very evening
> Our little one will say
> I need some shoes, dear mother
> And so does sister May
>
> Now it grieves the heart of a mother
> You everyone must know
> But we cannot buy for our children
> Our wages are too low
>
> Now listen to the workers
> Both women and you men
> Let's win for them the victory
> I'm sure t'will be no sin.

The words may have changed a little from performance to performance, but the sentiment did not. "Mill Mother's Lament" epitomized the resentments of Ella May and so many other women, and their aspirations for a better life for their children. Fittingly and tragically, it was sung at her funeral.[67]

Occasions such as this "jollification" became the main mechanism for reviving the strikers' spirits, of sustaining community: music was an essential component of them, and it was the women who provided it. The union songs that Beal and the others brought with them and earnestly tried to get the strikers to sing made no sense to these southerners. "Solidarity Forever," sung as it was to the tune of "John

Brown's Body," was in fact downright offensive. What the strikers did instead was adapt the traditional ballads and folk tunes of their common culture, writing new words for old songs. "Up in Old Loray," for example, was sung to the tune "On Top of Old Smoky," "Mill Mother's Lament," to "Little Mary Phagan." Daisy McDonald's "The Speakers Didn't Mind," a particular favorite, was sung to the tune of "The Wreck of the Old 97" and included these stanzas:

> They arrested the men, left the women alone
> To do the best they can,
> They tore down their tents, run them out in the woods.
> "If you starve we don't give a damn."

> Fred Beal and Sophie and all the rest,
> Are now best friends we know,
> For they came South to organize
> When no one else would go.

Historians of folk culture have explored the deeper meanings of these Loray songs, but for our purposes it is sufficient to say that while Ella May was not the only balladeer—as Vera Buch once said, "They all sang ballads"—it was her voice, her words, which were remarkable then and remain so today. They sang other songs too, of course. Amy Schechter, with her English background, proved to have a repertoire of bawdy musical ballads that the strikers loved to hear. "Oh girls, oh girls, take warning and never let it be / Never let a sailor go higher than your knee," she would sing in a broad cockney accent, to hoots of laughter from all present. Yet it was the songs of the local women— of frail eleven-year-old Odell Corley, whom the ILD dubbed the poet laureate of the strike; of the tall, strikingly beautiful Daisy McDonald; and, above all, of Ella May—that sustained the beleaguered band when most everything else seemed lost.[68]

A week later, there was another celebration at the tent colony, this time to mark its official opening. Seventeen tents had now been erected, each able to house twelve people. Again, there was music, dancing, and song. More ominously, there were also armed strikers mingling with the revelers. They had lost one headquarters building to violence, and they were determined not to lose another. On May 16,

Guards at the tent colony, just before Aderholt's death
(Courtesy Wide World Photos)

Roy Stroud, the secretary of the NTWU local, wrote to Governor
Gardner warning him of that fact. The strikers would defend the new
building "at all costs," he asserted, and it would be patrolled by armed
guards around the clock. Two experienced and tough northern unionists, Joseph Harrison and George Carter, both veterans of Passaic,
had arrived to help organize this activity. Beal did not entirely ap-
prove of these measures; nevertheless, by late May the new structure
was heavily guarded. A dozen men, usually "armed with shotguns or
other instruments of protection," slept there each night or patrolled
the perimeter once after sundown. They habitually stopped people in
the street to ask their business—something that bothered Gastonia's
police chief, Orville Aderholt. He agreed that the strikers had a perfect right to defend and protect their property, but "they did not have
a right to guard surrounding streets." Given the tension in the town
and the outrage of mill management at such behavior, violence was
always just around the corner.[69]

Though the building of the new headquarters no doubt raised their
flagging spirits and the presence of armed guards possibly made them
feel safer, the strikers in the colony could not have avoided succumb-
ing at times to the bleak belief that it was all over bar the shouting. The mill was now operating at near normal levels, and manage-

ment had made it abundantly clear that no more of the strikers could come back to work. Moreover, there was increasing dissension in their ranks about the NTWU's policy on African Americans. The Communist Party had declared the period between May 10 and May 20 to be National Negro Week, a time when the Party's commitment to racial equality would be reinforced. Nationwide activities were planned. In Gastonia, the NTWU representatives organized a highly publicized debate over the admission of African Americans as full members. The debate was held on May 10, and it was eventually agreed that blacks would be invited to join the Loray local and that the invitation would be extended not only to "Negroes who are now employed in textile plants as porters, sweepers, elevator hands and in similar jobs, but all Negroes be asked to join, including domestic servants, cooks and launderers."[70] Every leaflet issued by the strike committee would henceforth be addressed "To All Workers, Negro and White."

Given that African Americans comprised less than 1 percent of the Loray workforce, the widening of the membership qualifications at Party direction was intended to ensure that the local would have a token number of black members. If so, the result must have been disappointing. Local black leaders, particularly the clergy, warned their people against joining, and those invited to address strike meetings declined to do so, "saying that they do not propose to have anything to do with the local textile strike or union." Given that the decision to admit blacks was far from unanimous and cost the union a number of its most active members, the results must have been a bitter blow to its leadership, as well as a sober reminder of the way issues of race could always blur issues of class in the American South.[71]

Things were a little different in nearby Bessemer City's American Mill community, where blacks comprised nearly half of the workforce. Here attempts to recruit them to the NTWU's ranks were more successful, due in large part to the efforts of Ella May. Vera Buch was unstinting in her praise of Ella May's work with African Americans. Vera herself could make no headway with black workers at all; they would not even look at her, she said. But it was different when she took Ella May along. Ella May was a resident of Stumptown, so these African Americans were her neighbors; she relaxed with them on her day off, and they watched her children while she was at work. Moreover, she was no racist. "I know the colored don't like us," she once told Vera

Buch, "but if they see you're poor and humble like themselves, they'll listen to you." And listen to her they did, and some joined the union as a consequence. Buch believed that "she understood without argument the value of our union principles of racial equality," thus she was particularly dangerous to management, who may have eventually had her killed for that reason. (There is simply no evidence one way or another about who was responsible for May's death, and why.) But in any case, the way she had cast off racial prejudices again showed the singularity of Ella May's personality.[72]

Nowhere was the Party's rhetoric more at variance with reality than in the distorted way it treated the race issue. Story after story in the *Daily Worker* and *Labor Defender* emphasized the way striking workers enthusiastically supported the shattering of the barriers of race and caste in pursuit of the class struggle. In the pages of the *Daily Worker*, John H. Owens, the first black Communist to be sent to Gastonia, told of his enthusiastic reception there. As he spoke to the strikers, outlining the history of the class struggle, he sensed their apprehension turn to class solidarity. "'I have never heard a colored man make a speech before,' a soft voice said. I walked outside and sat down on some boards behind the strike headquarters. Ellen Dawson came out and shook my hand, said a sincere word of greeting and went into the hall. After that every striker was my friend . . . If Ellen Dawson vouched for me, I must be all right."[73]

But the reality was different. Owens did visit Gastonia, ready to make a speech, but the strikers would not let him. Vera Buch told the story: Owens "made one brief scared appearance at Loray," she remembered. "I recall him standing by the car looking apprehensively at all those white people surrounding him." Quickly he retreated to Charlotte, where he barricaded himself in his room until Beal got him out of town. Buch did not blame him, as she did others, for leaving the scene so quickly. "If ever anyone had a dangerous assignment," she agreed, "it was he." Not even the experienced and tough black organizer Otto Hall, Harry Haywood's brother, could do much good in Gastonia. He was sent down by the NTWU to replace Owens, but his work was inadvertently compromised from the start by Sophie Melvin. She met him in the street in Charlotte and, momentarily forgetting where she was, greeted him affectionately. The incident was noticed, and Hall's presence was thus marked. After a few days of fruitless endeavor, it was mutually agreed that Hall should return north. There was simply nothing he could do in Gastonia; in fact, his presence in the tent colony only stirred up trouble. So he departed, smuggled out of Gaston County in the rumble seat of an old Ford, just to be on the safe side. Legend (in the form of the *Daily Worker*) later had it that on the night of Aderholt's death, Hall had been saved from a lynch mob by a group of resolute white strikers who had secured his safe return home. The truth was clearly much less heroic.[74]

Despite all of the *Daily Worker*'s stories about African Americans addressing enthusiastic strike rallies, no black unionist ever mounted a public rostrum in Gastonia itself. Such an action was a virtual impossibility in the South of the 1920s. Even the slightest rumor that such a thing might happen carried with it real potentiality for strife. Beal knew this full well, and he vainly tried to persuade Weisbord to deemphasize the issue. The hostile press knew it just as well and gleefully seized upon it as often as they could. The union leaders had "had too much to say about the negro," the *Gastonia Daily Gazette* crowed gleefully in mid-May. "Albert Weisbord, secretary of the National, in particular, showed the poorest possible judgement on this question," as mill workers "back away fast when social equality with the negro is preached." In this the newspaper was correct. Nothing separated the strikers from each other, or from their leadership, more sharply than the race question. It was simply more powerful as a divisive force than class was as a unifier.[75]

For the Communists, insistence on pressing the issue of racial equality in a place as hostile as Gastonia became, as Theodore Draper said, "a trial of faith and courage." By their persistence, they "were trying to prove something to the world, to the Negroes, to the Comintern, and to themselves." From this perspective, the effort was much more important than the result, and to a degree the Party passed the test. It wobbled from time to time, but in the end the insistence on full equality remained firm. At the local level, though, the cost was serious dissension and disaffection. Paul Crouch insisted that this "ceaseless harping" on the race issue fatally weakened the Loray local and caused many original supporters of the strike to become even more vehemently antagonistic toward the NTWU than toward the mill owners.

It was ironic that on June 7, the night Aderholt was shot, the captain of the tent colony's guards, William Sedell, was in jail because he had been fighting with a fellow striker over racial equality.[76]

By the end of May, most observers considered the strike to be well over. The mill was working with a full crew, production had reached prestrike levels, and because the tent colony was located some distance from the mill village, those few holdouts who lived there were not visible. "Although Fred Erwin Beal, Carl Reeve and other leaders of the National Textile Workers Union still are in Gastonia," reported the *Gastonia Daily Gazette*, "little is heard of the strike." With great relief, the residents of Gaston County turned to other, more enjoyable things as summer approached. A popular new film, *The Trial of Mary Duigan*, had opened in town, and crowds flocked to see it. In nearby Charlotte, the thirty-ninth reunion of Confederate veterans provided ample occasion for parades, pageants, sentimental outpourings, and displays of southern patriotism. On June 5, six thousand people were "thrilled" by the Confederate pageant, in which one hundred local actors portrayed "The Rise and Fall of the Confederacy." The "contentment of the slaves" was particularly well depicted, the local drama critic thought. The textile strike? Why, it was "ended and over with in North Carolina, so long ago as to be an almost forgotten circumstance."[77]

But not by Fred Beal. He had learned much from the past three months. In particular, he understood that what had applied in Passaic or New Bedford did not necessarily hold true for the Carolina Piedmont. Just because many of the original strikers had returned to work did not mean that they were irretrievably lost to the cause. Too many had told him otherwise, had apologized for going back—"I just had to," they said. But they had assured him that they would come out again whenever he gave the call. The "unrest and dissatisfaction that caused the walk-out," recorded one observer, "is greater than ever." Nothing had changed. Beal now understood that "the scab of today was the striker of tomorrow," and he laid his plans for another mass walkout, scheduled for the night of June 7.[78]

3 THE SHOOTING

Mary Vorse, who had been in Elizabethton reporting on the strike situation there, returned to Gastonia on June 4. What she sensed, rather than saw, worried her profoundly. "Something's going to happen, Vera," she purportedly warned her roommate, Buch, "and perhaps soon. I can smell it. I smell danger here." Having delivered herself of this warning, she followed Reeve and Pershing back to New York—and safety. Strangely, at the time Vorse made no public mention of this premonition. Rather, in her descriptions of the scenes she found in the tent colony on her return, she emphasized the general sense of well-being that prevailed as spring turned to summer. The colony was "picturesquely set among woods near a ravine," she reported. Those living there looked well; they had gained weight, and the women's faces, so ravaged and anxious during the days of the evictions, were now rested. Sophie Melvin was working well with the young children, teaching them "organized play." Not even the presence of the heavily armed guards disturbed the general atmosphere of calm and tranquility. "It did not seem possible," she thought, "that further trouble should occur."[1]

Vorse did, however, remark on the number of prowlers around the colony and on the frequent threats from townspeople that the new headquarters would soon go the way of the old one. Indeed, the *Daily Worker* reported that the guards had loosed a few rounds at some prowlers and had apparently hit at least one, as "screams were heard." The guards were simply making good on their promise to shoot any of the "bosses' flunkies" who attempted to raid the colony, claimed the paper. In the absence of any corroborating evidence, the assertion that a prowler had been shot must be taken with extreme caution, yet it is true that the guards foiled at least one attempt to poison the colony's water supply, probably by the same person who had successfully fouled

Ella May's well a few days earlier. Despite the apparent collapse of the strike, the presence of the strikers, and especially of the NTWU leadership, was still a source of great tension in the county.[2]

Perhaps those who opposed the strike so vehemently shared Beal's conviction that "today's scab is tomorrow's striker," that the calm that had returned to Loray was an uneasy one and easily broken. The Manville-Jenckes intelligence officers certainly knew, through their spy network, that Beal was planning a renewal of the strike. Whether out of desperation, or from a conviction based on the knowledge that the discontent that prompted the original walkout had not been alleviated, Beal had come to believe that another one was possible. The fact that the *Daily Worker* consistently predicted this in early June provides some evidence that the idea was more than Beal's wishful thinking. Carl (then Karl) Reeve wrote on June 3, for example, that those workers "who have returned to work are not to be considered ordinary scabs. Most of them are friendly to the union, attend the union meetings and declare that only starvation" forced them back to the mill. The union leadership was "gradually educating" them into "the meaning of their strike-breaking," and many were ready to do battle again. Beal certainly thought so, and once again the key was to be the night shift. Acting on persistent rumors that the night workers would come out in a body after they had been paid on June 7, he decided to make it easier for them to do so by staging a mass rally that evening; then, defying the antiparade ordinance, pickets would march directly to the mill and call for their fellow workers to join them.[3]

June 7 was such a beautiful day that Gastonia policeman Tom Gilbert and his friend and former fellow officer Arthur Roach decided to take a few hours off. The grand parade of Confederate veterans was to be held in Charlotte; they decided it would be fun to see that and to do a little drinking on the way. Had the Gastonia strikers known that these two men were to be out of the district for a while, they would doubtless have been relieved, for Gilbert had often behaved particularly brutally toward them. Only a night or two before, during a run-in with him, "Red" Hendricks had been severely beaten. Roach, too, had a reputation as a drinker and a thug.[4]

The two men duly went to Charlotte, saw the parade, and slaked their thirst—or nearly so. On the way back to Gastonia the desire for more whiskey could not be resisted, and accordingly, they stopped to buy some at Pedro Melton's filling station, knowing that Melton was a sly-grog operator. When he claimed he had none to sell, the two became so incensed that they chased him into the Catawba River and fired several shots at him, then beat up his companion, J. C. Hensley. Fortunately for Melton and Hensley, two county police officers, John Irvine and Henry Mosely, were in the area. Hearing the shots, they rushed to the scene, pulled the shivering Melton out of the river, disarmed Gilbert and Roach, and ordered them "to return to the Gaston side of the river." This they did, but they were both in mean moods when they returned to Gastonia—spoiling for another fight.[5]

It was not long in coming, as Beal's plans for the walkout unfolded. The mass meeting that evening was more rowdy than usual, partly due to the presence of a larger number of company men and local police. Beal and Buch both had rotten eggs and rocks thrown at them as they addressed the crowd, and some alleged that at least one shot was fired. The policemen apparently "looked on and laughed." On his own admission, Beal then warned the hostile members of the crowd that if they persisted, they would get as good as they gave. Violence was in the air. Nevertheless, the strike leaders got their message across. They had reports "that there were some workers in the mill who wanted to come out," he told the crowd, and it was their duty to go and help them. Later he would deny that he at any time advocated entering the mill or in any way attempting to force people to leave their workplaces. "That would drive them away from the union when we wanted more members," he stated. Moreover, the mill was so heavily guarded that to try to enter it would have been stupid. All he did was urge people to show solidarity by marching to the gates. About two hundred people responded to his call and, led by Buch and Schechter, left for the mill. Beal, characteristically, did not go with them. Instead he returned to the new headquarters, and with the guards surrounding him, he began to catch up on his paperwork.[6]

The marchers did not get far. After about fifteen minutes, according to an eyewitness, they began to return "in straggling groups," with marks of violence upon them. Vera Buch hadn't wanted to go at all. Bitterly disappointed that once again the men had left the picketing to the women—"it was as usual just a small group of women, youth and children," she recalled—she determined that the march could not possibly have much effect on the situation in the mill. But it was too late to retreat. Off they went into the Carolina twilight, soon to be met by the "law." The police had lost all restraint. One of them, "a huge burly man," advanced on Buch, cursing. "His eyes were bulging," she remembered, "[and] his face was red." Seizing her by the throat, he started to squeeze her until she thought she would surely die. Tom Gilbert had a field day, bashing up several women, including the elderly Mrs. McGinnis, known to all as "Granny," who was on the ground searching for her glasses at the time. Several of those present later testified that they had heard him shout, as he hit her repeatedly, "I'm a full-blooded Irishman and I'll fight till I die," and "If anybody don't believe I'll fight a woman as quick as I will a man, just let her get in my way." The whiskey had done its work. Irene Corley swore that she heard him yell, "Come on, boys. Let's go down and kill every one of this ———. It's just as well to do it now as later."[7]

The police violence had its effect. The marchers scattered in all directions, but most made their way back to the safe haven of the tent colony or the union hall. That much is certain. What happened in the next few minutes, however, will always be open to conjecture. The situation is made even more problematic by the widely varying accounts of the two strike leaders, Beal and Buch, whose reports differ for reasons of both political disagreement and personal antipathy. Buch said she went back to the union's headquarters, briefly told Beal what had happened, and began writing an account for the *Daily Worker*. All was calm again, she said, the marchers having dispersed. Beal's account, rather, was of commotion, of wounded men and women, and of panic at the approach of the Committee of One Hundred. Then there was shooting—both Buch and Beal agreed on that. Buch said they fell to the floor and stayed there until the firing stopped. They heard the sound of a car driving off at high speed, and then all was quiet again. Nervously venturing outside, they found Joe Harrison, one of the guards, pale and bleeding profusely from wounds in his arm and thigh.[8]

What had happened? Two trials later, no one can yet be sure, though certain basic facts seem incontestable. It is reasonably certain that a car carrying Gastonia police chief Orville F. Aderholt, deputy chief Adam Hord, deputies Gilbert and Charles Ferguson, and sometime deputy Roach arrived at the headquarters. There the policemen were met by four guards—George Carter, Joseph Harrison, William

Police chief Orville Aderholt and National Guard commander Major Stephen Dolley (Originally published in the Labor Defender*)*

McGinnis, and Louis McLoughlin. Carter asked Aderholt if he had a search warrant, but before he could answer, Gilbert, claiming that no warrant was needed, seized Harrison's gun in an attempt to disarm him. Meanwhile, Roach, none too steady on his feet, made as if to enter the union hall. Aderholt went after him, took his arm, and was leading him away when the shooting began. Who shot first will never be known. But when the volleys stopped, four officers—Aderholt, Gilbert, Roach, and Ferguson—and Harrison lay wounded. Aderholt died the next day. A tall, gaunt man who was easily recognizable by the large black hat he always wore, he had treated the strikers reasonably decently and, indeed, may have gone to the union hall mainly to keep an eye on

Gilbert and Roach. If so, he paid dearly for his sense of duty. The Gastonia community and the Loray management now had their martyr.[9]

Again, Buch and Beal disagreed on what happened next. Buch said she and Edith Miller drove Joseph Harrison to the hospital; Beal said he did, along with K. O. Byers, his personal guard, and Ruby McMahon, a striker. He then made his way to Charlotte by taxi, he said, both to avoid lynching and to talk with Tom Jimison about what to do next. After spending the night with Jimison, Byers and Beal moved on to Spartanburg, South Carolina, where the law eventually caught up with them.

The same law had caught up with Buch, Schechter, and Melvin somewhat earlier. In their version, after dropping Harrison off at the hospital, Buch and Edith Miller went to Mrs. Perry Lodge's guest house. Lodge was a strike sympathizer, and a number of the NTWU people had stayed there. They had not been there long when the building was surrounded. They were arrested and taken to a cell in the city jail, where they were soon joined by Sophie Melvin and Amy Schechter. Buch was relieved to find herself in jail; at first she had thought she was in the hands of a lynch mob. Melvin told her that Beal had set out for Charlotte to seek legal aid, but Buch was unconvinced. To her, his disappearance seemed to represent yet another example of a man deserting his post in a crisis.[10]

It was a long night for the four women strike leaders. They were soon joined by other local women, who told them of the "reign of terror" presently occurring in Gaston County in the shooting's wake. Once the events had become known, Major Bulwinkle had taken command. Prominent Gastonians were deputized "to assist in arresting the officer's assailants." The deputies scoured the country for strikers. They rampaged through the tent colony, ripping up the floorboards, tearing down tents, terrorizing the women and children, and separating mothers from their children in their desire to break the last vestiges of NTWU resistance. Gangs of men searched the nearby houses and woods for fugitives, bringing in "adherents of the organization by the dozen." Major Bulwinkle proved his mettle in no uncertain manner by personally bringing in George Carter, the guard who had originally challenged Aderholt. By the end of the night, more than sixty men and women were in jail, mainly on charges of assault with a deadly weapon and intent to kill. Many of them showed obvious signs of the beatings

Major A. L. Bulwinkle, alleged leader of the Committee of One Hundred
(Line drawing by Fred Ellis, originally published in the Labor Defender)

on their faces and bodies. Of the strike leaders, only Beal had escaped arrest. The women officials of the NTWU were all in jail, as were the guards and the most prominent of the local strikers. The tent colony stood deserted. The mob had done its work well.[11]

Beal was soon arrested in Spartanburg; on his way back to Gastonia, he survived what he described as a lynching attempt. He was then taken to the Monroe jail for safekeeping. There he gave his first interview, in which he took pains to explain that he "was not trying to run away when they found me in Spartanburg." He had "gone there for a much-needed rest over Sunday" and had always planned to return to Gastonia to join his comrades. Few believed him then, and from the perspective of more than sixty years, his flight does appear suspiciously like a failure of nerve. Vera Buch, admittedly no friend of Beal's, always followed this line, alleging that the account of the night's events Beal provided in *Proletarian Journey* had been fabricated in order to refute the persistent charges of cowardice raised against him.[12]

Certainly the mob's initial failure to locate Beal was one reason why Gastonia remained at a flash point for the next few days. Another was the emotional tide that swept the community as a result of the police chief's funeral. More than five thousand attended the ceremony at Gastonia's First Baptist Church, "the mill owner standing beside the mill worker and many Negroes filling one of the galleries." "Strong men wept," it was reported, as they were reminded of the "scene of Friday night when the officer they were honoring was shot in the back at the headquarters building of the Loray strikers." Few there heeded E. J. Sox's adjuration to resist vengeance. There was even shooting during the funeral itself. George Moore, a special deputy sworn in the night of the shooting, was hit by a fellow officer as they both pursued "four suspicious-looking men." In this tense atmosphere, Gastonia took on the atmosphere of a closed city, as Charlotte Wilder found out when she arrived there on the morning of June 9. She was a teacher at Smith College and had come to do field research for a project on mill towns. She had scarcely registered at a local rooming house before she was taken to police headquarters; the police detained her for an hour while her luggage and room were searched. That same day, a New Jersey man stopped at a local hospital for treatment for a minor ailment. The doctor on duty advised him to get out of town as fast as he could. "People from New Jersey aren't popular around here," he warned. Though Gastonia's atmosphere was reported to be calm after the funeral, it was a calm imposed by the mob.[13]

The *Gastonia Daily Gazette* was far from calm. In the wake of the Aderholt shooting, it lost all remaining restraint in its call for vengeance, and its tone both reflected the spirit of the community and animated it. Very quickly the paper had decided that the police chief's death was the result of "a deep laid plot"—that the strikers had deliberately lured the officers to the strike headquarters for the simple purpose of murdering them. "The electric chair should claim every one of the number who participated in the shooting," the paper railed. The "arch-murderer" of the "bunch [of] Russian Anarchists" was Fred Beal. Incidentally, the *Daily Gazette*'s editor believed that he, too, had been marked for death: he claimed to have been invited to the tent colony on the night of the shooting, ostensibly to see a documentary film. The cry for retribution was unrestrained. "The blood of these men cries out to the high heaven for vengeance," shouted another editorial. "The community has been too lenient with these despicable curs and snakes from the dives of Passaic, Hoboken and New York." The Communists had "shot down as brave and as good a man as ever lived," it said, and it urged that "this display of gang law not go unavenged." The Gastonia community was given a steady diet of this type of invective in the days following the shooting, together with an insistence that the city be protected from any further intrusion of pernicious outside influences. "Plainclothes men should meet every train, bus and jitney entering the city," the editor advocated, to see "that every person entering can show satisfactory reason for being there." The *Daily Gazette*'s lack of restraint at this time was one reason why Jimison and the defense team believed their clients could never receive a fair trial in Gaston County.[14]

The district's leading newspaper, the *Charlotte Observer*, was similarly unrestrained in its apportioning of blame for the tragedy, attacking the "foreign agitators" who had disturbed a "contented" community. Like the *Daily Gazette*, the *Observer* believed that Aderholt had been deliberately ambushed. It was, the paper asserted, "a well-planned attempt at slaughter of these officers of the law." The "menace" must be "rounded up" and removed, preferably "through processes of law." Predictably, the *Daily Worker* called on the "Workers of the Nation" to defeat the "framed-up" murder charge against the strikers. "Hundreds of workers from surrounding towns" were "flocking to Gastonia to protect the strikers," the paper exulted; it called the incident not an ambush but a "well-planned" police attack that went wrong only because of the guards' resolution in defending their territory. Had they not done so, there would have been a general massacre.[15]

Of North Carolina's major newspapers, the *Raleigh News and Observer* provided the most balanced coverage of the days following the Aderholt shooting, and the most sensible editorial comment. Deploring the hysteria and calls for violence, the paper pointed out that those under arrest were entitled both to a fair trial and to "the presumption of innocence until they are proved guilty." Attacking the *Gastonia Daily Gazette* directly, the editor thought that "at any other time, such editorial utterance would fall flat by the weight of its own hysteria" but that in Gastonia, given the town's current atmosphere, "it may serve to inflame the public mind further" and was therefore to be utterly condemned. Picking up on this theme, the *News and Observer*'s liberal columnist Nell Battle Lewis began to sound the refrain she would return to consistently in the following months. Deploring the killing, she pointed out how the laws of North Carolina had consistently failed the strikers. The Gastonia authorities, she claimed, had sanctioned the current violence by refusing to punish those who had previously committed violent acts against the striking workers. "What is there in that record," she asked, "to have made the strikers think that they could secure justice under North Carolina law[?] . . . It operates blatantly and shamelessly in favor of the economic group which opposes them." She posed this question: when the law fails, as it did in Gastonia, what else can be expected but violence? Lewis's passionate, angry columns in support of the strikers' rights were to earn her great calumny in some North Carolina circles, but they stand out today as reflecting a courageous, balanced engagement with the wider issues of class and economic hegemony that lay at the strike's core.[16]

Moreover, she had her supporters, both within North Carolina— where her allies included Frank Porter Graham—and outside its boundaries. The veteran socialist Margaret Dreier Robins sent her one hundred dollars to put toward the strikers' defense fund. In the accompanying note she praised Lewis for her courage and urged her to keep up the good fight. It had always been her experience, she told Lewis, "that the American people believe in fair play and that they will fight for it the moment they understand the issue. You write so simply and with such passionate love for fair play that you will convince others—you and fair play will win." Thus encouraged, Lewis kept punching away.[17]

Of course, the killing of Aderholt and the consequent roundup and arrest of the strike leaders did not go unnoticed outside the region. Demonstrations in support of Beal and his lieutenants took place in several northern cities, and some of those demonstrations, including the one in Detroit, ended in violent clashes with the police. Most were organized by the Communist Party or its agencies. A few strikers who were not in jail were quickly transported northward to help in such affairs, for the events of June 7 certainly forced the Party, despite some misgivings, to devote much more time, energy, and resources to the "city of spindles." Though the mythic influx of workers from the surrounding counties to defend the strikers, a phenomenon reported by the *Daily Worker*, did not actually occur, that of Party officials from the north certainly did. They came to take the places of their NTWU comrades now in jail and to prepare for the next phase of the struggle: the defense of the jailed strikers and the publicizing of their cause throughout the United States—indeed, throughout the world. Those who arrived quickly on the scene included James Reid, national president of

New York demonstration in support of the Gastonia strikers (Originally published in the Labor Defender*)*

the NTWU; Weisbord, who was on his way out of both the NTWU and the Party, though he did not know it at the time; Alfred Wagenknecht of the Workers International Relief; Juliet Stuart Poyntz, executive secretary of the ILD; Bill Dunne, editor of the *Daily Worker* and a committed Fosterite; Walter Trumbull, a member of the ILD's national committee and reportedly a nephew of Connecticut's Republican governor; and, making brief return visits, Paul Crouch and Ellen Dawson. The literature they freely distributed on their arrival indicated that they were here for the long haul and that upcoming proceedings in the "Gaston and Mecklenburg county courts would be made the battle-ground of the party for many important issues."[18]

Of these new arrivals, the most important were Wagenknecht and Juliet Poyntz. Wagenknecht had vowed to reestablish the tent colony as soon as possible, and certainly the need was urgent. The tents had all been dismantled and stored by city officials, and there was literally nowhere for the few residents who remained in the area to go. The *Charlotte Observer* reported, "Two thin and weary mothers with children hanging on to their shabby skirts sat in the open glade where they have made their homes for several weeks" and watched the tents being folded away. They were in despair, their men were in jail, and they had been sleeping in the woods. Fortunately, their husbands were released a day or two later, but the accommodation problem remained urgent. To Wagenknecht's credit, he battled so fiercely with local officials and a hostile community that he quickly secured the release of the impounded tents and was also able to rent some land in Arlington Heights, outside the Gastonia city limits, where the tents could be erected. On June 17 he proudly announced that reconstruction of the tent colony had begun. In vain the *Gastonia Daily Gazette* protested, urging county authorities to dismantle and remove the tents to prevent "another tragedy." The NTWU, meanwhile, had decided not to relocate in Gastonia but to move its headquarters to Bessemer City, where regular union meetings were still being held. Local residents reported that "harangues" were "going on every night, presumably by local speakers," as the national leaders were all in jail. There had even allegedly been a black speaker "who is trying to organize the colored folks of Stumptown." It was "like a nightmare," the *Gastonia Daily Gazette* exclaimed. "A nation-wide movement on behalf of the imprisoned thugs and murderers is being undertaken." Gastonia's fight to cleanse itself of this evil influence was far from over.[19]

The International Labor Defense was a key component of this movement. Founded in 1925, the ILD was a "radical legal action group that specialized in representing jailed union members, immigrants, political activists and members of minority groups." The man most responsible for its formation was J. P. Cannon, but after his expulsion from the CPUSA in 1928, the ultimate control of the ILD passed to J. Lewis Engdahl. As historian Charles H. Martin has written, "The ILD's guiding philosophy was its concept of mass defense or mass protest." Basic to this concept was the notion that "since working-class defendants inevitably faced a hostile court system, legal manoeuvres alone could not win an acquittal." Rather, courtroom defense had "to be complemented by a mass protest movement that would mobilize the general public on behalf of the accused." It was only through this dual battle, in the courts and on the streets, that victory could be won. The ILD brought this policy to its involvement with the Gastonia strikers. In the months ahead, the concept would cause violent disagreement within the defense legal team, particularly with Tom Jimison and his associates, who bitterly resented ILD attempts to dictate defense strategy. Moreover, in the end, the mass protest movement became little more than a sustained attack on the South, its

Mobilize
For
Gastonia

**A MILLION
SIGNATURES!**

**$50,000.00 FOR DEFENSE
AND
RELIEF**

JOIN THE
INTERNATIONAL LABOR DEFENSE

If you are interested in the growth
and development of the International
Labor Defense you should become a
member at once. Not only should you
as an individual join, but you should
also get your fellow-workers to join.
Get your neighbors and your friends
to join. The initiation fee is 25c, the
dues are 15c per month. Five members constitute a branch. Get five or
more of your shop-mates or friends
together who want to help the I.L.D.
Send in the names together with the
initiation fee and you will receive a
charter. *Remember that without organization the working class can accomplish nothing. Organize into the
I.L.D.*

Above and overleaves: *Three of the ILD's appeals for aid to save those accused of
killing Chief Aderholt (Originally published in the* Labor Defender*)*

people, its culture, and its institutions, mainly through the pages of
the *Daily Worker*, whose most inflammatory pieces were thoughtfully
reproduced by the *Gastonia Daily Gazette*. This was satisfying for
some readers in the northern cities, perhaps, but of little value to the
defendants in the Charlotte dock.[20]

Juliet Poyntz, the ILD's executive secretary, was the person most
responsible for the application of ILD policy in Gastonia. She was
another of the impressively credentialed women who took part in this

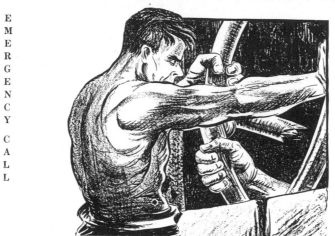
Gastonia drama. Born into a wealthy Nebraska family, she had graduated with an M.A. in history from Columbia, had spent two years at Oxford, and had taught history at Barnard. Proud of her English heritage and name—"Poyntz is just an old English name, as you will find out by reading Shakespeare's comedies," she once told reporters—she was also a dedicated Communist. Eventually she was directed to end

THE MURDER OF SACCO and VANZETTI MUST NOT BE FORGOTTEN!

Save the Gastonia Prisoners!

THE TRIAL STARTS JULY 29th

THE RIGHT OF THE WORK-ERS OF THE ENTIRE SOUTH TO ORGANIZE AND STRUG-GLE FOR BETTER CONDI-TIONS IS M E N A C E D.

———

The RIGHT OF WORKERS TO DEFEND THEMSELVES AGAINST M U R D E R O U S RAIDS OF THE MILL OWN-ERS' POLICE AND STRONG-ARM MEN IS AT STAKE.

NOW—15 SOUTHERN TEX-TILE WORKERS—MEMBERS OF THE NATIONAL TEXTILE WORKERS UNION — ARE CHARGED WITH M U R D E R THEY FACE THE E L E C T R I C   C H A I R. EIGHT OTHERS FACE LONG YEARS OF IMPRISONMENT.

———

THE MILLIONS OF WORK-ERS IN THE WHOLE OF AM-ERICA ARE CHALLENGED!

The Gastonia Strikers Must Be Saved from Electric Chair!

NOT ONE MUST BE SENTENCED TO PRISON!

ALL 23 INNOCENT MEN AND WOMEN MUST BE UNCONDITIONALLY RELEASED! THE DEFENSE OF THESE HEROIC STRIKERS IS Y O U R CAUSE. RALLY TO THE SUPPORT OF THE INTERNATIONAL LABOR DEFENSE.

Millions of workers must voice their demands—a million signatures be gathered on the petitions.

$50,000 MUST BE RAISED.

Rush all Funds to
Int'l Labor Defense

140 E. 11th St.—Room 402—New York City.

INT'L LABOR DEFENSE (National Office)
80 E. 11th St., Room 402, New York City.

I enclose $............... for Gastonia Defense. I further pledge
$............... per week.
Name ....
Address ....
City and State ....

her involvement in open Party activities in favor of secret work, which she did throughout the 1930s. What eventually happened to her remains a mystery: she walked out of her room one June morning in 1937 and simply disappeared, never to be seen again. She had told friends that she was disillusioned with the Party and ready to break from it, and the assumption of most scholars, as well as at least some of her

Party colleagues, is that she was most likely murdered by the KGB.

By this time, as Vera Buch believed, she may even have become a double agent. In 1929, however, she was at the height of her public career in the Party, courageous and articulate, an orator of "force and power" and, according to Tom Jimison, also "utterly unscrupulous" and so dedicated to the notion of impending world revolution that she was perfectly willing to let the Gastonia defendants "go to the electric chair as martyrs in the class struggle" if that would in any way help the larger cause. Poyntz made it clear from the outset that the ILD's dual policy would be aggressively followed in Gastonia. "The Gastonia trial will take its place in the history of the labor struggles in America," she asserted in her first press statement, "beside the Sacco-Vanzetti case. Around the Gastonia strikers will be formed the iron ring of workers defense." This defense would be conducted not merely in the courts "and by legal advisors, but by the mass action of the American working class." [21]

The linking of the events unfolding in Gastonia with the execution of the two Italian anarchists, still a raw nerve among American liberals, was something the ILD shrewdly played upon as the legal proceedings approached. Of course, the Communists were not the only group in America anxious to ensure that no repetition of the Sacco-Vanzetti outrage occurred. The American Civil Liberties Union, which had been involved in Gastonia since the events of April 18 and which had retained Jimison initially, now increased its financial and emotional support, and Jimison reported regularly to its executive director, Forrest Bailey. The ACLU continued to pay Jimison and to meet the expenses of the associates that he engaged to help him: J. F. Flowers; his law partner, W. H. Abernethy; and ex-judge Frank Carter, "perhaps the most liberal and intelligent lawyer in the State." Most important of all, the ACLU negotiated with the first of the "outside lawyers"— those with national reputations—who were eventually to come to Gastonia. This first lawyer was John Randolph Neal from Tennessee, chief counsel for the defense at the famous "monkey trial," the Scopes trial of 1925. Both Clarence Darrow and Arthur Garfield Hays, the nation's leading civil liberties lawyer, had also been mentioned as attorneys likely to lend a hand, but Jimison preferred Neal. A southerner himself, Jimison wanted lawyers around him who understood the South.

By this time Poyntz and the *Daily Worker* routinely referred to Jimison as "Attorney Jimison of the International Labor Defense." Totally absorbed in preparing the strikers' case, he probably did not notice, and if he had, he might not have realized the significance of the proprietary remark. Yet it was emblematic of the bitter jurisdictional and ideological divisions that would eventually mar every aspect of the defense effort.[22]

Within days, Jimison had become convinced that the best line of defense was that of self-protection: Aderholt and his fellow officers had clearly entered the strikers' premises illegally, after having broken up their picket lines "by the usual methods of police brutality." He was of the opinion that the police had fired first. "If the strikers shot at all," they had done so not only in defense of their premises and civil rights but also "in defense of their own lives." His prime task was to get the prisoners out of jail, and for that purpose he had issued writs of habeas corpus to force an early hearing, in effect a preliminary hearing, at which the state would have to present its evidence, thus forcing the release of many of the seventy-one people currently in custody, as there could be no possible case against them. But even at this early stage, he expected as many as twelve to be charged with murder. Feeling in the town was still intense, he said, and he needed the protection of the sheriff whenever he went there. Quoting a "negro cleric I once knew," he said "the mill interests seemed to be 'hell-bent and damnation sprung,' on sending Beal and four or five others to the electric chair." To this end, "officers and managers" of Manville-Jenckes had appeared before the city council the previous evening and insisted that the city employ its attorney, Major Bulwinkle, as a special prosecutor, even though the council had already retained "the entire Bar of Gaston County" as well as "two of the most notable criminal lawyers" in the state to assist the solicitor.

It was a ghastly situation, and when the cases came to trial Jimison would certainly need help. As it was, the destruction of the tent colony gave rise to numerous civil issues that he simply had to ignore, as he was working "twenty hours a day on the defense of those who are imprisoned." It was going to be a hard struggle. Moreover, the strikers would certainly always be up against "the perjured testimony" of "sorry whites who hope to curry favor with the mill-owners." What had not yet crossed his mind was that some of the defendants would insist on perjuring themselves as well, for the good of the cause and for advancement in the new, Fosterite hierarchy of the Party.[23]

The application for habeas corpus had the result Jimison expected. By the middle of the week, the number of strikers still held in jail had been almost halved, to thirty-seven. The others had been released either completely, for lack of evidence, or on bail on lesser charges. By the time the hearing began, on June 18, the number had been further reduced to just twenty-three, fourteen of whom had been formally charged with murder and nine with assault with intent to kill. Judge W. F. Harding, the presiding official at the Charlotte hearings, immediately made it clear that he was less interested in having the prosecution show why they should not be released than in throwing the burden of proof on the defendants. The evidence adduced was predictable and provided a preview of future trials. The state produced eyewitnesses who testified that the strikers had fired first, that the attack was unprovoked, that the officers had gone to the colony simply in response to a phone call from an unknown woman and, most damning of all, that both Beal and Buch had repeatedly urged the armed guards to "shoot to kill." Tom Gilbert and Otto Mason were both quite specific as to who fired the first shot. It was, they agreed, W. M. McGinnis. The defense claimed that all was quiet when the officers appeared; that though some of the strikers did possess weapons, these were purely for defensive purposes; and that no one had given a shoot-to-kill order. Amy Schechter testified that Beal and Buch were both in a small union office when the shooting started and had remained there throughout the affray, along with the Millers, Sophie Melvin, and Schechter herself. During that time, no weapons were fired from the union hall, as the state alleged.[24]

Schechter was cross-examined by Clyde Hoey of Shelby, known as the "silver-tongued orator of the South." In his old-fashioned frock coat and with his flowing silver locks, he looked almost like a caricature of the old-style southern lawyer, but he possessed one of the finest legal minds in the state. His cross-examination provided another preview of what the defense team had to expect, and it helped explain Jimison's decision in favor of Neal rather than Arthur Garfield Hays or even Clarence Darrow, because the issue Hoey raised had more to do with the Scopes trial than the Sacco-Vanzetti trial. "Did she believe in God,"

he wanted to know. Jimison predictably objected, Judge Harding over-
ruled him, and Schechter eventually replied that she did not. "Well,"
thundered Hoey in response, "You don't regard the oath you have just
taken on the Bible" to have any meaning. He went on to ask her about
what she believed to be the best form of government. Her response—
that while she did not wish to substitute the Russian for the American
form entirely, she nevertheless believed in "government by a majority
of the population, who happen to be workers and farmers"—was just
what Hoey wanted to hear. He questioned Edith Saunders Miller, too,
about her religious beliefs. Like Schechter, she replied that she did
not believe in God, or that the Bible was God's "inspired word," though
she took pains to point out that she did not raise these matters with
the children she worked with. The *Gastonia Daily Gazette*, the Gastonia clergy, the Gaston County mill owners, and Major Bulwinkle—
who was described by the *Daily Worker*, in one of its better phrases,
as looking "like a well-bred bullfrog"—all had been emphasizing for
months the alien and fundamentally subversive nature of the belief
systems of these northern interlopers. Now it was part of the official
courtroom record, admitted as evidence by the presiding judge. Small
wonder that Juliet Poyntz likened the attitude in that Charlotte courtroom to that of a "heresy trial," one "conducted in the medieval spirit
of entrenched autocracy." Belief in God, she said, or rather nonbelief,
would be one of the main points on which the strikers would be tried.
Like that of Sacco and Vanzetti, this trial now bore the unmistakable
imprint of John T. Scopes—a fight over fundamental spiritual and cultural values. It was scarcely surprising that Jimison expected such a
long, hard battle.[25]

Having listened to the evidence, Judge Harding had no doubt where
his duty lay. The evidence showed, he said, that the officers went to
the camp in response to a phone call, thus they acted entirely within
their responsibilities. There was no trouble at the tent colony until
Gilbert attempted to disarm a guard, again entirely within his legiti-
mate duties. Then the shooting began. The first shots clearly came
from the union hall, he believed, and he thus ordered fourteen strikers
to be held without bond on charges of murder. These were Beal,
K. O. Byers, W. M. McGinnis, Louis McLoughlin, George Carter,
Vera Buch, Joseph Harrison, J. C. Heffner, Robert Allen, Russell
Knight, N. F. Gibson, K. T. Hendricks, Amy Schechter, and Sophie

Clyde Hoey, attorney for the prosecution (Line drawing by Fred Ellis, originally published in the Labor Defender)

Melvin. Eight others—Ernest Martin, Walter Lloyd, C. M. Lell, Clarence Townsend, D. E. McDonald, Robert Litoff, C. M. Pittman, and Clarence Miller—were charged with assault with a deadly weapon and released on $750 bond. Inexplicably to some, Edith Saunders Miller was not charged; she and Caroline Drew were the only member of the NTWU local staff not to be. Drew had been released earlier, having proved conclusively that she had been in Bessemer City at the time Aderholt was shot. The others went back to jail to await trial at a special session of the Gastonia Superior Court, beginning on July 29.[26]

With the inquest behind it, the accused behind bars, and the trial still weeks away, Gastonia settled into an uneasy, early summer calm. Even the *Daily Gazette* quieted down, reserving its outbursts for the new tent colony's dwellers; for the *Daily Worker*, whose crippling financial difficulties it tended to see as an act of the Most High; and, increasingly, for Nell Battle Lewis. The use of her Sunday *News and Observer* column, "Incidentally," as a means of raising funds for the strikers' defense particularly incensed the editor. Lewis was concerned that though "these strikers are our own people," most of the expressions of support for them came from outside the South. Guilty or innocent, they were "entitled to a fair trial," and she invited North Carolinians who felt likewise—those who had sympathy with the strikers' "fundamental aims, which are nothing more or less than better conditions of labor and life"—to contribute to a defense fund that Lewis would establish and administer. Remember, too, she wrote, "the failure of the law" in April, "the blackjacks and the bayonets," the "women choked," the "unpunished mob violence." But most important, she urged her readers to "remember . . . most of them are our own people." The *Gastonia Daily Gazette* reprinted the column with little comment, save to sneer at the "short-haired woman-lawyer journalist from Raleigh"; in its own words, the paper found the column "so disgusting that we are letting it speak for itself." Nevertheless, the *Daily Gazette* had lowered its voice. Like other southern newspapers, it even allowed itself to be distracted briefly by a national matter that was of great concern to southerners. Mrs. Hoover had invited Mrs. Oscar De Priest, wife of the first African American to be elected to the House of Representatives since Reconstruction, to join her and other congressional wives for tea at the White House. The regional outrage was enough to displace Gastonia as front-page news, if only briefly.[27]

For those held without bail, the time passed extremely slowly. (Their number soon increased to fifteen with the capture in Gaffney, South Carolina, of Delmar Hampton, who had allegedly been guard captain the night Aderholt was shot.) For the women, at least, life in the county jail was a great improvement over the conditions of their original confinement, at least physically. Vera Buch recalled that the food was plentiful and good, the cell was clean, and the jailer and his wife, Mr. and Mrs. Tom Hanna, were friendly. Hanna was from Ohio and was an ex-prizefighter. He frequently assured them that they were safe with him. Nevertheless, initially they could hardly help but feel lonely and abandoned, for they had no news of the world outside and no visitors. Where were their comrades?, Vera would ask repeatedly. "Where were Albert, the ILD, Wagenknecht, and the others who should have helped?" Eventually Juliet Poyntz did arrive; she explained that their friends had tried frequently to see them but had been denied access. Only then did the feelings of abandonment begin to dissipate. The women eventually developed a routine. They talked

The Gaston County jail (Originally published in the Labor Defender)

a lot, the three of them, and they got to know and to like each other better. The tensions between Schechter and Buch melted away, and both were protective of the "cherubic" Melvin, who actually needed no protection. Buch's mother sent them packages of books—a Russian grammar particularly interested the press—so they read and studied. She also sent dress material, and they sewed prolifically: they made dresses, they made tops, and they made, Mrs. Hanna told the press proudly, "lovely underclothes." Sophie, who had worked for a time in the garment trade, was particularly adept. She recalled making a "very smart" skirt for Amy and, for Fred Beal, a pair of trousers that was hardly big enough to fit a doll. (Fortunately, he appreciated the joke.) And they sang. Mrs. Hanna loved to listen to them. Amy had a most "cultured voice," she said. "You should just hear her sing 'Old Black Joe,' and 'Tell My Mother if You See Her to Come Home.'" Mrs. Hanna did not say whether she ever heard them sing snatches of the poems that Vera Buch said Ella May sent to them frequently. In their cell nearby, the men prisoners could hear the women singing, and they often sent along requests via Hanna. These the girls would sing at the top of their voice. Sometimes they would help their jailer with his paperwork, and both Sophie and Vera did typing for him. He would bring the work to their cell and simply leave it there, often along with his keys. More than once they had to remind him to lock them in for the night. The weeks in jail, then, for the women, were not unbearable, though they were undoubtedly tedious. Buch even described them as "peaceful," at least until the pretrial publicity began.[28]

A *New York Times* reporter who visited them in jail wrote that they had absolutely no complaints about their treatment, especially since Hanna had allowed them to decorate their cell walls with cheerful prints. "Everybody in this building has been kind to us," reported Melvin, with "a wealth of curly hair falling down to her shoulders." The "round faced, bobbed haired" Buch, who was doing her laundry when the reporter arrived, was quick to concur. Even the shy Amy, who "lurked in the background during the interview," agreed that she "was not troubled by her predicament." They were all pleased, however, to talk with someone from New York, after their long weeks surrounded by southern accents and southern ways.[29]

For the men, things were not quite so comfortable, as Buch well knew. "We are much better situated than the boys," she admitted to Mary Vorse. Things were harder for them: they were crowded together in a single cell, and at times the other prisoners were far from friendly to them. Yet they too, as they got to know each other better, developed a sense of companionship, a camaraderie borne of adversity as well as commitment. Beal and the youthful J. C. Heffner, who had just turned seventeen and was deeply religious, spent hours reading biblical passages aloud to each other. George Carter, of Mispah, New Jersey, one of the men the NTWU had sent to join the strikers' guard detail, devoted a block of time each day to trying to teach the illiterate Bill McGinnis to read and write. Beal, like Buch, remembered the time in jail as having truly positive aspects.[30]

Though time hung heavy on the hands of the prisoners, that was scarcely the case with their lawyers. Jimison was pleased with his team, especially now that Frank Carter had agreed to join them. But even with Neal on board, there would be "but five of us to meet the seventeen who represent the Philistines." Recognizing that the best chance for the defendants was to have the trial shifted from Gastonia, on the grounds that the town was so inflamed against his clients that it would be impossible for them to be treated fairly there, much of the

WE MUST FIGHT ON!

By FRED ERWIN BEAL

(*A Statement Dictated In Jail Especially For The Labor Defender*)

THE FRAME-UP IN GASTONIA IS AN ATTEMPT TO CHECK THE GROWTH OF THE N. T. W. U. THAT HAS SUCCEEDED IN ORGANIZING THOUSANDS OF SOUTHERN TEXTILE WORKERS FOR STRUGGLE AGAINST THE MOST MISERABLE CONDITIONS.

THE BOSSES HAVE USED EVERY METHOD AVAILABLE TO SMASH OUR UNION. THEY HIRED GUNMEN AND THUGS AND WRECKED OUR FORMER HEADQUARTERS DESTROYING FOOD INTENDED TO FEED NEEDY STRIKERS.

WE MUST FIGHT ON IN SPITE OF THE TERRORISM AND FRAME-UP OF ACTIVE STRIKERS. THE WHOLE LABOR MOVEMENT MUST GET BEHIND THE VICTIMS OF THE BOSSES TERRORISM AND FRAME-UP.

Fred Beal's statement from jail (Originally published in the Labor Defender*)*

defense team's effort involved securing affidavits and collecting evidence to that end. The *Gastonia Daily Gazette* proved to be a useful source; this was perhaps one of the reasons why, too late, it moderated its editorial stance. By this time the defense had compiled an impressive dossier of *Daily Gazette* editorials, all designed to show that in a community so incited to violent action, a fair trial was impossible. The move for a change of venue was supported by the state's liberal elements, led by Nell Battle Lewis. Given that Gaston County's "legal officers have been the open enemies of the strikers," she argued, and that mob violence had been officially sanctioned there, to hold North

Carolina's "most important trial for many years" there would be ludicrous. The whole United States, indeed the world, would be watching. Moreover, she agreed with Juliet Poyntz that "the attitude of the prosecution exhibited at the habeas corpus hearing suggested that it may very likely turn into a heresy trial"—a trial of the defendants' opinions rather than their alleged complicity in Aderholt's death. If so, the trial would leave "a stench and a stain" on the state, and if movement of the venue could in any way help prevent this, then it must be permitted.[31]

Of course, the trial's judge would be the key figure in determining where it would be held. The defense team had little confidence in Judge H. Hoyle Sink, who had originally been given the case, and were delighted when he asked to be replaced on the grounds of his mother's serious illness. Jimison was even happier when Governor Gardner selected Judge M. V. Barnhill, of Rocky Mount, to replace Sink. Barnhill, a relatively young man with a reputation for fairness on the bench, had recently ruled that public authorities had a duty to provide equal public transportation facilities for white and black citizens alike, a decision that made him a liberal in North Carolina terms. Then, to top it off for the defense, Judge Thomas J. Shaw sent both Gilbert and Roach to be tried on assault charges arising out of the fracas at the Catawba River on the afternoon of Aderholt's death, describing their behavior as "disgraceful." This, of course, hardly helped their credibility as witnesses. By mid-July, despite the vigorous denial of the prosecution that a fair trial could not be held in Gaston County, most observers conceded that "the Sacco-Vanzetti case of the South" would be tried somewhere other than Gastonia—perhaps in Shelby, with its large and comfortable courthouse, or in Charlotte, in neighboring Mecklenburg County.[32]

Was it the "Sacco-Vanzetti of the South," or a rerun of the Scopes trial? John Randolph Neal obviously saw elements of both. As he formally announced his acceptance of a place on the defense team, he pointed out that "never before in America have so many people been on trial for their lives in connection with one killing," and he expressed certainty that "the whole United States would be listening in on what occurs in Gastonia." Referring to the habeas corpus proceedings, and answering charges that the defense was trying to turn the trial into a media circus, he argued that it was actually members of the prosecution who "have attempted to digress and utilize the radical beliefs of the defendants to prejudice the public" against them. "God and Communism will not be on trial in Gastonia on the 29th of July," he asserted. But the defendants' opinions upon these and other questions would be. "The mill owners, the prosecution and . . . the press" had all used their opinions to prejudice the Gastonia community. "It is precisely the defense counsel which has insisted that the defendants should not be convicted because they are strikers, unionist, radicals, Communists or atheists, or whatever their opinions may be." Jimison and his defense colleagues were delighted with Neal's involvement and welcomed the increased visibility his presence gave them. Only Nell Battle Lewis sounded a note of caution. Despite his great ability and his southern roots, he was still "a foreign lawyer," and she did not think out-of-state lawyers had a place in this trial, which was essentially about state issues, about North Carolina's failure to deal adequately with the "great social questions" that the state's "Industrial Revolution" had raised. But Neal was better than either Darrow or Hays, she conceded; at least he was "a neighbor from over the mountains."[33]

The International Labor Defense was also very busy in the weeks before the trial. Its main concern was to implement the second aspect of its strategy—the concept of mass defense. To this end, rallies were held throughout the United States at which strikers, including workers like Clarence Miller who were out on bail on assault charges, spoke on the inequities of the mill system and of North Carolina justice and of the need to "save the victims of the Gastonia conspiracy." Mother Bloor took teenage strikers Elizabeth McGinnis and Binnie Green on a national tour to publicize the causes on the ILD's behalf. A mass mailing soliciting funds was planned for the first week of July but had to be postponed when the postal service declared the envelopes unmailable because "Smash the Murder Frameup Against the Gastonia Strikers" was stamped on the front. Party, ILD, and NTWU officials continued to come South in such profusion—both to help organize the defense and to do the work of those in jail—that it was widely reported that the Communist Party was planning to establish its permanent southern headquarters in Gastonia, a rumor that the Party did nothing to discount and that pleased the city's good citizens not at all. Nothing came of this rumor, of course, although a southern office of the ILD was established in Charlotte, headed by Trumbull. Beal was replaced by Hugo Oehler, with Clarina Michelson and Ben Wells to support him.

Finally, the ILD announced its plan to hold a southern conference of the NTWU in Bessemer City the day before the trial was due to start; William Zebulon Foster would be the keynote speaker. This was to be the high point of the mass defense strategy. As such, it transfixed the Gastonia community—and irritated Jimison and his team intensely.[34]

Serious problems had already developed between the ILD and the courtroom lawyers over defense strategy, in particular over how far were the trial lawyers to be bound by Party dictates. The ILD had always claimed publicly that it was running the defense effort. It now began to do so privately, and this was bound to cause friction with the ACLU, to say nothing of the local lawyers in the defense team. Of particular concern was the ILD's tendency to release frequent bulletins commenting on the various legal issues to be raised in the trial, always without prior consultation with Jimison. These bulletins were usually violently critical of the local community, its leaders, and of North Carolina justice generally; they were often picked up by the *Daily Worker* and then gleefully reprinted by the *Gastonia Daily Gazette*. By mid-July, the ACLU and the ILD were openly hostile, the ILD having publicly described ACLU suggestions that it tone down its stridency a little as "a surrender to the opposition." A month later, Forrest Bailey himself went public, wondering "if some form of intelligent control could be exercised over what the *Daily Worker* prints about the case during the next few weeks." But by this time the ILD had cost the defense team its most prestigious local member. Just before the trial was scheduled to begin, Judge Frank Carter bailed out. He was at pains to make it clear that he still had faith in the cause of the defendants and believed them to be the victims of a brutal tyranny rarely witnessed in the South—"a ruthless purpose, amazingly supported, to smother heresy, religious, industrial and political, in its own blood, which savors more of the fifteenth than the twentieth century." But he could not conscientiously remain with a defense team that intended to inject "issues in the case other than the evidence regarding the slaying." He would not be party to making the defendants martyrs to a larger cause. The defense was to be plagued with these basic issues of control and purpose in all the trials of 1929.[35]

Like the lawyers, Gastonia's city council was busily preparing for the trial. The experience of Dayton, Tennessee, during the Scopes trial had taught a valuable lesson. There was money in trials, and if publicity could not be avoided, at least it could be turned to the community's advantage. Thus, when reporters from the North started to arrive, including Joe Shaplen from the *New York Times*, Don Wharton of the *Herald Tribune*, and Harry Lang of the *Forward*—thirty press people in all—they found that the *Daily Gazette* had opened a branch office for their benefit, complete with typewriters furnished by the chamber of commerce. It was available to all, even to the representatives of the *Daily Worker*. Welcoming them, the *Daily Gazette*'s editor said he felt certain that they "would be eminently fair in their reports of the forthcoming trial." Gastonians were urged to welcome the outsiders, to "take them into their homes" or "to take them out to a typical Gaston County dinner, fried chicken, roas'n'ears, corn on the cob, country ham . . . peach ice cream." It was all very cozy, and the visitors appreciated it. When the county's solicitor, John Carpenter, received a cablegram in German from a group of Berlin workers, which no one on the prosecution side could read, Joseph Shaplen translated it for them. Predictably, it opposed "the industrial and police terrorism and class justice" to which the strikers had been subjected.[36]

What had happened to the strikers who were not in jail and had not already left the county? Most of them probably moved into the new tent colony, and while Hugo Oehler's claim that union meetings were being held there daily can be dismissed for the mere puffery it was, some union activity nevertheless persisted, despite the climate of oppression. From time to time the newspapers carried reports of rallies and protest meetings, and there were no doubt many unreported gatherings where Ella May, Daisy McDonald, and others sang their songs and spoke of their dreams for the future. When the NTWU headquarters moved to Bessemer City, the center of the remaining union activity was also relocated. The *Daily Worker* told of a July 6 meeting there that was attended by nearly five hundred people; the crowd was addressed by Poyntz, Bill Dunne, Violet Hampton, and W. W. Beal, Fred's aged father, who had come south in solidarity with his son and presumably for love and concern as well. Ella May was the subject of a speech at that rally. Wes Williams, the local NTWU president, spoke of a young widow who had recently joined the local. This woman had lost four children due to poverty and malnutrition and had asked to be switched from the night to the day shift so that she could care more adequately for what remained of her family, but her request had been

Strikers' children in the tent colony, selling the Labor Defender
(Originally published in the Labor Defender*)*

callously refused. This could only have been Ella May, though she was
not technically a widow. Already, the facts of her life were being subtly
altered.[37]

No doubt many of the strikers from the tent colony joined their fellow unionists in Bessemer City on July 28 to hear Bill Foster, winner
of the latest round of the faction-fighting that plagued the Communist
Party in 1929. The *Charlotte Observer* reported that there were 280
people in attendance. Foster urged them not to give up the fight. The
union was here to stay, he said; the Gastonia strike was but the open-

ing round of a struggle that would soon see a militant organization of
textile workers spreading across the whole region. Binnie Green, back
from her tour, also spoke, to great applause.[38]

Some union activity continued, then, but of more importance was
the fact that sympathy for Beal and his co-workers still ran high. An
anonymous correspondent to the *Gastonia Daily Gazette*'s editor let
him know why in no uncertain terms. "The chief fact that you need
to let soak in," he wrote, was that "your paper has made more Communists in this section than Beals [*sic*] and the reds that have come
here at least a thousand to one, you could have averted all the real
trouble that Gastonia has had, just by taking a stand for the working
class." But the paper never would, nor would the "crowd" whose views
it represented. That was why "the working people of this county stand
almost to a man for the strikers" despite their communism: Beal and
his colleagues had at least taken that stand.[39]

The number of workers who gathered about the courthouse to await
the trial's opening was testimony to that continued support. Long before the appointed opening hour, the small courtroom was packed.
The "white" section was quickly filled to capacity, so spectators were
soon forced to crowd "into the Jim Crow gallery." They were mainly
mill folk, a sympathetic journalist wrote; "the stamp of generations of
poverty" was on them. They looked "bleached out," he thought, exud-
ing "the odor of long hours of toil."[40]

Harriet Herring remarked that "the people who crowded the courtroom" that hot summer's day were obviously working people—"cotton
mill people, some in their Sunday clothes, but many in their overalls."
The number of defendants had now grown to sixteen due to the last-
minute addition of Clarence Miller, and when they were brought in,
"there was then a great deal of waving, bowing, smiling and greeting
between them and their friends, many of whom they had probably not
seen for weeks." Vera Buch was clearly touched at their reception. "I
wish you had seen the spontaneous demonstration of the union members in the courtroom," she wrote to Mary Vorse. "At every recess of
the court they flocked around us and nearly ate us up in their joy at see-
ing us." Hazel Mizelle, writing for the *Charlotte Observer*, also noted
the preponderance of textile workers in the crowd, adding disapprov-
ingly that many of the men were wearing overalls; in that and other
ways, she said, they typified the spirit of "the great unwashed," the

sort of shiftless people who were always "just here and there," often out of work and "living in makeshift homes." Not your better sort at all. Cora Harris thought the onlookers were a "pathetic group," a motley crowd of "flappers," in their "brief skirts, colorful blouses and chokers, bracelet and hats at jaunty angles," older women "with deep lined faces," and men uncomfortable in their Sunday clothes. As they sat there in the summer heat—"a torrid blanket of warmth that lay over judge, jury, prisoners and spectators"—Mizelle and Harris, like Herring, could not help but notice the joy with which the crowd greeted the prisoners, "the warm embraces, moist kisses, friendly pats on the back and excited conversations." Some of the reunions were genuinely touching. "God bless you my boy," Eva Heffner reportedly cried as she gathered her son, the youthful J. C. Heffner—whom the *Charlotte Observer* described as being "revered among the cotton mills of Gastonia"—to her bosom across the barrier of the wooden rail. She then "kissed him tenderly." The strike may have failed, but the faithful still clearly regarded its leaders as heroes.[41]

There was particular interest in the women defendants: they were described as if they were appearing at a gala premiere rather than in the dock. Sophie Melvin looked ravishing in "powder blue," which "set off perfectly the natural beauty for which she was praised by so many of the people outside the courtroom," wrote Mizelle. Inside, the spectators allegedly gasped at her prettiness. The frock and "her chestnut bobbed hair" set her off as "the most attractive of the female contingent under arraignment." Buch looked stylish as well, "in sleeveless green washable silk," and even Amy Schechter had taken some trouble for the occasion. She was also wearing blue and had tamed her unruly hair so that it fell over her ears in an orderly fashion. Revolutionaries though they were, it was doubtless reassuring to some to realize they were women as well—real women, who cared about "women's things." With masculine savoir faire, their jailer asked that their late appearance in court be excused, as "they had not yet completed their toilet" at the trial's due starting time. "All women were alike," he told reporters; they all wanted to look their best in court—even Communists.[42]

Neither the male defendants nor their lawyers were subject to such scrutiny as the women. The *News and Observer*'s Fleet Williams thought they looked collectively "more like a group of college boys and girls" than people facing possible execution. Harrison was de-

Sophie Melvin, charged with murder
(Originally published in the Labor Defender*)*

scribed as a "bush-haired labor organizer" from Passaic, and Beal's flaming red hair was a subject of some press comment, but in general there was more interest in the dress of the prosecution lawyers. Hoey, the "silver-tongued orator of the South," was in his customary frock coat, with a "deep-red rose in the lapel," his flowing gray hair neatly trimmed for the occasion. The liberal journalist Paul Porter described him as affecting "the mannerisms and adornments of Henry Clay," but Porter thought he ended up "looking more like a doctor in a traveling medicine show." It was solicitor John G. Carpenter who occasioned the most sartorial comment. "The Beau Brummel of this judicial district" wore a relatively conservative white linen suit on the first day, "a deep lavender zinnia" in the lapel, but on day two he looked particularly "snappy" in a dark blue coat, white flannel trousers, and black and white sports shoes, topped off with a red boutonniere. Bulwinkle, too, looked resplendently military. Porter thought there was a serious point to all this costuming: to impress the jury with the gravity of the occasion and the power concentrated on the prosecution's side.[43]

By day two, Carpenter's appearance was perhaps the most exciting aspect of the drama, for the trial itself was a complete anticlimax. Jimison and the defense team had done their work exceedingly well. A succession of witnesses attested to the climate of opinion in Gastonia, particularly to the view that the Committee of One Hundred was "going to take care of the defendants if they were acquitted." H. G. Gulley, a private detective employed by the defense, produced as evidence a sample of the leaflets the Loray Mill had recently had printed; these leaflets were, he said, "designed to fan sentiment against the strikers." Finally, a selection of twenty-four of the *Gastonia Daily Gazette*'s more intemperate remarks, and the testimony of Jimison himself about the threats against his own life he had recently received while visiting his clients, all served to convince Judge Barnhill that the defendants could not get a trial in Gastonia that "would have every appearance of fairness." Accordingly, he ruled that the trial should be held in Charlotte, with August 26 as the likely commencement date. Proceedings were then adjourned. Barnhill's decision was widely and lavishly praised, both in the South and elsewhere. The *News and Observer* thought it vindicated North Carolina justice, the *New York Times* dubbed him "a just judge," and even the *Gastonia Daily Gazette*, while asserting that a fair trial could have occurred in the city, nevertheless agreed that moving it was doubtless for the best. The community, having breathed a sigh of "genuine relief," could now get on with its normal business, "rid of the menace of the agitators," for they would be unlikely "to again try to foist their doctrines and beliefs on this community." There were only a few grumbles at Barnhill's decision.[44]

Thus the reporters left for home and the defendants returned to jail—or rather the men did. The prosecution had decided not to press for the death penalty against the three women; they were to be charged with second-degree murder, with bail at five thousand dollars each. They protested, of course, but only for the record. They were really delighted to be leaving jail and North Carolina. Buch and Schechter were soon on their way north, to be the featured speakers at ILD rallies and fund-raisers throughout the nation. Sophie Melvin decided to remain in the South for a while. She attempted to address the North

Labor Defender *cover, July 1929. Beal is in the center. Tom Jimison is on the right, Joseph Harrison on the left. Vera Buch appears over Beal's right shoulder, with Amy Schechter behind her. (Originally published in the* Labor Defender*)*

Carolina Federation of Labor's annual convention, and when she was
predictably refused, she held her own rally at the Wake County Courthouse; there she lambasted both the AFL and its affiliate, the United
Textile Workers of America, for having sold out to the bosses, and she
called on the workers to continue their mass protests. She and her co-
defendants would not get a fair trial, she said, "unless the workers of
the world take immediate steps to exert mass pressure. They are the
ones who can influence Judge Barnhill." Mass defense was still quite
central to the ILD's legal armory.[45]

Tom Jimison said after the trial had been shifted that he hoped to get
some sleep. He had been working extremely hard and was exhausted.
He could not afford to relax for long, though, for after the aborted
trial, Fleet Williams commented on "the stupidity and worse" of the
defense, particularly of the ILD's propaganda. It was, he said, hardly
conducive to the best interests of the defendants to be constantly referring to the proceedings as a "trial to legally lynch workers"; the defendants really needed protection from such friends "almost as much
as they needed protection from their enemies." Forrest Bailey at the
ACLU agreed. Despairing of being able to cooperate with the Communists, he and his board had decided to engage additional defense
counsel, quite independently of the ILD. Increasingly, the names of
Clarence Darrow and Arthur Garfield Hays were being mentioned as
possibilities, yet there were influential local supporters like Nell Battle
Lewis who still bitterly opposed the engaging of any further outside
legal help, wanting instead the addition of "an able experienced North
Carolina lawyer . . . to the defense team." Jimison, caught between
these opposing forces, knew that there was little chance that a unified
defense could be prepared in just four weeks. So did Fred Beal, but
still, they had to try.[46]

What of the remnants of the strikers, who by now formed only a
small, beleaguered band? There was little they could do except go
back to the tent colony and wait, in conditions increasingly described
as deplorable—with "poverty and rags, hunger and disease" preva-
lent. Neither Oehler nor Caroline Drew could deal with the situation, their opponents alleged: relief supplies were totally inadequate,
and they themselves had reportedly told the residents it was time
to move on. This was not so, Drew angrily retorted, though she did
admit that some colony dwellers would be sent to other counties and

states to "do organizational work for the union." Moreover, Kate Burr Johnson, North Carolina's welfare commissioner, visited the colony on August 23 and effectively ended the talk about squalid living conditions and malnourished infants. On the contrary, the children looked well cared for, she reported, while generally she found the colony "clean and well kept and well drained." Still, it was clear that not only was the strike at the Loray Mill well and truly over, but the NTWU's presence in Gastonia was also marginal and unlikely to change, despite the stalwart people—like Daisy McDonald, Bertha Tompkinson, C. W. Saylors, and Lorella Byers—who had been with the union since the beginning and were still there, in the little tent colony, as the date for the second Aderholt trial approached.[47]

Meanwhile, frightened janitors at the Charlotte courthouse claimed to have seen the ghost of the slain Orville Aderholt there, lurking in a cellar below the courtroom.[48]

4 TRIAL AND TERROR

As one can see in their memoirs, Vera Buch and Fred Beal's recollections of the signal events in which they were both involved in 1929 were often at variance. One thing the two leaders agreed on, however, was the confusion and ill-preparedness of their defense team. Both of them blamed this confusion on forces outside Jimison's or even the ILD's control. Beal said that the Communist Party leadership was split down the middle over Gastonia defense policy in 1929, as it was over most everything else. Party "right-wingers" insisted that the defense be based on the notion that the defendants had all been framed, that they had not fired their weapons at all, and that Aderholt had been shot by his own drunken associates, while the Dunne-Foster group, which was slowly becoming dominant within the Party, took the opposite view. The fact that the strikers fired their weapons should be frankly acknowledged, they argued, even lauded, and the defense should be based on their absolute right to do so in order to protect their union headquarters and living space. Beal said the ILD simply did not know which group to obey. Buch essentially agreed with Beal as to the split in the Party hierarchy over their defense. She believed that the ILD representatives were also split and that the prospect of a unified defense strategy emerging was therefore minimal.[1]

Certainly the Party's disagreements were clearly reflected in the way the *Daily Worker* discussed the issue. Initially, the shooting was portrayed as a "frame-up" pure and simple; "Charge Thirteen with Murder in Gastonia Frame-up" was a typical headline in the weeks following the police chief's death, and that may well have been the thrust of the defense team had the July trial proceeded. The legal staff of the ILD was working for a change of venue and a delay in proceedings "in order to more completely expose the ruthless, unscrupulous legal methods of the prosecution with the frame-up [*sic*] evidence," the paper reported in late July. After the shift in venue, however, the group's emphasis changed. From then on, "self-defense" was the only line of argument presented whenever the legal proceedings were discussed. "The Gastonia prisoners are today, as Sacco and Vanzetti were for seven long years, in the shadow of the electric chair," said an editorial on the eve of the second anniversary of the Italian anarchists' execution. "[They were] charged with murder, because they dared defend themselves against an assault of police thugs and gunmen who attacked their tent colony with the object of destroying it and murdering the strikers and their friends." The strikers had simply been defending what was theirs, and they had done so with such resolution that the "capitalist exploiters" were determined to have them killed.[2]

In the long weeks leading up to the trial, it became clear that the ILD expected little from the legal proceedings: the best defense was still, according to ILD officials, the mass defense. The American justice system would not save those accused from "class murder"; only the "mass action of the working class of the United States and of the world" would do that. Everyone must make a commitment, urged the writer John Dos Passos. The "least any man can do is to make it known as widely as possible which side of the fence he is on in this fight" and then act resolutely on that statement. "The mass strength of the American working class," said the ILD's national secretary, J. Louis Engdahl, "will save the brave members of the National Textile Workers Union and their sympathizers from the fate of Sacco and Vanzetti." To the end of mobilizing the American working class, rallies were held throughout the United States in August, while the executive of the International Red Aid, in Moscow, issued an appeal "to the workers of the world" to ensure that a "mounting wave of working class protest" prevented "the mill-owners' hangman" from doing his obscene work. It is, of course, difficult to gauge the extent of national and international support that such appeals generated, and doubtless the *Daily Worker* exaggerated both the size and the frequency of demonstrations throughout the United States and the world. Yet the extent to which the non-Communist press also reported frequently on such meetings indicates that the mass defense strategy had moved Gastonia firmly onto the international stage.[3]

Historians William and Christina Baker, who have studied international reaction to the events in Gastonia, have concluded that many of the rallies, parades, and riots that occurred throughout the world between August and October 1929 were organized by local Communist Parties as their particular contribution to mass defense. Britain's Communist Party was particularly active in getting people into the streets in support of the defendants. Nevertheless, concern for their fate ranged far wider than Party circles. Liberals generally were sensitive that another Sacco-Vanzetti case was in the making, while laborers all over the globe saw some connections between what had happened in Gastonia and their own situation. British miners, for example, had gone through their own particular form of stretch-out, while textile operatives there had for years been losing economic ground due to the twin burdens of wage cuts and longer hours. They viewed Gastonia, then, "in practical rather than ideological terms"—as something that could happen to them. "In truth," the Bakers wrote, "the Gastonia episode provided points of international identification with just about every aspect of radical politics and working class experience," and this accounted for the intense interest abroad. American tourists that year were often made uncomfortable by this concern. Mrs. Edwin C. Gregory, Senator Lee Overman's daughter and the former state regent of North Carolina's Daughters of the American Revolution, returned to her home in Salisbury, North Carolina, quite disgusted with all the attention the foreign press had paid to Gastonia. "I couldn't pick up a newspaper in Europe that didn't have the Gastonia disturbances spread all over the front page," she complained bitterly. She thought the defendants should be "deported," doubtless for ruining her trip.[4]

Three interlocking points were made repeatedly at these rallies held in the United States during August, meetings that were often addressed by the three women defendants. One was that militant workers could expect no justice from capitalist courts. The change in the trial's venue meant nothing; it was certainly no guarantee of a fair trial. The Charlotte courts, said Amy Schechter, were just as firmly under the control of the mill owners as those in Gastonia, and all that had happened was that a veneer of fairness had been provided where none, in fact, existed. "If we are saved from the vengeance of the mill owners, it will be by the power of a growing union," she declared, "and by the mobilization of the workers of America," not by capitalist jus-

GASTONIA HEARD AROUND THE WORLD

Some of the Many Tokens of International Solidarity

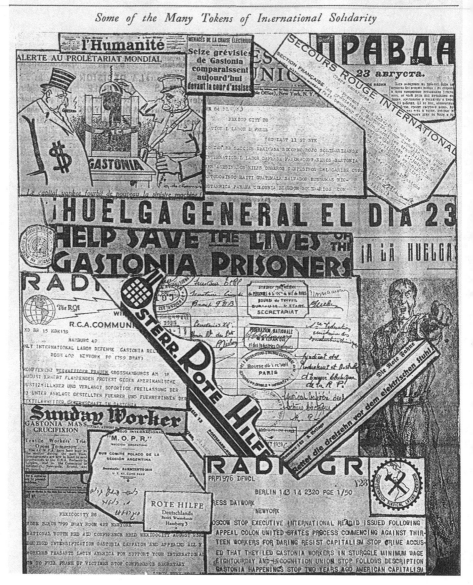

International support for Gastonia workers (Originally published in the Labor Defender*)*

tice. For Jimison and his associates, busily trying to put together a defense that would stand up in the "capitalist courts" of Charlotte amid a hostile community, such remarks were not exactly helpful.[5]

Second, the fact that August 23 was the anniversary of the Sacco-Vanzetti execution gave the ILD a superb point of comparison and a rallying cry. "Sacco-Vanzetti Week" now became "Sacco-Vanzetti Gastonia Week." Rallies were held throughout the world on August 23, both to remember the two martyrs and to show solidarity with those facing the same fate. It was too late for Sacco and Vanzetti, but at least their memory served to inspire those who fought against the mill owners, those "class enemies" who were "striving to burn alive the Gastonia prisoners."[6]

Emphasis on the class nature of the Gastonia struggle was the third constant of the ILD's mass defense strategy. In speech after speech, article after article, broadsheet after broadsheet, the ILD stressed that the events of 1929 were part of a pattern of class warfare that was breaking out all over the world. The prisoners were "class war prisoners," nothing else, and to save them from "class murder," members of the international working class must again "vent their fury against the murderous hirelings of American imperialism." For this reason, the defense of the Gastonia sixteen had been and would continue to be "conducted along clear class lines." If this meant parting company with other supposed friends of the prisoners, so be it. The nation's liberal newsmagazines, the *Nation* and the *New Republic*—to say nothing of the *New York Times* (the "harlot of privilege," the *Daily Worker* called it)—joined groups such as the ACLU to advise a more moderate approach. The *Nation* was particularly trenchant in its attacks on the ILD. "Unfortunately, too, the Gastonia defendants have some theatrically-minded friends, who are more zealous than wise," asserted one unnamed columnist, "and insist upon dramatizing the case as the prologue to world revolution." According to the writer, this tactic was stupid: more than that, it placed the lives of the defendants in danger. "We hope," he wrote, "that the Communists will prune their appeals of all phrases that may be interpreted as threats." After all, "events of the last two weeks had proved that North Carolina justice was not dead." Joseph Shaplen, writing in *The Survey*, made the same point. "In general, the *Daily Worker* and the International Labor Defense have given the impression to newspaper men and outside sympathizers of the defendants, that they were more interested in proving the existence of a 'frame-up' than in the acquittal of the accused men and women," he contended. Liberals should vigorously oppose their strategy, not only because the case was "an important episode in the struggle for the improvement of labor conditions in the South" but also because sixteen innocent people faced the possibility of heavy prison sentences. There was hope, however, particularly in the "fine manner" in which Judge Barnhill had handled matters so far. The defendants might still be saved through court action, provided that calmness and mutual respect prevailed.

The Communists would have none of that. The liberal journals and individuals were really "class enemies" anyway. All of them—especially the Socialist leader Norman Thomas, a "sniveling preacher"—had placed their faith in the proper working of the capitalist justice system for Sacco and Vanzetti, and look at the result. Sacco and Vanzetti went to their deaths "because of the meddling of the liberals," and this would not happen again. In the class war that had overtaken Gastonia—William Dunne's "citadel of the class struggle"—there was no place for the "meddling" liberals or the "yellow" socialists.[7]

As historian Theodore Draper has explained, the emphasis on the class-based nature of the Gastonia struggle made perfect sense to a group of revolutionaries who believed implicitly that world revolution was imminent. To Bill Dunne, "the sharp struggle reaching the point of armed conflict, furnishes irrefutable proof of the process by which the inner contradictions of capitalism in the imperialist period bring on economic struggles which speedily take on a political character." The world crisis of capitalism, of which Gastonia was a potent symbol, was at hand, and the time had to be seized without hesitation or compromise. Moreover, from the vantage point of more than sixty years, Party journalist Liston Oak's analysis of the affidavits presented to the court in July—an analysis which showed, he said, that sentiment for and against the strikers was "divided on class lines"—is hard to refute. The "capitalists," the mill owners, the middle class, the police, the courts, and the preachers all wanted them dead; their fellow workers and the small shopkeepers with whom they did business were overwhelmingly on their side. Certainly, the demonstrations in the courtrooms and the real affection with which the three women were greeted when they came out on bail early in August are indicative of that view.

The Communists were wrong on many things—their worldview, their analysis of American capitalism, their insistence that class solidarity would transcend racial antagonisms in the South. On the essentially class-based nature of the divisions in the Gastonia community, however, they were right.[8]

Of course, for Jimison and his team, who were struggling to get a defense ready before the trial's opening on August 26, the ILD's mass defense strategy and the split with the ACLU that ensued was a major handicap—all the more so since Arthur Garfield Hays, the ACLU's chief counsel, had at last agreed to assist at the trials. For local liberals like Nell Battle Lewis, the ILD rhetoric was a disaster. She had taken up the cause of "the forgotten eight," the local men on trial along with the union leadership and those who had come from other parts of the country to help out. "They were simply Gastonia mill-workers who wanted better wages and conditions," she argued, and now they were in danger of becoming sacrificed to the class war. All she got from them was a rebuke and a profession of faith in the ILD's tactics, but she remained unconvinced. The ILD propaganda would "incite bad feeling," to the detriment of the defendants, she insisted; besides, though she was emphatically "not a participant in the 'class war,'" she nevertheless wanted justice for the mill workers. There were many like her, she said. The ILD did not know what it was talking about.[9]

Indeed, many other North Carolinians did feel like Lewis. William Terry Couch of the University of North Carolina Press, for example, was outspoken in his support for justice for the strikers, though he deplored the sensationalism and downright lies of the ILD. In an attempt to coalesce such people into a body of support for the strikers and a counterweight to the ILD, the ACLU encouraged the formation of the North Carolina Committee of Liberals, later called the "Fair Play to the Gastonia Strikers" Committee. Elizabeth Yates Webb of Washington, D.C., daughter of a prominent North Carolina judge, headed this group, which aimed to provide "intelligent" and "balanced" support for the Gastonian defendants. Nell Lewis was a charter member. Others to sign up included Couch; John H. Cook, dean of the North Carolina College for Women; D. Elton Trueblood, dean of Guilford College; and Elbert Russell, dean of Duke University. Most of those who joined were either academics or clergymen. Several distinguished North Carolinians, including Howard Odum and Mary O. Cowper, declined the invitation. Despite Webb's best efforts and all her good intentions, the committee, which did nothing more significant than produce a mailing list, was no effective counter to the extremes of the ILD and the *Daily Worker*.[10]

Nevertheless, a few members of the committee did do more than merely allow their names to be used. One of these was the Reverend Ronald Tamblyn, a Methodist minister from Greensboro. He made a visit to Gastonia to see for himself what was happening there, then spoke of the disturbing situation to "the two thousand girls at the North Carolina College for Women." The girls were interested, concerned, and sympathetic; an opposite reaction came from Bernard Cone, the president of the Proximity Manufacturing Company, who was quick to summon the Reverend Tamblyn to his office to voice his displeasure at the tenor of Tamblyn's remarks. Nevertheless, Tamblyn continued to speak to his congregation, to local civic groups, to anyone who would listen about the need for balance and fair-mindedness in dealing with the strikers and not remain "comfortably indifferent to the great iniquities practiced in the name of law and society upon innocent folk." Sadly, he believed that he had made little headway, except perhaps among the young. Their elders remained overwhelmingly convinced "that Beal and the whole crowd . . . should be taken out and hung to the first tree."[11]

Once again, the nation's press drifted into North Carolina, this time to Charlotte. Courtroom seating had to be altered to accommodate "the greatest group of news and magazine writers ever to cover an event in that city." Again, the major northern dailies—the *New York Times*, the *New York Herald Tribune*, and the *Baltimore Sun*—had sent representatives. The left-wing press was also there, as were the liberal newsmagazines. Liston Oak was to cover the trial for *Labor Unity* and Bill Dunne for the *Daily Worker*, while Oak's wife, Margaret Larkin, had been engaged by *Survey Graphic*. The wire services had their representatives, and there were people representing foreign publications. Mass defense had worked; the trial was a major news event.[12]

Of course, Party members poured into Charlotte as well, augmenting the numbers of those already in the area. The usual array of pre-trial rallies and picnics took place. At one of these gatherings, Bill Dunne provided his opponents with a free hit when he told the white audience that "he had rather have his sister marry a negro than a loafing white man." Even the *Daily Worker* conceded that the remark had caused consternation and that several of the audience had left forthwith. The *Gastonia Daily Gazette* thought the episode indicated just how bankrupt the NTWU had become, as did David Clark. "The Communists may harangue until judgement day," he wrote in the *Southern Textile Bulletin*, "but they can never convince the cotton mill operators of the South that negroes are their equals." Juliet Poyntz took time off to do a little recruiting in Hickory, North Carolina, aiming to form an NTWU branch there. She and a British-born organizer, Ben Wells, held a meeting at a "negro tabernacle," urging the eleven whites and 150 African Americans who attended to "fight shoulder to shoulder . . . for better wages, shorter hours and the abolishment of child labor." Few were disposed to do so, and the minister who had provided the venue later apologized to his community, saying that he had no inkling that it was to be "a communist affair." Incidentally, the speakers allegedly "failed to make a hit with either race." [13]

Margaret Larkin had a happier experience. She attended an ILD-NTWU picnic in the woods at Mount Holly just before the trial began. There, for the only time in her life, she heard Ella May sing. It was a transfixing moment. The songs just "bubbled" out of her, she reported, just poured from this "slight figure with brown, bobbed hair, a firm profile and a very thorough smile." People crowded about the singer, chuckling at the attacks on the bosses in her lyrics, nodding as she sang of the hardship and meanness in their lives. "Her full, throaty voice gave the songs in mountain style, with an odd sort of yip at the end of each line that delighted her audience," Larkin wrote. "Purtiest singing I've ever heard," remarked a woman striker when Ella May had stepped down, and Larkin was inclined to agree. Thus began her quest to retrieve Ella May's "ballets" and make them part of America's folk song heritage. [14]

Charlotte was in the grip of scorching summer weather as the trial began on August 26. Soon the Mecklenburg superior courtroom became "as hot as an oven and rather smelly." These unpleasant conditions, however, did not deter would-be spectators, many more of whom turned up than could possibly be accommodated. The *Gastonia Daily Gazette* reported that several thousand were unable to gain admittance and that "scores" who had gotten in but were unable to find seats also had to leave. As with the abortive first trial, Harriet Herring thought that most of those present were "very sympathetic with the strikers," though she was only able to talk to a handful. "Oh I hope they turn them all loose, don't you," remarked the "vivacious mill woman" seated next to her. "Three elderly working men" sitting near her were also "very talkative about the whole situation" and very sympathetic toward the defense lawyers. Mill people in general were in support of the strikers, said one of them; "you could hardly find a working man who was not." The man "had much to say about the stretch-out system—especially as put in by Manville Jenks [*sic*]," which he blamed for all the "trouble" at Loray. As they parted that evening, he repeated what he had earlier claimed—that "you could not find any of the working people about Charlotte and Gastonia who were not for the strikers and for the union" and that "they preferred this National Union to the one at Marion [the UTW]." Anecdotal as they may be, these remarks are evidence that Beal and his associates, despite all the forces arrayed against them, had at least captured some hearts and minds.[15]

There was little to interest the spectators on the trial's opening day, consumed as it was by legal argument. They did find some amusement at an overzealous deputy's refusal to let the smartly attired women defendants take their place in the dock: thinking they were spectators, he brusquely shoved them away. At the end of all the argument, however, the defense had scored two important victories. First, Judge Barnhill greatly narrowed the scope of the state's case when he struck out a portion of the bill of particulars first filed on July 29; he ruled that this passage, which related to the alleged conspiracy, was far "too vague and indefinite to permit the defendants to prepare their defense." Jimison was "jubilant," believing that up to three-quarters of the state's evidence would now be excluded. Second, Barnhill rigorously reaffirmed what would be admitted as evidence. "I shall restrict the evidence to what happened on the grounds and will permit no evidence of any conspiracy except to resist the officers on the night of June 7," he ruled. Testimony "would be restricted to events bearing directly upon the shooting." These were important rulings in favor of the defense, as was Barnhill's decision to permit Jimison and his team to examine prosecution witnesses before their evidence was heard. No wonder Carpenter "vigorously resisted" the amending of the bill of particulars, and no wonder the defendants appeared "jaunty in spirit" as Barnhill gave his ruling. The defense needed a boost. Barnhill had already rebuked

Jimison over a slanderous ILD press release which had appeared over his name but which he had never seen, while the newspapers were full of stories "of differences of opinion between the defense counsel and the ILD, over whether it was to be considered a simple murder trial, or an episode in the 'class war.'" Jimison was having his troubles with Hays as well. Celebrated as the defense's "big gun," Hays displayed a willingness to assume that mantle, and his attitude profoundly irked the North Carolina lawyers and Neal, who believed that they had done all the hard work and that they, not the latecomer, thus deserved any accolades. As Forrest Bailey, Hays's close friend, earlier wrote in an irritated tone, "Those who are already in, especially Tom Jimison, not excepting John Neal, are anxious to have a monopoly of the prestige which they think this case will gain for them." The defense, then, remained split in serious and complicated ways.[16]

The prosecution had no such problems about unity, and they made an imposing array. There was the suave Hoey with his flowing gray locks, his cutaway coat, and his jaunty boutonnieres, and there was the "breezy" Carpenter. Sophie Melvin recalled that as she and her future husband, Si Gerson, were strolling to the courtroom each morning, they would often meet the dapper solicitor. "Good Mawnin', Miss Melvin," he would invariably greet her, doffing his hat and bowing elegantly, "you are looking perfectly charmin' this morning." He would then proceed inside to prosecute her. Other members of the prosecution included E. T. Cansler, one of the state's most able trial lawyers; Major Bulwinkle; R. Gordon Cherry, state commander of the American Legion; George B. Mason; A. C. Morgan, Gaston County's solicitor; A. E. Woltz; and various lesser lights of the Gastonia bar. All of them, said Nell Battle Lewis, were "staunch defenders of the faith," committed to the values and culture of the mill owners and ready to demand the death penalty for those seen to be challenging them.[17]

The trial now became hopelessly bogged down in the tedious process of jury selection. Because thirteen of the defendants were accused of a capital crime, the defense had a huge number of peremptory challenges—168 in all—and the prosecution had 58. Moreover, because of the events of the past months, most of the potential jurors had already formed opinions as to the guilt or innocence of the accused and could thus be excused for cause. Day after day, the tedious process of examination of prospective jurors went on. The jailer's five-year-old tow-

John Carpenter, Gaston County solicitor (Line drawing by Fred Ellis, originally published in the Labor Defender*)*

headed twins Jennie and Sylvio McGinnis would draw a name from the venire box, then the prosecution would question the people about their occupation, as they wanted no mill workers or union men on the jury, and the defense would question them about their connections with mill management, the extent of their property ownership, and their religious affiliations. Both were interested in opinions already formed as to the defendants' guilt or innocence. Day after day went by in this manner. The reporters became bored, and the defendants likewise. Vera Buch kept her nose buried in a book, while others slept. Only Clarence Miller "took enough interest to advise the counsel" and to wave at friends and supporters. Few prospective jurors "furnished relief from the drab proceedings." One such was J. G. Campbell, a Charlotte newspaper vendor, who kept the court in an uproar with his quirky answers to the questions put to him. He was a Presbyterian, he told Jimison, because he was "afraid of water" and thus had had to leave his family's Baptist faith. Joseph Shaplen reported that Campbell was "a fiery little man, who with arms akimbo showed great relish in telling the court and counsel that nobody ever made up his mind for him." He put on an "amusing" entertainment, which Barnhill eventually put a stop to, much to the disappointment of the bored reporters.

Perhaps because of his gift for the wisecrack, both sides passed him. Later they would bitterly regret having done so. Not until September 4 was a jury finally chosen, after the examination of more than six hundred potential jurors. Until then, wrote Raleigh journalist Fleet Williams, "the trial had served no useful purpose except to highlight the need for jury reform." It was the opinion of the reporters present, however, that in the final analysis, the defense had done rather better than the prosecution. There were two textile workers on the panel, four small farmers, two union members, and no managers. Now the trial could at last begin.[18]

The hearing of the prosecution's evidence had barely started when there was a sensational development. Medical evidence on the extent of the injuries to Aderholt, Roach, Gilbert, and Ferguson was being heard when, on a signal from Carpenter, the courtroom doors were opened and a life-sized wax effigy of the slain police chief, dressed in a ten-gallon hat and the blood-stained clothes he had been wearing the night of June 7, was wheeled into the courtroom. The effigy's entrance caused pandemonium—"a half-stifled wail" from Aderholt's widow, consternation in the jury box, laughter from the reporters present, and angry objections from the defense. Carpenter said that he needed the figure in order to explain the nature of Aderholt's wounds, but Barnhill would not listen. He ordered the effigy to be removed forthwith, both from the courtroom itself and from the adjacent office areas, though the clothes were admitted as evidence. Normal proceedings were then resumed, but already, reported the *Charlotte Observer*, "[the effigy's] gruesomeness had had a telling effect on the jury."[19]

This bizarre stunt had apparently been inspired by a popular Broadway play of the 1920s, *The Trial of Mary Duigan*, which had recently been filmed and had had a long run in both Charlotte and Gastonia. In the film, though, it was the defense that used a dummy, dressed up in the victim's clothes, to prove that the diminutive Mary could not possibly have struck the fatal blow. The prosecution really had no reason to pull the stunt, which was "new to courtrooms of this or any other state," except for its sensational effect. The effigy, incidentally, was no hastily constructed affair but had been carefully molded over the previous three weeks by a Gastonia lad, at a cost of one thousand dollars. He had worked secretly in the courtroom's basement, which explained the reported sightings of Aderholt's ghost.[20]

The state's evidence followed a fairly predictable pattern, or so the *Daily Worker* thought. The witnesses provided "a maze of perjury and contradiction," which was hardly surprising, given that the trial was merely a show, masking "the real issue of class against class." The result was a foregone conclusion, the paper predicted, the legal lynching of the "leaders of the textile workers." There was certainly a predictability to the prosecution's witnesses. All of those who, like "star witness" Otto Mason, claimed to have seen the whole incident were present or former employees of the Loray Mill. And all of them told essentially the same story: that Beal had previously urged the strikers to "get to the mill" and force the night shift out, if necessary; that the strike guards had fired the first shots; and that they had done so at the urging of Beal and Buch, who could clearly be heard shouting "Shoot him" and "Do your duty, guards" as the struggle between Gilbert and Harrison began. They were all adamant that it was McGinnis who fired the first shot; Tom Gilbert even asserted that it was McGinnis's first shot which hit him. The deputies who testified all agreed that they had gone to the strike headquarters in response to a then-anonymous telephone call (now known to have come from Mrs. Walter Grigg) about trouble there, and that Aderholt had been shot as he walked away from the building, having dissuaded Roach from entering it. They all emphatically denied that they had had any part in dispersing the picket line earlier in the evening or that they had threatened to kill the strikers.[21]

In cross-examination, the defense concentrated its attack on a few specific points. First were the confessions Carter and McLoughlin allegedly made the night of the shooting. The defense said these were involuntarily obtained, the result of severe beatings. Sophie Melvin took the stand to testify that she had been in the cell next to McLoughlin, along with Schechter and Buch, and that they had heard repeatedly "scuffling, banging, shouting," and screams of pain. Sheriff L. M. Allen of Cleveland County, to whom the confessions were allegedly made, denied any duress, though he did admit he had failed to warn either of them that the confessions could be used against them in court. Judge Barnhill nevertheless allowed their admission as evidence.[22]

Next, the defense took pains to throw doubt on the characters of Gilbert and Roach, and to that end the incident at Pedro Melton's filling station was vigorously explored. Both denied drinking that day, either in Charlotte or at Mrs. Grady Moore's on their return to Gastonia, where Gilbert allegedly was seen drinking "cherry wine." Both of them, in fact, claimed not to have touched alcohol for several years, though both admitted to having police records for violation of the prohibition laws. Adam Hord, the only policeman present who was not injured, was also forced to admit to several arrests for drunkenness in the past as well as to having been charged with killing an unarmed boy. Furthermore, under cross-examination the police witnesses admitted three important contentions: that they had had no search warrant when they entered the perimeter of the tent colony; that there was no disturbance there when they arrived—that all was quiet; and that no one knew who fired the shot that had killed Aderholt. In fact, Roach admitted, "I don't think any man could say who shot whom. They were just shooting, that is all." That, together with the contradictions the defense was able to point to in the prosecution evidence—for example, Grace Duffie, another Loray employee, testified that she heard 150 shots being fired, about ten times more "than the number fixed by any other witnesses"—left the defense reasonably confident that after three days of sustained prosecution attack, the case had not been established. Not even the evidence of Deputy Sheriff W. P. Upton— that when he went to the union hall ten minutes after the shooting he found Buch, Melvin, Clarence Miller, and Schechter there, all busily cleaning up cartridges—was thought to be particularly damning.[23]

Fleet Williams was inclined to agree. Some essential facts had been established, he wrote in the *News and Observer*. Aderholt had been shot in the back; there had been a telephone call to the police station, made by Mrs. Walter Grigg, who was disturbed by the disorder of the regular union meeting; there was no continuing disorder on the grounds when the officer arrived. These facts were beyond contention, but the prosecution had established very little else. True, both McGinnis and McLoughlin had admitted to firing shots, "but the testimony is all to the effect that Chief Aderholt was unhurt after these two shots had been fired." There was no evidence that either Carter or Harrison, the other guards present, had even fired their weapons. Though the state certainly had more evidence to present, Williams thought it would have to be much stronger than that so far heard in

Arthur Roach, wounded in the attack on the strike headquarters (Line drawing
by Fred Ellis, originally published in the Labor Defender)

order to secure a conviction, for the defense obviously had some strong
cards to play. In particular, he expected both Roach and Gilbert to be
thoroughly worked over.[24]

Joseph Shaplen was of a similar mind. The prosecution, he thought,
had singularly failed to produce any evidence of a conspiracy to murder
Aderholt, nor had they done much of a job of "incriminating each of the
defendants individually." Some of the state's witnesses were, to put it
mildly, distinctly suspect. Mrs. Duffie, for example, had conveniently
remembered witnessing the shooting only after getting her job at the
mill, where her father also worked. She had been "encouraged" in her
recollections by Major Bulwinkle. Shaplen thought that the suddenly
jaunty Jimison, who had taken to appearing in court in a "flaming red
tie" with a red buttonhole to match, may well be correct in his predic-
tion that once all the prosecution evidence had been heard, the court

would order that the charges against several of the defendants be dismissed. The rest, he thought, would eventually be acquitted.[25]

There was to be no further presentation, however, by either side. When the lawyers, the defendants and the spectators were finally seated on the morning of September 9, they were greeted with the news that J. G. Campbell, the newspaper vendor whose wisecracks had so brightened up the jury selection process, had become unhinged, a "raving maniac." His behavior had become a matter of concern as the trial proceeded; he had spent a lot of the time "squirming in his seat and rolling his eyes," his state of mind hardly helped by his fellow jurors, who reportedly teased him unmercifully, subjecting him to all sorts of "petty annoyances." Over the weekend his condition had deteriorated so markedly that he had had to be confined to a cell, where "he shouted and prayed and scraped the floor with a tin cup." Judge Barnhill had examined Campbell at 5 A.M. that morning; Campbell had "patted" the judge's feet and murmured "here is our good old judge" before again becoming violent, "crying to be shot, to be released, to be buried with his face down, and reinforcing his outcries by pounding a tin cup on the hard stone." Earlier he had had to be dragged out from under a bath, whereupon he had threatened to shoot three of his rescuers. Barnhill had reluctantly decided that there was nothing to do but declare a mistrial.[26]

Jimison was furious, immediately issuing a statement blaming the state for the aborted proceedings. "The effigy of Aderholt the State brought into court the first day simply scared him to death," he said, and the result was "a calamity which has robbed the defendants of acquittal for the state has put in no case and what it had to add was cumulative." His anger was vindicated by the remarks four of the jurors made to the press. They "would have voted to turn them [the defendants] loose," they said, the state having failed to prove its case—at least up to that point. A. F. Parker, one of the jurors, confirmed this decades later. "There wasn't a doubt in the world that the police was drunk when all that happened," he told an interviewer, and that was another reason they had been leaning toward acquittal.

Whether the sight of Aderholt's effigy caused Campbell to break can never be known. Certainly he had been terrified by its appearance— "his stricken eyes almost popped out of their sockets." But it transpired that he had long been considered simpleminded and that there was a history of insanity in the family. Moreover, his fellow jurors, bored and recognizing Campbell's eccentricities, had teased him constantly during the days they were sequestered together. "We were all locked up and had to have something to do, so picked on him, I guess," recalled one of them more than forty years later. "Shouldn't have done it, I guess." But they did. They tied his shoestrings together, sewed his pants up, hid his bedclothes, and generally made Campbell's life miserable. Both sets of lawyers had known of his simplemindedness but had passed him, thinking the other side would object. As for the eventual outcome of the new trial, now scheduled to begin on September 30, the view was divided. "It is an old adage that all delays in criminal trials benefit the defense," Fleet Williams thought, but this case might prove an exception, in that the defense had had a much better jury selection. The *Daily Worker* believed such speculation to be irrelevant. The delay was a mere glitch in the ruling class's "own machinery for a legal lynching."[27]

So the reporters again started for home; the male defendants went back to jail; the three women, still on bail, went off to Charlotte to dine with Amy's rich lawyer brother Frank at his Charlotte hotel, refusing "to wear anything but plain clothes in the dining room"; and Gastonia went on the rampage. Citizens who, on the evening of September 9, retreated to their front porches after supper "to catch some cool air" witnessed a most peculiar sight. A long line of cars, 105 in all, snaked through the city led by a motorcycle policeman, identified by many as Charles Ferguson. Drivers blew their horns, waved American flags, and shouted patriotic slogans as they "roared through the town," ignoring all the red traffic lights. According to Nell Battle Lewis, there was no doubt about who had organized this strange procession: it was the Committee of One Hundred, "which is said to be sponsored by the Manville-Jenckes Company." Angered beyond endurance at the termination of the trial, and fearful that the Communists might yet go unpunished, these strike opponents were about to vent their frustration in no uncertain fashion.[28]

First the convoy made its way to the NTWU headquarters, allegedly looking for Schechter, Buch, and Melvin. Disappointed by their absence, the mob members ransacked the place and did the same to the Bessemer City NTWU building just to make their point, shouting "long live 100 per cent Americans" while they worked. Next they surrounded Mrs. Perry Lodge's rooming house, where many NTWU organizers and Party officials stayed during their Gastonia visits. Inside were Ben Wells, a Lancashire-born NTWU official who had recently arrived in Gastonia; C. D. Saylors, a local organizer; and C. M. Lell, a Loray striker, still to be tried on the assault charges arising out of the events of June 7. About one hundred men crowded into the house, both Mrs. Lodge and Wells later testified, and Mrs. Lodge knew many of them personally. They were singing the grand old hymn "Praise God from Whom All Blessings Flow," but their intentions were neither Christian nor pacific: they shouted that they would shoot every organizer "who came down here." Wells was dragged to the front porch, an American flag was draped around him, and he was forced to make a speech denouncing the NTWU. They were then bundled into a car, and the mob set off for Charlotte. Halfway there, the convoy stopped and Wells was told to call Hugo Oehler in Charlotte to arrange a meeting, presumably so that he too could be captured. Wells complied but gave an obviously fictitious address, thereby alerting Oehler to the danger. Back in the car, Wells was repeatedly asked "how much the ILD paid to knock Mr. Campbell in line," and when he scoffed at the stupidity of the question, he was beaten so savagely that he lapsed into unconsciousness. All three men, including Wells, were able to identify several Loray Mill executives among their captors.[29]

The convoy made straight for Charlotte. At a crossroads just outside the city, it split into two groups. About fifty cars proceeded into the city. First they drove to the local ILD headquarters; finding no one there, they then went on to Jimison's law office and demonstrated noisily outside before moving on to his apartment and vowing to lynch him if he showed his face. Again frustrated by his absence, they then went to the Walton Hotel, looking for Bill Dunne, but once more their quest was in vain: Dunne had prudently absented himself for the evening. Their anger partially spent, the tired and disappointed men, "most of them dressed in white shirts," then returned to Gastonia, to the vast relief of the many Charlotte residents whose sleep had been disturbed by their racket. They had not disturbed Charlotte's finest, however. The night's police blotter contained no mention of the mob's presence in the city.[30]

A second group of the vigilantes had a much more satisfactory time of it. They drove through Concord, in neighboring Cabarrus County, and stopped at a lonely spot about eight miles out of the town. There they dragged the three unionists from the car and, after much talk about lynching them all, ordered Lell and Saylors to whip Wells with ropes and wooden posts. The men refused, so some of their captors set upon Wells themselves, hitting him repeatedly, mainly with tree branches. Fortunately, they were interrupted by R. B. McDonald and E. F. Leigh, local farmers out on a possum hunt. McDonald called his dogs, and the abductors fled in their cars, leaving a sorely bruised Wells and a shaken Lell and Saylors to make their way on foot to Concord, where they reported the matter to the local police before returning to Charlotte by train.[31]

The reaction from the defense lawyers to the night of violence was, predictably, one of outrage. Neal issued a statement bitterly critical of the Committee of One Hundred, calling it further proof "that a reign of terror which existed prior to the June 7 raid, and which still exists, forced the union members to defend themselves." The mill organizers were, he said, "determined to smash the union and get rid of the organizers at any cost." The Communists viewed the proceedings similarly; "Mill Thugs on Murder Raid," screamed the *Daily Worker*'s banner headline. Its Gastonia correspondent, Sender Garlin, told of "how the bloodthirsty posse of Gastonia is challenging the whole working class." One thing was already certain: the thuggery would not upset plans to hold a huge mass meeting in South Gastonia the following Saturday, September 14. This gathering would go ahead "in spite of the threats of mill murder gangsters," and a "powerful workers' defense corps" would be there to prevent further trouble.[32]

Outside the South there was extensive coverage of the night of violence. Newspaper editors, many of whom had just finished praising Barnhill and the way he had raised the level of southern justice, now hurriedly returned to the more familiar sport of South-bashing. The *New York Times*, less censorious than most, thought "the outburst of the rioters" proved not only that Barnhill had been right in changing the trial's venue but also that it strengthened the view "that the Gastonia murder and the Charlotte trial neither begin nor end the difficulties. They arise from the fact that the South has been newly industrialized, and is in the midst of struggles and workers' claims which were fought out in other parts of the nation when smokestacks began building among the farms." The night had brought disgrace not only to the state but to the "entire nation," decried the *Indianapolis Times*; moreover, it was simply another page in the story of Gaston County violence. "Have local authorities and police ceased to function?," the paper asked. "The mob spirit has been growing daily under the eyes of the police. . . . What are they doing to prevent the mob from carrying out its lynching threats next time?"[33]

Liberals in North Carolina were asking the same questions. The *News and Observer* was both angered and saddened by what had happened, believing the state to have been "disgraced." It was "a sad reflection upon law when men can be spirited away from a town like Gastonia and escorted by a caravan of automobiles through Charlotte without arrest, beaten and left on the highway." The *Greensboro Daily News* thought the violence simply reflected "the prevailing hate" in the Gastonia community, a climate that had "been carefully built up these many months" and would be very hard to remove. Where were the police on the night of September 9? Leading the parade. John A. Livingstone, Washington correspondent for the *News and Observer*, thought that the mad juror had become a symbol for North Carolina's collective state of mind: "It is excited, fearful and strained . . . a mind marked by violent prejudices." Moreover, if the aim of the violence had been to frighten the Communists out of Gaston County once and for all, then it had proved shockingly unproductive. Rather than frighten them, the mob had given the Communists precisely what they needed, "a fillip to a dying cause." More violence would surely follow, he warned, and it would not be long in coming.[34]

There were, however, those who excused the mob's action, to some degree at least. The *Charlotte Observer* was inclined to downplay the significance of the violence, calling it "simply a gathering of people excited over recent events, with no definite purpose in mind." The mob action should, however, serve as a reminder of the "wrought-up condition of the minds of the working people in the territory affected by the Communist agitators," something the state's liberal elements should particularly bear in mind, as should the Communists, who were preparing for their Saturday rally. The *Gastonia Daily Gazette* was much more direct. The good citizens of Gastonia had had all they could stand of the "reds" in their midst. The incidents on Monday night had to be seen in the context of occurring in a community that had "reached breaking point" and would no longer put up with "the sort of trash that is uttered by these reds." If they came back to South Gastonia on Saturday afternoon, they did so at their own risk and "in the face of the most determined opposition from the citizens of that community." They were not wanted, and "though they have been run away two or three times without suffering physical violence," this situation was likely to come to an end. The "good people" of the community had been "law-abiding" for long enough, the paper warned, pointing out that in many other southern counties, including any in South Carolina or Mississippi, "these organizers would have been hanging at the business end of a rope long before now." Gaston County's scrupulous adherence to law and order throughout the long ordeal had prevented this sort of event from happening so far, but it was unlikely to do so any longer.[35]

Given the escalating climate of violence, the state was forced to take some action. John Carpenter promised a full inquiry into the incident and vigorous prosecution of any alleged perpetrators—a claim that the Communists, at least, took with a very large grain of salt, because Saylors insisted that both the solicitor and Bulwinkle had been members of the mob on the night in question. Nevertheless, fourteen men were promptly arrested and charged with "conspiracy to kidnap, kidnapping, assault with intent to kill, imprisonment and false arrest." Roach, Gilbert, and Ferguson were among them. The rest were all employees of the Loray Mill, including the superintendent, A. G. Morehead, and the mill's physician, Lee Johnson. All were held on bonds of one thousand dollars each, pending preliminary hearings before Judge Shaw. The Loray Mill posted bond for all of them.[36]

On the same day, eight NTWU members were also arrested in Charlotte after police raided an apartment there and allegedly "uncovered an arsenal of guns and ammunition." Lell and Saylors were among their number, as was Dewey Martin and a recent arrival in the district, George Saul, who was said by police to be from Colorado, where he had "been directing miners' strikes." Though the ownership of shotguns and rifles was certainly no crime in North Carolina, the men were arrested and charged with "conspiracy to overthrow the government"; because they were Communists, the official logic went, that could have been their only purpose in collecting the weapons. Doubtless, the guns would have first been used at the meeting in South Gastonia on Saturday afternoon. To the *Gastonia Daily Gazette*, the arrest of these men bore out its long-held contention that "this gang was bent on murder if need be" and were coming to the Saturday rally "prepared to kill"—an allegation, incidentally, that the Party representatives failed to entirely deny. Rather, Liston Oak confirmed that the guns were to have been used at the mass rally to protect the speakers, and the *Daily Worker* said the meaning of the raid on the apartment was clear: to deny the workers the right to protect themselves. "The mill owners and their murderous vassals, the police, and private thugs and gunmen, are preparing one of the most monstrous blood-baths for workers in the history of the country," said the paper, and the arrests and arms seizures were simply part of the preparation for the expected "measure against defenseless workers." The workers would nevertheless defend themselves against the ruling class's hired guns, the paper maintained, though by what means was not entirely clear.[37]

The behavior of the Loray Mill management on the morning of September 14 bore out the *Daily Worker*'s mordant analysis. According to II. W. Branch, a Loray worker and one of the very few members of the Committee of One Hundred ever to talk publicly about the activities of that body, the mill's intelligence officer gave him a pistol, twenty rounds of ammunition, a note to his foreman saying that he was absent from work "serving a good cause," and explicit orders "to do everything necessary to break up the union meeting." He knew many others who were similarly armed and instructed, he said, and by midday the streets of the city were being patrolled by armed bands whose members were determined that no unionist would pass. The tension, the menace in the air, and the certainty of violence were pervasive, and it was doubtless for this reason that Dunne, Oehler, and the Party leadership decided that discretion was, after all, the better part of valor. Deciding at the last minute to abandon the meeting, they retreated hastily to Washington, D.C. They decided so late, however, that there was no time to adequately warn those who planned to attend. Tragedy resulted.[38]

The first to discover the change in plans was ILD publicity director Liston Oak. He had set out by car for the meeting, which was due to begin at 3 P.M., along with his wife, Margaret Larkin, Mary Heaton Vorse, and the driver, NTWU member A. E. Grier. When they reached the meeting place, they found that a crowd of two thousand, led by twenty-five heavily armed deputies, all members of the American Legion, had blocked off all access to it. Oak urged Grier to try and pierce the cordon of people, but this was a mistake. The crowd, obviously hostile, now surged out of control. Fortunately, the police then arrived. Oak and Grier were arrested, Oak on a charge of carrying a concealed weapon, which he did not deny. The women, badly shaken, were escorted to safety. Oak was extremely glad to see the police. He feared that had they not arrived, he would have been lynched.[39]

Meanwhile, also unaware of what had happened in Gastonia, a group of twenty-three Bessemer City union members set off for the rally in a truck specially hired for the purpose. Most of them were standing on the open bed enjoying the fall sunshine. Among them was Ella May. On the outskirts of Gastonia, the truck was stopped by a large band of angry men. They ordered the driver, George B. Lingerfelt, not to go any farther, but instead, "on pain of death," to turn round and return to Bessemer City. Lingerfelt, who had simply been hired for the day, was in absolutely no mood to argue, and did as he was bid. Eyewitnesses differed as to the details of what happened next, but the following factual outline seems uncontestable. After Lingerfelt turned the truck around and drove off, a sizeable number of cars followed him fairly closely. Just after the convoy had crossed the Bessemer City overpass, one of these cars suddenly speeded up and cut in front of the truck. Lingerfelt could not stop in time. Instead he careened into the car, hitting it with considerable force before coming to a halt. Some of those in the bed of the truck were thrown onto the highway as a result of the collision, but not Ella May. She was still standing in the truck when "the remainder of the mob came up," got out of their cars, and began firing their shotguns and pistols. Ella May was hit by a single bullet as she stood there; she said something like "Lordy they have shot me," then collapsed. Death was instantaneous, the bullet having destroyed the large aorta and then lodged in her spine. Most of the other unionists fled into the woods to evade the hail of bullets, but Charlie Shope tenderly helped carry the body of his "cousin" to a nearby cabin. From there it was duly collected and removed to the city morgue.

Shope then went home to try to explain to Ella's children what had happened to their mother. This time the state did not even wait for the completion of the coroner's inquest before taking action. The day after Ella May's death, it was announced that seven men were being held on charges of "conspiracy to slay" her. They included F. T.

Ella May's orphaned children. Left to right: *Albert, 3; Myrtle, 11; Chalady, 13 months; Clyde, 8; Millie, 6 (Originally published in the* Labor Defender*)*

Morrow, the driver of the car; Lowery Davis, Troy Jones, and Theodore Smith, who were in the car with him; L. M. Sossoman and Will Lunsford, who allegedly were in the group that surrounded the truck; and, oddly, Lingerfelt. All except Lingerfelt were Loray Mill employees, and Baugh, the mill's manager, was there at the arraignment to make bail for them all.[40]

The reaction came from all over the world. For liberal North Carolinians, it was but another sickening part of the ongoing nightmare. "The State of North Carolina stands shamed and disgraced by this inhuman crime," thundered the *News and Observer*. "The humble woman sought to improve the conditions under which she worked sixty hours a week to find bread for her five children," and for this she had been slain. Frank Porter Graham, a professor of history at the University of North Carolina and soon to become its best-known president, thought "her death was in a sense upon the heads of us all." And to think that those who killed her rejoiced in their Americanism! "Americanism," he thought, "was not riding in cars carrying men and guns that day, barring the common highway to the citizens of the State." Rather, "Americanism was somewhere deep in the heart of this mother who went riding in a truck toward what to her was the promise of a better day for her children." Ella May was the true American. If she had flirted with "alien doctrines" and false promisers, "it is we who are responsible for the void of leadership into which they came." The false Americans were the ones who had murdered her.[41]

As for Nell Battle Lewis, she was heartsick. Mary Vorse, who had returned to Gastonia to cover the trial, had spoken to Ella May a few days before her murder, and she now lent Lewis the notes she had made of that conversation. From Vorse's notes Lewis reconstructed the story of Ella May's life and an explanation of her commitment to the NTWU, which she ran in her "Incidentally" column under the bitter headline "A Triumph of North Carolina's Industrialism." The union "was a light in a dark sky" for Ella. "In it she saw some hope for herself and her children, the possibility of a fuller life." That was why she stuck with it, despite the blackjacks and the beatings, and why she was so determined to attend the Saturday rally—more determined than the leadership, as it happened. There was the truck, the "gang of angry, threatening men, the chase," Lewis wrote, then "a sharp halt. A volley of shots, agony tearing suddenly through Ella May's breast. The children . . . the baby . . . Dear Jesus, what will happen to them now?" Lewis could not answer the question.[42]

Outside the South, there was a wealth of editorial and other comment, much of it predictable South-bashing. A survey of the titles of some of the pieces indicates their general tone—"A Regrettable Mob Act," "Where the Brute Reigns," "A Southern Reign of Terror," and "Time to Stop Lynching" are just a few examples of the scores of columns commenting on the Gastonia violence. A very few reached beyond fairly standard condemnation of mob action and of the failure of local law enforcement to search for any wider meaning for her death. Gerald W. Johnson thought he had found it. "For a few weeks at least," he wrote in a moving obituary, Ella May "had lived." She had found in the union "a light—a will of the wisp perhaps, or the lurid mouth of hell, if you insist, but at any rate, a light, and she followed the gleam. . . . Shot down like a mad dog on the highway she may have been," but at least she died believing in something, "and if it happened to be the wrong thing," it was still belief. Moreover, in her death there was a warning for "the Christian gentlemen of North Carolina," those who had deliberately unleashed the "Tarheel beast" that killed her. She was gone, but her people were still there, "and if these drab and colorless ones are capable of such belief, what may not come of it?"[43]

"Now gentlemen," Johnson concluded, "club that to death if you can. Electrocute it if you can. Shoot it down on the highway if you can. For it isn't Ella May Wiggins that faces you now gentlemen. It is the sense of justice of an outraged people, which cannot be murdered by mobs. Faith did not die on the highway, nor is the world's belief in decency buried under Bessemer City clay."[44]

Whether Ella May was deliberately murdered on the specific orders of the mill management or simply the tragic victim of a mob slaying can never be known. Vera Buch was convinced of the former, arguing that her ability to bring African Americans into the NTWU had so incensed the mill owners that they ordered her killed. Others believed that her position as the strike's balladeer had marked her for special attention when the time came. Johnson's moving column showed that it did not matter. Deliberate or not, her shooting had made her a martyr, a symbol of the deeper meaning of the Gastonia struggle.[45]

The Communists immediately grasped this concept and quickly sought to capitalize on it. Announcing that it had taken full control of the funeral of the "Fearless Class War Fighter" who had been deliberately murdered by the "mill owners' gangsters . . . because of her tremendous influence on the workers," the Party called for a one-day strike throughout the land to remember her, and mass protests to mark her death. Nor were her children forgotten. They would be sent to the Young Pioneers School in Philadelphia, the Party said, to be "trained for leadership in the class struggle." Thousands of leaflets were quickly distributed to announce the protest.[46]

Ella May Wiggins, just twenty-nine years old, was buried in Bessemer City on Tuesday, September 17. Though Bill Dunne called it "one of the most impressive demonstrations of militant mass protest against the murderous terror of the bosses' black hundreds that has ever been seen in the South," the reality was, as W. T. Bost of the *Greensboro Daily News* wrote, that "it was a battle between Karl Marx and John Wesley and John Wesley won." The one-day strike did not occur, and there were no demonstrations, just a simple graveyard ceremony held in the pouring rain and conducted by the Reverend C. J. Black of the

International Labor Defense

Membership Card

Name *Ella May*

Branch *Bessemer City*

City *Bessemer City, N.C.*

Date of joining

(signature) .... Sec'y

Ella May's ILD membership card (Originally published in the Labor Defender*)*

First Baptist Church. The Bessemer City undertaker, Frank Sisk, had insisted on this arrangement. "We want this thing done right," he explained, and there was nothing the ILD people could do about it.[47]

True, her fellow unionists Dewey Martin, Wes Williams, and C. D. Saylors all spoke at length about her work for the NTWU, how she had joined the union "and worked to better the conditions of the working people" and how she had "given her life for the betterment of her fellow workers." But Engdahl, Dunne, and the other Party members present were all kept in the background, and it was the Reverend Black who had the last words. He read from John 14 and First Corinthians and, inviting all present to be "men and women who fear God," prayed for peace and for Ella May's orphaned children as the plain pine coffin was lowered into the red clay of the grave. "Brother Black had conducted a communists' funeral, and buried a dead sister exactly as a Christian," said Bost. "And Roger Williams had registered a triumph over Marx."[48]

Unquestionably the funeral's most moving moment came as the coffin was being lowered. As Ella's children, drenched and bewildered, scattered flowers on its lid, Kathy Barrett, a friend and fellow striker, stepped forward and sang "Mill Mother's Lament" in her clear voice. One stanza—

> It grieves the heart of a mother,
> You everyone must know,
> But we cannot buy for our children,
> Our wages are too low

—led Robert Thompson of the *News and Observer* to muse that this lament was the key to Ella May. She "was no more a Communist than she was a capitalist," he later wrote. "She joined the union, just as she no doubt joined the church at some time in her life, in the hope that it would in some mysterious way, improve the lot of herself and her children." Of all the thousands of words written about Ella May Wiggins both at the time of her death and subsequently, these are the ones that still ring truest. Her five children were sent not to the Young Pioneers school in Philadelphia but rather to the Presbyterian orphanage at Barium Springs, North Carolina. The Communists lost that battle as well.[49]

Those who had hoped that Ella May's death might at least bring an end to violence in the Gaston County area were disappointed. In the early hours of the morning after her funeral, three armed men came to the home of Cleo Tesneair, an NTWU organizer, in neighboring Kings Mountain. They abducted him, drove him across the South Carolina border and, somewhere near Gaffney, forced him from the car and into the woods, where they "flogged him unmercifully." They were from Gastonia, they told him, "and we're going to clean out this damned union." At the same time, another group dynamited the speaker's stand on a Kings Mountain lot that the NTWU had recently rented. Tesneair eventually made his way home, not severely hurt, but scared and shaken. There were the usual cries of outrage. "The fascist gangs of the mill barons have added another hideous crime to their

Ella May's children mourn at her funeral. (Originally published in the Labor Defender)

bloody record," said the *Daily Worker*. Both Governor Gardner and the ACLU offered rewards for information leading to the conviction of the perpetrators, but no one ever came forward. It was yet another of the unsolved acts of violence that disgraced the Gaston County area in 1929. It was also the last. Tesneair's abduction and beating marked the end of the pattern of systematic violence against NTWU members that had begun in the early morning of April 18.[50]

The explanation for this denouement is not hard to find. The NTWU had decided to abandon Gastonia, to end any pretense that a strike at the Loray Mill still existed. On September 23, the fifteen families still residing there were told that the tent colony was to be taken down, that the strike was over, and that they should find employment elsewhere. It was unnecessary to add that the strike had been lost, for the residents had known that for a long time. Mattie Hughes spoke for them, of their confusion, their broken dreams, and their regrets, to the curious reporters who had hurried to the colony on receiving the news. In

April she had been a spinner at the Loray Mill, earning twelve dollars a week, and she had been one of the original strikers, because she had believed she needed more money. Yet as she reflected on her life since then, she now knew they had not been too badly off. She and her family had a bathtub and running water in their mill house, she was paying off the furniture at one dollar a week, and yet she still had five dollars a week left after all rent and food bills had been paid. "We got along just fine." But she had struck with the rest and had not worked steadily since. True, her old life had been hard; she had had all the "cooking and housework to do" on top of her twelve-hour shift at the mill. "But, oh, God! I wish I had my job back," she cried. She and her family would have to uproot themselves now, she thought, and head for somewhere "where they would appreciate a good spinner and a God-fearing woman." Perhaps she would find that place, perhaps in South Carolina. All the women were worried for their future and for their families. The NTWU had nothing left for them, nothing at all. Four days later, the colony and its inhabitants were gone, and no one knew for sure where. Nothing symbolized the failure of the Gastonia strike more poignantly than the dramatically swift dispersal of these last human remnants of the union in which they had once so fervently believed.[51]

Though the abduction of Tesneair brought the violence in Gaston County to an end, its legacy still had to be dealt with. Sitting as an examining magistrate, Judge Thomas J. Shaw lost no time in conducting a preliminary investigation of those arrested for the abduction and beating of Lell, Saylors, and Wells. After hearing a great deal of eyewitness testimony, including that of the three victims, he ordered seven men bound over for trial in both Gaston and Cabarrus Counties, declaring as he did so that what the mob had done was "a disgrace to Gaston County." Those so indicted were A. G. Morehead and William Pickering, superintendents at the Loray Mill; Manville-Jenckes employees Dewey and Tom Carver, Smiley Lewis, and Carl Holloway; and Horace Lane, overseer of the Myers Mill in South Gastonia. As always, Baugh was on hand to provide the $7,500 bond required for each.[52]

In the course of his inquiry, however, Judge Shaw had given the defense lawyers for those accused of Aderholt's murder a real shock. Wells had testified at considerable length about his abduction and flogging and had even identified some of the perpetrators. Then, abruptly, the defense lawyer, Plummer Stewart, asked him if he believed in God.

"Nope," said Wells. What about the literal truth of the Bible? Again Wells answered, "Nope." "Do you believe that if you would tell a lie that God would punish you even in this world or the hereafter?," continued the persistent Stewart. "Nope," Wells replied for a third time, though he added that his own convictions would force him to tell the truth. That was enough. "He's disqualified himself your honor," declared the attorney, and so he had. Judge Shaw explained to the bemused Britisher that under an ancient North Carolina statute, which had never been repealed, nonbelief was sufficient grounds for the impeachment of a witness. Wells's testimony was thus disqualified. It had no effect on the inquiry, since there was more than enough evidence from good God-fearing men to secure the indictment, but it did pose disturbing questions for the Aderholt defense. Would the Communist defendants be able to testify in their own defense, as presumably they, too, would run up against this problem? For Bill Dunne, the meaning of Shaw's ruling was clear: the state had "declared an open season on atheists."[53]

Then there was the coroner's inquest into Ella May's death. It was still far from completed on September 25, when the coroner, J. F. Wallace, ruled that it be continued until October 19 because of the impending clash with the Aderholt trial. As he did so, he added another Loray Mill employee, W. M. Borders, to the list of those accused of conspiring to kill her. By this time a host of different witnesses had told very different stories about the sequence of events on the day she died. "A red headed man with a floppy panama hat" had shot her, claimed one witness. No, it was a bare-headed blond fellow, said another. The "weazened-face, blue eyed little mountaineer" Charlie Shope had told the most connected story of the shooting. Still dressed in the blood-stained garments he had worn on the day, for he had no others, he described how "Miss Ella May" had fallen into his arms, crying "Lord-a mercy, they done shot and killed me." "I caught her and Roy Carpenter helped me hold her up," he said, simply, but he knew she was dead. About fifty shots had been fired in all, he thought, first at the truck and then at the strikers fleeing across open fields to the shelter of the nearby woods. A number of other witnesses, however, claimed to have seen no evidence of violence at all that day, either in Gastonia or on the road to Bessemer City. Clearly, the truth of her slaying was going to be hard to reach if, indeed, reaching it were even possible.[54]

Finally, there was the next Aderholt trial, due to begin on September 30. Mass defense was still the ILD's main emphasis; the rallies and propaganda continued with even greater intensity, now that there was a martyr to rally behind. The defense team was purged of those lawyers least acceptable to the ILD, which was, after all, supposedly providing the funds.[55] Jimison was replaced as chief defense council by J. Frank Flowers, something to which he agreed readily, though he retained only "a minor role" in the revised setup, about which he was much less happy. More importantly, the celebrated Arthur Garfield Hays would not be returning to Gastonia. The attorney issued a statement pleading pressure of work elsewhere, but those close to him knew that he had found the experience of the first trial so disagreeable that he simply could not face a repeat dose. It was "a great relief to feel free of the Gastonia case," he told Roger Baldwin. Of his fellow counsel in Charlotte, "the most charitable way I can put it," he said, "is that they have their way of doing things and I have mine." He had been more explicit to Forrest Bailey. The first trial "was the most trying situation in which he ever found himself as a practicing lawyer," he admitted, and there was no way he was going through that again. Moreover, he had not appreciated the reception some of the locals had given him. "There goes that Jew with the three Republican names," they would shout after him in the street, "Arthur, Garfield, and Hayes!" The defense had urgent financial problems as well. In short, it was in serious disarray, as Beal and his fellow defendants well knew.[56]

The prosecution had no such concerns. They had streamlined their bench; six of the lawyers present at the earlier trials were no longer deemed necessary. They had had the experience of having already presented some of their evidence and had been able to refine their attack as a consequence. Moreover, there was the element of surprise. Rumors were persisting despite official denial that in order to make conviction certain, some charges would be reduced and others dropped altogether. Would that be the case?[57]

5 THE VERDICTS

Gastonia's year of drama had not ended. The drama's location had merely shifted from the streets and open spaces of the city to the courtrooms of Gaston, Mecklenburg, and Cabarrus Counties. Besides the second Aderholt trial—or third, depending on how those few days in July were viewed—those indicted for the kidnapping and flogging of Ben Wells had to appear in the courts of two counties, and the attempt to bring the alleged killers of Ella May to justice had barely begun. It was a busy time for the region's lawyers.

Liston Pope called the second trial "rather an anticlimax," given that all Communist activity in Gaston county had now ceased. Certainly the presence of a mere fifty spectators in the courtroom at the trial's opening supported this view, and the quiet opening provided a real contrast to the rowdy scenes just a month earlier, when people had clamored for admission. As rumored, though it seemed to surprise the disorganized defense team, the state immediately announced that it would be seeking guilty verdicts of not more than second-degree murder against only seven of the sixteen defendants—Beal, Miller, McGinnis, Carter, McLoughlin, Harrison, and Hendricks. The remaining nine, including the three women, were free to go—nol-prossed with leave. The assault charges were dropped against all except these seven. The reduction of the number of the defendants and in the severity of the charges meant a corresponding reduction in the number of peremptory challenges available to the defense during jury selection—from 168 to 28. All others had to be for cause, and this change was bound to ensure that there would be no repeat of the torturous process of the earlier trial. It was also believed that the reductions would make a conviction more certain. Certainly the Communists thought so. True, it was a retreat "compelled by the mass pressure of the working class," argued the *Daily Worker*, but it was also "a retreat made in order to get a more savage punishment of the workers than could well be obtained otherwise." The need for mass defense, therefore, was greater than ever. Further, though much had changed between the trials, the legal issue remained unaltered. It was still that of unlawful conspiracy among the strikers, out of which had resulted the murder of Chief Aderholt. Now it was simply a conspiracy of seven, not sixteen.[1]

Liston Pope believed that an analysis of the "economic alignment of the witnesses" who appeared for the prosecution and defense revealed something of the class-based nature of the conflict that had so shaken Gastonia. The prosecution was to present forty-nine witnesses, "of whom 14 were law-enforcement officers or members of their families, 10 were professional people (including 1 minister), 8 were merchants, 10 were skilled workmen and craftsmen, and 5 were ordinary mill workers." No fewer than ten were employed by the Loray Mill at the time of the trial, and only one had been, briefly, an NTWU member. Of the twenty-two defense witnesses, on the other hand, all but two "were, or had been, mill workers or organizers for the NTWU." It was not surprising, commented Pope dryly, that "in view of this alignment of witnesses, . . . the evidence presented by the two sides was highly contradictory in character."[2]

Much of it had also become familiar, having all been heard before. Again the prosecution aimed to prove, this time without the aid of a dummy, that Aderholt had been shot in the back; that the police had been enticed to the tent colony as part of a prearranged plan; that the strikers had fired the first shots; that they had been exhorted to do so; and that the police had simply been returning fire. Thus the first few days were largely taken up with evidence already presented at the mistrial. Otto and Eunice Mason again testified that they heard Beal exhort the crowd to go to the mill and drag people out if necessary; that Aderholt, on his arrival at the tent colony, inquired what the trouble was and was informed that "it was none of your damned business"; that Harrison had pointed a gun at Tom Gilbert; that a struggle ensued; that Buch and Beal could be heard shouting "Shoot him, shoot him"; that McGinnis fired the first shot; and that, after the first shot, noise and confusion reigned. Other witnesses again identified McLoughlin as having fired after McGinnis, and they agreed that neither of these shots had killed the police chief. "Red" Hendricks was also identified as having fired at the police, and all the witnesses agreed that they had heard Beal exhorting his guards to shoot. The alleged confessions of McLoughlin and Carter were again admitted as evidence over the vigorous objection of the defense team. Mrs. Grigg once more talked about her phone call. Connie Neal said Hendricks had come to her house after the shooting, "white as could be and plumb scared to death." He had implored her to let him hide in her closet, but she refused. The defense, of course, once again drew attention to the fact that all the witnesses heard so far were or had been employed by Manville-Jenckes and that Mason had been a company spy for quite some time.[3]

Roach, Gilbert, Ferguson, and Hord essentially repeated the testimony they had given earlier. Again Gilbert identified McGinnis as the person who wounded him. Again, the events that occurred at Pedro Melton's filling station were given a thorough airing on cross-examination, as the defense spared no effort in blackening the characters of the two officers involved. Roach, in particular, was subjected to a scathing attack by Jimison that went far beyond the allegation of frequent drunkenness and past violations of the state's liquor laws. The lawyer produced an "old one armed man" who alleged that Roach had seduced two young girls in Grover and Smyrna, North Carolina, and had then promised to pay the man to keep one of them "during the period of her confinement" but had not come across with the money. Jimison also charged that Roach had been forced out of the Gastonia police force "for accosting couples on the highways at night and extracting money from them." Roach denied the accusation, maintaining that the reason he had to leave was that he "got in some trouble about slapping a pet Negro." He had been sworn in as a special deputy on the night of June 7, however, and was glad to have been so, because he hated the unionists and wanted them out of Gastonia. "We don't need any Russians in North Carolina that don't believe in God," he asserted from the stand.[4]

The revelation of these details from Roach's murky past was one of the two highlights of the trial's first days; it even topped the remarkable allegation that Adam Hord, while drunk, had once slept in a church—with his horse alongside him. The other was the arrival in Charlotte of the "labor jury." This group of ten men and two women, which included two African Americans, had been elected at a recent conference of the Trade Union Unity League (TUUL). Its purpose was to listen to the evidence and render its own verdict, which would then be submitted to various groups the league represented. The jury included several local NTWU members, including Daisy McDonald, but it was the presence of its two black members, Sol Harper of the TUUL's Negro division and Charles Frank of the American Negro Labor Congress, that occasioned the most comment as they filed solemnly into the Charlotte courtroom—two days after the trial had started. The selection of the blacks, said a TUUL representative, "expresses the absence of racial prejudice among the white workers who helped select them" and "their general solidarity with the struggles of the southern working class."[5]

Solidarity or not, the group could not be permitted to remain in the courtroom proper, or, rather, the two African Americans could not. They were quickly told to remove themselves to the balcony forthwith, in accordance with North Carolina ways. Noisily the whole twelve trooped out and, after posing for photographers, moved upstairs, where they sat for the rest of the trial. David Clark believed it was proper for them all to be there, "because people who associate with negroes on such terms of equality are no better than negroes." Clark believed the "labor jury had been sent to Charlotte as a deliberate effort to insult the people of this section and to cause more trouble," a view with which at least part of the defense team heartily agreed. Neither the furor engendered by the presence of this "jury" nor the publicity and press coverage surrounding the southern NTWU rally in Charlotte on October 12, which had racial equality as its main theme, did the cause of the defendants much good, no matter how well they fit the parameters of ILD mass defense theory.[6]

Nevertheless, the defense was reasonably confident as it came to present its evidence, which it had not had the chance to do at the mistrial. The plan was to show that the strikers had good reason to fear the police, given the escalating level of violence in the community—violence directed exclusively at them. The lawyers wanted to prove that Gilbert and Roach were particularly antagonistic toward them and that on June 7 the two were both so drunk as to be out of control. There had been no plot to lure the police officers to their deaths; rather, the police had arrived unannounced, had trespassed on the colony's grounds, and had begun the shooting. In returning their fire, the guards were simply defending their property—an action that, ironically, Aderholt had earlier conceded they had the right to undertake.[7]

Thus the defense produced a parade of witnesses to substantiate its account of the night's events. Several, including various members of the Corley family, testified about the state of Roach's and Gilbert's sobriety that evening, while H. A. Strange said he was certain that after the parade had been broken up, he had heard Gilbert shout, "Let's go down and kill them all out. This is the best time we will ever get. I have been aggravated with them as much as I intend to be." Both Gladys Wallace and Saylors testified as to previous threats by Gilbert to kill them all, again when he was drunk. In their accounts of the minutes before the shooting, the arrival of the police, and the tussle between Gilbert and Harrison, defense and prosecution differed little, except on the crucial point of who fired the first shot. Wallace, Saylors, Paul Sheppard, and Katie Corley all were adamant that the police had shot first, and without provocation, as Beal and Buch had *not* cried "Shoot him, shoot him." Only after the police had started shooting, they agreed, did the strikers retaliate.[8]

In cross-examination, the prosecution lawyers did their best to move the emphasis away from the facts of the case to the beliefs of the defendants. Indeed, Cansler specifically requested that the lawyers be permitted "to ask the same questions as those admitted by Judge Thayer in the Sacco-Vanzetti trial," thus confirming what the defense lawyers had always contended, that the state wished to make the defendants' beliefs the trial's central issue. They were at first unsuccessful. When Dewey Martin was testifying, the prosecution attempted to introduce the racial issue: Cansler asked him whether a "negro, Otto Hall," had ever shared a speaker's platform with him. The defense objected, whereupon Cansler argued that the prosecution considered it an impeaching question—that the testimony of anyone who advocated "the social equality of whites and Negroes" should be disregarded. Barnhill, after hearing argument, ruled against the prosecution; the race issue would not, therefore, be brought into the trial. The defense, much relieved, went on with its plans to put all the defendants on the stand.[9]

There was another issue pertaining to belief, however, on which the judge had not yet ruled. During the cross-examination of striker Katie Corley, the daughter of striker Gladys Wallace, Corley was asked about her ILD membership and, specifically, whether the organization was an arm of the Communist Party. The defense objected strenuously, arguing that matters of belief were of no relevance to the court, and after hearing argument, Barnhill reserved his decision on the question. When he gave it, the character of the trial changed. To some, like Liston Pope, the real issues of the trial had never been conspiracy or murder but "the Communist attitudes toward politics, race, unionization and religion." To allow these issues to be introduced openly into the trial was inevitably to influence the minds of the jury against the defendants. Right from the first inquest and the questioning of Amy Schechter, the defense lawyers had thus fought to prevent such matters from being discussed, and they had largely been successful. They had thought they had an ally on the bench and had fashioned their strategy accordingly. But they were wrong.[10]

It was during the questioning of Fred Beal that Barnhill announced his decision, which was clearly an attempt to find a middle way between the two extremes. There was to be no unrestricted questioning of the witnesses; the prosecution was banned from asking questions concerning their membership of, or affiliation to, any particular association, including the Communist Party. However, the defendants could be questioned about their personal beliefs and convictions, not for impeachment purposes but to enable the jurors to gauge what manner of person they were listening to and to assist them in determining how much weight to place on each defendant's evidence. The prosecution lawyers were less than satisfied at the limits placed on them, and the defense was aghast that the door had been opened at all. The judge, having made up his mind, would not be moved. A witness who took the stand in his own defense laid "himself open to cross-examination as to his own utterances and acts," he thought, "but the examination must be confined to that scope." Moreover, a Communist, with his or her primary loyalty given to the Soviet Union, should not necessarily "determine to be tried as a loyal citizen of the United States." This was enough to cause the *Daily Worker* to trumpet "Judge Barnhill Rules Workers Are Not Citizens" and to prompt other, more sober citizens to worry that the heresy trial, or the Sacco and Vanzetti repeat that they had hoped to avoid, was not now upon them after all.[11]

The questioning of Fred Beal proceeded along these lines. Though he was on the stand for five hours, much of the time under cross-examination, and though he answered all questions of fact freely and volubly, Beal was extraordinarily vague and evasive when questioned about matters of belief. He talked about the events of June 7: how he lay on the floor during the shooting and thus had had no clear idea of what was going on; how he had not been in the parade but in the union hall working on the accounts; and how he had taken Harrison to the hospital before traveling to Charlotte by taxi to see Jimison. He told of his arrest in Spartanburg, his return to Gastonia, and his fear that he might be lynched on the way. He was, he admitted, "scared" of the Committee of One Hundred. Beal told, too, of his arrival in Charlotte in January 1929 and of his general organizing activities in the area. He professed no hostility toward Aderholt; rather, he claimed that the police chief was probably trying to limit the trouble caused by his drunken deputies when he was shot. Try as they might, the prosecution lawyers could not build up a picture of a crazed and violent revolutionary. When confronted with copies of articles purportedly written by him, and explicitly advocating violence, that had appeared in the *Daily Worker* or *Labor Defender* in recent months, he either denied authorship altogether or claimed the articles had been rewritten before publication. He had never ever advocated violence, he averred, either in Gastonia or elsewhere. When asked if he favored the overthrow of the United States government by force or violence, he explicitly said no, nor did he support the abolition of the United States Constitution. It was simply not a very revolutionary performance. As Fleet Williams reported, he successfully "parried all questions of Communism," which the terms of Barnhill's ruling enabled him to do. The prosecution, perhaps despondently, did not even raise the question of his religious belief. Williams was sure Beal would probably have claimed he was still a Methodist.[12]

The next witness, however, made no attempt to mask what she held to be true. This was Edith Saunders Miller, Clarence Miller's wife, who had been sent by the Young Communist League to work with the tent colony's children. The defense put her on the stand to corroborate Beal's account of the events of the shooting, and she was able to do so. However, under the delighted cross-examination of the prosecution team, she also did much more. She was asked what she taught the children. Did she tell them that they needed "a government of workers and farmers," as in the Soviet Union? "Yes," she said. Had she discussed the flag with them? "When the workers and farmers got control of this government they would have a flag of their own," she said, and it could well be the flag of the Soviet Union. She had also taught the children about the evils of capitalism, including the cruelties of their own situation. Soldiers were always used by mill owners against strikers, she said; what they had seen in Gastonia was typical of the whole world, but it was a world about to change.[13]

Miller was equally forthcoming about her religious belief—or lack of it. Under the "watchful eye of J. Louis Engdahl," and to the despair of the defense lawyers, she emphatically denied belief in a Supreme Being; instead, she affirmed her conviction that man "controls his own destiny." The defense objected, but in vain; Barnhill this time decided to permit the line of questioning for impeachment purposes only. The prosecution's purpose was somewhat different, as the defense well knew. It was never impeachment, but rather, as Neal said in a despairing final plea to the judge, "to get into the minds of the jury that the defendants hold these ideas." Whatever faint hope their clients had of acquittal, Neal and Jimison knew, had died with Miller's testimony. The defense decided, therefore, to put no more witnesses on the stand.[14]

Fred Beal always believed that Edith Miller had been told by the Party to testify as she did. Right to the end, he said, the Party had been divided as to whether to use the witness stand as a vehicle to "propagate" Communist principles, given that conviction was a certainty anyway, or whether to avoid antagonizing the jury any more than necessary. He and the other defendants had all been told not to mount the soapbox and to avoid propaganda. According to Beal, Engdahl had apparently given just the opposite set of instructions to Miller at the very last minute because the Party had decided to make what political capital it could out of the trial. Later Beal was predictably bitter about what Miller had done. She had, he thought, been more concerned with gaining "the commendations of Stalin's lackeys in New York and Moscow" than with the prisoners in the dock.[15]

Vera Buch's account tends to agree with Beal's, though for quite different reasons. She argued that the trial came at a time when the factionalism that had so riven the Party throughout the year had come to a head. She, Weisbord, Beal, and many more were on the way out in Party circles; others, like the Millers, were on the way up. The trial was a device through which the Millers could be recreated as heroes. Thus Miller was given a starring role at the June 7 shootout, when according to Buch he had not even been in Gastonia at the time—an argument that is hard to believe, given the testimony of Deputy Sheriff Upton, who claimed to have arrested Miller at the union hall. Much of the defense evidence at the trial was also perjured, Buch said. The prosecution was not the only offender here. As for Edith Miller, she was "a collaborator in the fabrications of the Party," but as far as her testimony was concerned, she may have been acting under the instructions of her organization, the Young Communist League, rather than the Party itself. The YCL, Buch said, was regarded as being much more radical, more militant, more "leftist" than the parent body, and in her responses from the stand, Miller may have been speaking for them.

Whatever the case, the Party quickly capitalized on her testimony. The *Daily Worker* praised her to the skies. She had gloried "in the opportunity to use the sounding board of the courtroom to convey a real Communist, a real proletarian challenge to the fascist reaction," exulted the paper, "knowing that only by so doing can the proletariat receive the enlightenment that equips them for the struggle to victory." Implicitly contrasting her testimony with that of Beal, the *Worker* pointed out that Miller had not accepted "the opportunist conception of trimming principles for some supposed illusory advantage" but had rather "sought to tear off the blindfolds of religion and capitalist ideas from the masses." She had indeed done "her Communist duty." Incidentally, the Party never disputed that the instructions given to Miller differed from those given to the other defendants, nor that they had been kept from the defense lawyers. The reason for the change, said Party officials, was not for propaganda purposes, nor was it to create martyrs. Rather, it was to broaden the grounds of appeal to a higher court should a guilty verdict be brought down.[16]

The defense lawyers were less concerned about the reasons for Miller's decision to testify as she did than about containing the damage she had done. But that was to prove impossible, given the decision not to call further witnesses. Instead, their alternative theory of Aderholt's death had to be confined to their closing argument. It caused quite a sensation nonetheless, as the contention was that Aderholt could well have been shot by one of his own men—to be precise, Adam Hord. Aderholt had been killed by pellets from a sawed-off shotgun, Thaddeus Adams argued, and Hord was the only man present to have carried such a weapon. Aderholt was shot in the back. Hord, who had admitted to going behind the union hall in his search for miscreants, could have done that. "His own crowd did it," Adams alleged, while they were "running around trying to find people." The defense also concentrated on Roach and Gilbert, arguing that the firing had occurred only after the "two drunken policemen," acting completely without authority, had invaded the union's property. Aderholt, in fact, was portrayed less as an aggressor than as a victim of Hord's reckless gunplay and, above all, Tom Gilbert's drunken thuggery. McCall contemptuously called Gilbert "the bloody Irishman of Gastonia, who'll fight a woman as quick as a man." He and Roach had planned the raid on the union hall, McCall said, which had resulted in tragedy. "The blood of poor Aderholt is on Roach and Gilbert," he closed.[17]

Given the limited evidence, the defense lawyers did not do a bad job of showing "reasonable doubt." They were no match, however, for the combined histrionics of the prosecution team. "The silver-tongued orator of Shelby," Hoey himself, "without malice, without hate, without even bitterness in my heart," urged the jury to find all the defendants equally guilty. Jack Newell, with his talk of "Bealism and gunism," contended that "little children were taught to disrespect the government of the United States." The dignified Cansler spoke of Aderholt's voice "appealing to you today from eternity." And above all, the prosecutors had Solicitor Carpenter on their side. Liston Pope, with considerable understatement, commented that in his closing address the solicitor took to the brink the wide latitude "allowed in summations in North Carolina courts." During the course of his two-hour address, Carpenter acted out the tragedy, impersonating Aderholt. He sobbed; he prayed; he lay on the floor; he seized the hand of the weeping widow, until Barnhill made him release it; and he handed her Aderholt's bloodied coat, imploring her, in breaking tones, to "take it home." He praised the chief as "this stainless Christ-like chap," and he excoriated Beal and his fellow defendants as a "traitorous crowd, coming from hell." His impassioned appeal to the jury included the poetic questions,

> Do you believe in the flag of your country,
> floating in the breeze, kissing the sunlight,
> singing the song of freedom. Do you believe in
> North Carolina? Do you believe in good roads, the
> good roads of North Carolina on which the heaven-
> bannered hosts could walk as far as San Francisco.

Into this peaceful land had come Beal and his "fiends incarnate, stripped of their hoofs and horns, bearing guns instead of pitchforks." They had brought "bloodshed and death," but now they stood at the bar of justice. There was only one answer the people could give. In a parody of the instructions Beal allegedly gave his guards that fateful night, the solicitor urged the jury, "Do your duty, men; do your duty." [18]

Carpenter's extraordinary performance occasioned much comment. Outside the region it was pictured as another example of the odd folkways that confirmed the South as a region apart—a place "Where Oratory Still Witches"—while within the state, liberals were disgusted. Calling his performance "nauseous burlesque," the *News and Observer* said the solicitor had made a "prostitution of the trial." Prostitution or not, Carpenter's antics seemingly did not offend the jury, which brought in a verdict of guilty on all counts after less than an hour's deliberation. Under the circumstances, the verdict itself was scarcely a surprise. What was surprising was the severity of the sentences Barnhill imposed, particularly on those from out of state. Beal, Carter, Miller, and Harrison were all sentenced to seventeen to twenty years; McGinnis and McLoughlin to twelve to fifteen; and Hendricks to five to seven. Beal reportedly fought back tears when these draconian sentences were announced. Bond, pending the expected appeal to the state supreme court, was set at a very low level: $5,000 for the first four, $2,500 for McGinnis and McLoughlin, and only $2,000 for Hendricks. The *Gastonia Daily Gazette* was appalled. Though its editors approved the verdict and the sentences, they believed that the paltry bond level had negated the effect of both. The defendants would soon be "scot free[,] . . . never to be heard from again in this country." [19]

Predictably, the defense lawyers quickly filed notice of appeal, and in doing so, they clearly signaled the grounds. "These boys were convicted because the jury were made to hate their beliefs," said Flowers. The verdict had come so rapidly that the jury could not have considered each defendant separately, as they had been charged to do. They had, instead, been motivated by prejudice, "which warps our conceptions and obscures our judgement." [20]

Though the jury had quickly found the defendants guilty of conspiracy to murder Chief Aderholt, the question of who actually fired the fatal shot was never addressed and remains open to this day. Though the defense introduced its alternative theory of the killing—

Fred Beal in jail (Originally published in the Labor Defender)

that Aderholt was shot by Adam Hord—almost as an afterthought, it gained wide currency surprisingly quickly. In *The Mind of the South*, W. J. Cash asserted that Aderholt was killed "quite probably by a gun in the hand of one of his own officers." Robert L. Williams and Elizabeth Williams, joint authors of a study of the strike, repeated the assertion, adding that the killing might even have been deliberate, as Hord had designs on the police chief's job. Frank Sisk, the Bessemer City mortician who arranged Ella May's funeral, agreed that there was much talk after the killing that Hord had done it to secure his own advancement, while Mareda Cobb was in no doubt at all as to who the real culprit was. Aderholt had not been shot by the strikers, she told an interviewer many years later, but by "the cops"; everyone in Gastonia said so at the time. Surprisingly, even Aderholt's daughter came to agree. Adam Hord could well have killed her father, she told Christina

Baker. They had not gotten along well for some time; besides, Hord was an ambitious man who coveted the police chief's position. If so, he must have been sorely disappointed, for he was not chosen to succeed Aderholt. Tom Jimison added a new dimension to the speculation when, in 1935, he asserted that the man who actually shot Aderholt was never brought to trial. He knew who it was, he said, but because of his past association with the defendants, he could say no more than that. Many others knew who the real culprit had been, he continued, "including some of the attorneys who presented the case."

Despite Jimison's unsubstantiated assertion, it is still most probable that no one then knew who fired the fatal shot and that no one can know now. Of the police officers at the scene, Hord alone was armed with a shotgun loaded with number 4 shot, the type that hit Aderholt. Moreover, the police chief could easily have stepped into his line of fire as he directed the drunken Roach away from the union hall. Nevertheless, the camp guards were using number 4 shot as well, and they too were shooting in Aderholt's direction. Any one of five people, including Hord, could have hit him, and he could even have been hit by more than one blast. No one will ever know.[21]

Not everyone approved of the jury's verdict, of course, or of the means by which it had been reached. In London, a pitched battle took place near the United States Embassy: police vigorously dispersed more than five hundred Communists who had gathered to protest the verdict. Women screamed and fainted, reported the *New York Times*, as police charged the milling mass of demonstrators blocking the entrances to Victoria Station. Earlier, the demonstrators had marched from Nelson's Column singing the Red Flag and distributing leaflets denouncing the verdicts as an "even more ghastly crime" than the execution of Sacco and Vanzetti. Within the United States, the ILD was active in promoting similar demonstrations and expressions of outrage; in particular, the group emphasized that the life and martyrdom of Ella May provided inspiration for the continued struggle. The *Labor Defender*'s November issue ran an article that May herself had purportedly written just a few days before her murder, in which she asserted her belief that "we are going to have a union in spite of what the boss says," together with a photostat of her membership card and an ILD appeal to "Fight in the Spirit of Ella May for the Freedom of the Gastonia Prisoners."[22]

More generally, and especially outside the South, the raising of the religious issue received much critical comment, as did Judge Barnhill—who a short time earlier had been the hero of the hour—for permitting its introduction. The ACLU bitterly accused Barnhill of "transforming a murder trial into one of heresy." Moreover, he had not needed to do so, as yet another North Carolina judge had explicitly denied the validity of the 1777 law. Over in Cabarrus County, presiding over the trial of those accused of flogging Wells, Saylors, and Lell, Judge A. M. Stack rejected the contention that nonbelief was grounds for impeachment. Whatever the 1777 statute may have said, it had been invalidated by the Fourteenth Amendment to the Constitution, with its guarantee of equal protection under the law. So there had been room for doubt, the defendants' supporters argued; Barnhill could have taken another course and must therefore take the blame for the "heresy hunt" into which the trial had degenerated. "It seems to me," wrote Heywood Brown in the *New York World Telegram*, that "the disposition of the American press to concede that the Gastonia trial would not be another Sacco-Vanzetti case was much too hasty. Judge Barnhill of North Carolina has made himself fit to lace the shoes of Massachusetts Webster Thayer, and to wear them too." Most of "the greatest leaders of world thought" could not have testified in the trial, given Barnhill's ruling, he argued, and certainly most modern religious leaders would have found their credibility impeached. "North Carolina, there she stands, mired in a bigotry which has not abated in one hundred and fifty years."[23]

Judge Barnhill, however, did not share this perspective. Speaking to the Rocky Mount Rotary Club, in his only public comment on the trial, he ridiculed the defense's contention that the "policemen stood up and shot each other." This was a "fake defense," he thought, mandated by "Communistic influences." The only proper defense, the *"real* defense," was that of self-defense—that the defendants had acted as they did out of fear of the mob. Had their lawyers stuck to this line of argument, he thought, and followed it through, at best Beal and his companions would have been found guilty only of manslaughter, presumably at his direction. Instead, the ILD had triumphed over the local defense counsel, most obviously in its insistence that Edith Miller take the stand. "The hypocritical act of the witness kissing the bible" and then repudiating its contents a few minutes later had had an indelible effect on the jury, and for this the ILD stood responsible, not the trial judge. He had had to allow the state the right to question her as to her religious beliefs; North Carolina law, as he saw it, dictated no other course. But it was the ILD who insisted that she take the stand in the first place.[24]

Barnhill's critics were at one with the *Gastonia Daily Gazette*, however, in the belief that the seven prisoners would not long remain in jail. There would clearly be an appeal, and pending it, they would soon be freed on bail. Everyone who believed this was wrong, for the bitter disputes between the defense lawyers now became noisily public. One result of this wrangling was to delay the provision of bail money. Jimison had made his attitude clear even before the trial had finished. He did not wait for the verdict; instead he departed for a family vacation. But he was holding $15,000, which had originally been the bail money for the three women defendants and was now expected to be used to free at least some of the seven prisoners. But with Jimison away and out of contact, this could not be done. Some money was found from other sources, and Hendricks was the lucky beneficiary. The six others remained in jail.[25]

Nor did the situation change on Jimison's return. He refused to release the $15,000, saying that it had already been attached for debts owed by the ILD, including his own and Neal's fees. Moreover, a private detective, H. G. Gulley, whom the ACLU had employed in order to assist the defense lawyers, had not been paid either. Thus the money would not be released until these debts had been settled. In taking this position, Jimison had brought into the open a dispute that had simmered below the surface at least since the mistrial and had further soured relationships within the defense team. Despite all the appeals for funds and the fanfare over their mass defense efforts, the ILD had not been good about paying the lawyers, especially Jimison, who had been on the case the longest. In September, Engdahl had returned his bill for $3,000, saying that while he did not dispute its accuracy, the money was not there to meet it. "I must ask you, therefore, to reduce your fee to what we can pay," he stated, offering him instead "a straight fee" of $1,000. The other lawyers had similar problems. Indeed, at one stage Thaddeus Adams had insisted on being paid in advance to avoid further "misunderstanding or difficulty in collecting." McCall had received no money either, and the whole defense effort had been handicapped by the ILD's failure to make good on its long-standing promise to provide money for stenographic assistance. To the ILD, convinced that the revolution was at hand, all this squabbling about money seemed needless, petty, and selfish, but for the southern lawyers—especially Jimison, who had spent most of his year on nothing but Gastonia matters—it was their livelihoods.[26]

Once the dispute had become public, it swiftly became more rancorous. Jimison, Abernethy, and Neal issued a joint statement pointing out that their quarrel with the ILD involved much more than money and included the ILD's conduct at the trial—for example, the insistence on placing Carpenter and Bulwinkle in the mob that flogged Wells, and the deliberate exploitation of the defendants "in order to raise money to spread Communism." In so doing, the attorneys argued, they were inflaming local opinion against the defendants so as to prejudice what slight chance they had of acquittal. The men raised the matter of the "labor jury" as a case in point. The group arrived late, left early, and yet "rendered a verdict in which the trial judge was held up to ridicule and roundly condemned," again without any thought of the effect on the defendants. The lawyers were sorry that the defendants were still in jail. On the other hand, at least they were being protected from further "public exploitation."[27]

The Communist response was no less heated. The *Daily Worker* accused Jimison of having deserted the cause of the workers and joined the other side. "First among these fakers is none other than the cheap lawyer-actor T. P. Jimison," wrote Si Gerson, "whose very name is a stench in the nostrils of militant workers," for he "went over bag and baggage to the side of Manville-Jenckes and the capitalist class— where he always belonged." The defendants, of course, blamed him for their remaining in jail. Neal rushed off to New York to try and persuade the ACLU not to provide more bail money until there were ironclad guarantees that the defendants would not be further exploited. The ACLU eventually responded by bringing suit against Jimison, while Adams and Flowers bitterly excoriated him as a turncoat and a liar. Meanwhile, the defendants remained in jail much longer than necessary. Not until mid-December was the last of them, Carter, released. Predictably, he attacked Jimison and Neal for having kept him there so long. It was a sad, bitter ending to what had started in April as a genuine attempt to provide assistance for an exploited and harassed group.[28]

*Delegates at the general conference of the National Textile Workers Union,
held in Charlotte, North Carolina, October 12 and 13, 1929.* Seated, left to right:
*Solomon Harper of the American Negro Labor Congress and member of the
"labor jury"; Albert Totherow, a Gastonia striker; Russell Knight, a released
Gastonia defendant; J. Louis Engdahl, ILD executive secretary; Bill Dunne,
southern representative of the Communist Party; William Z. Foster, secretary
of the TUEL; and Sophie Melvin.* Standing, left to right: *Liston Oak, ILD
publicity director; George Maurer, southern organizer for the ILD; Dewey
Martin, NTWU organizer (Originally published in the* Labor Defender)

    Even though the Aderholt trial was over, the drama in the region's
courtrooms was not. Indeed, even as Edith Miller was proclaiming
her nonbelief, the same issue was being raised in Concord, in Cabarrus County's superior court, where the seven men accused of assault-
ing Lell, Saylors, and Wells were arraigned. There, as I noted above,
Judge A. M. Stack took a position opposed to both Barnhill and Shaw
and ruled out the questioning of any witness as to his or her beliefs,
even for impeachment purposes, on the grounds that the Fourteenth
Amendment prohibited it. Thus Wells was free to testify, but he was
not there to do so; after his earlier experience, he had thought there
was no point to it. Nevertheless, the state built up a good case against
the four men, all Loray Mill employees, whom the grand jury even-

tually sent for trial. Mrs. Lodge gave evidence of what had happened at her house, and both Lell and Saylors testified at length about the events on the road and the flogging itself. They were easily able to identify many members of the mob, while R. B. McDonald and E. F. Leigh, the possum hunters, described how they had broken it up. The defense lawyers, led by Bulwinkle, dismissed the whole thing as a frame-up, "a diabolical plot, hatched up to perpetrate a fraud upon North Carolina," and offered evidence to show that the defendants were all at work in the mill that evening. As the *News and Observer* sarcastically observed, the defendants "vigorously contended no crime had been committed at all and that the State witnesses kidnapped and flogged themselves." Judge Stack privately described the defense argument as "absurd," but the jury accepted it. The four were acquitted after only forty-five minutes of deliberation. Wells was right to stay away.[29]

Much the same thing happened a week later, in Gastonia, where the defendants had been indicted on kidnapping charges. There they did not even come to trial; a Gaston County grand jury found no true bill in the case, and that was the end of the matter. The action passed almost without comment, because on the same day the grand jury also reported its findings on Ella May's killing. The coroner's jury, having been pursuing a fairly leisurely investigation since mid-September, and having added two more names to the list of those indicted—Horace Wheelus (originally reported as Wheeler) and Jack O. Carver—turned the matter over to the grand jury on October 23. The jury went about its work with a will, examining no less than forty-two witnesses before deciding that there was insufficient evidence to indict anyone for the slaying. Judge Sink, who presided, pronounced himself "amazed" at the decision, which, said the *Charlotte Observer*, "clears the docket of every charge arising out of the labor troubles that have disturbed this section since April 1."[30]

For many in North Carolina, the rest of the country, and the international liberal community, the overwhelming response was not amazement but disgust and anger. The contrast between the savage sentences handed down to the Aderholt defendants earlier in the week and the freeing of the alleged slayers of Ella May was too stark to ignore. "So it seems to be true," thundered the *News and Observer*'s managing editor, Frank Smethurst, "the blood of Ella May Wiggins is as futile as her life. Yesterday Gaston County washed the hands of her blood as

Cover of the Labor Defender's *memorial issue for Ella May (Originally published in the* Labor Defender)

easily and indifferently as a mob of its citizens shot her down more than a month ago." Titled "Ella May Wiggins Doesn't Count," Smethurst's editorial was widely reprinted and praised; Heywood Brown thought it deserved a Pulitzer Prize. The outraged Nell Battle Lewis wrote, "Nothing so shamelessly contemptuous of the rudimentary standards of public decency has taken place in North Carolina within my memory." She declared that nothing the ILD had said or done over the past months "surpasses this bare fact."

For Frederic Nelson of the *New Republic*, the issue was broader than the refusal to punish the "wanton" shooting of a helpless woman, reprehensible as that was. "It was Samuel Butler I believe, who wanted to know why sexual immorality in English fiction is so much more seriously condemned than homicide," he wrote with all the anger he could muster. "North Carolina might ask herself by what processes of mind she has come to consider a ragged little Union meeting so much more criminal than murder, kidnapping, flogging, false arrest and arson." Throughout the state and nation, there were similar expressions of outrage, while in several European cities, crowds reportedly burned Judge Barnhill in effigy. Within North Carolina itself, the outcry focused increasingly on Governor Gardner; many people demanded that he take vigorous action to ensure that Ella May's killer be found and dealt with. As Frank P. Graham wrote in a personal appeal to him, "The worth of a human life, the right of free assembly, the even processes of the law, the self-respect of the people of North Carolina are all on trial in this case and cannot be dismissed by a grand jury." The case could not be allowed to rest, for as Mrs. E. M. Land, president of the North Carolina Federation of Women's Clubs, told the governor, "before the world of thinking, intelligent people, North Carolina is on trial."[31]

During the unfolding of the Gastonia drama, Governor Gardner had shown no great sympathy toward either the Loray strikers or the defendants in the Aderholt murder. A textile mill owner himself, and brother-in-law of Clyde Hoey, his sympathies had clearly lain with mill management and those who supported it. "I am thoroughly of the opinion that drastic steps should be taken to rid this state of their presence," he had written to Senator Overman in September with reference to the ragged rump of Communists still working in the Gastonia region; he was also bitterly critical of both the *Greensboro News* and the *Raleigh News and Observer* for their sympathy toward the strikers. Both papers, he complained to a friendly editor, had taken great "delight" throughout the long year in "impugning" his sincerity and "misinterpreting my motives." Yet he could not ignore the strength of feeling engendered by the grand jury's decision, or the pressure on him to take further executive action. "A Reward Is Not Enough," said the *News and Observer*, referring to his offer of four hundred dollars for information leading to the conviction of the killers. "We have the right to expect more from the State of North Carolina." "More" was soon forthcoming. On October 28 Gardner announced that he had appointed Judge Pender A. McElroy of Marshall to reopen the case, sitting as an examining magistrate. "The state would exhaust every resource at its command to secure the indictment, conviction and punishment of those guilty of this crime," the governor declared. Gardner's action was exceedingly well received, except in Gastonia. The *New York Times* praised him for restoring "North Carolina's good name" and thought he was "shouldering responsibility with high public spirit. . . . If the Governor prevails in his crusade for equal privileges for all before the law, the facts will yet be developed in open court." [32]

Judge McElroy lost no time in getting going. He began hearing evidence on November 4. The attention of the press, however, was caught not so much by him as by Gaston County's deputy sheriff, M. V. Wiggins, described by the *News and Observer*'s Charles Parker as "a lank mountaineer." He was one of the first officers to arrive at the scene of Ella May's slaying and, since then, had allegedly been "tirelessly engaged in gathering evidence" against her slayers, including material which had not been presented to the original grand jury. He was obsessed with removing a blot "from the state's fair name," he told reporters, and had also been greatly moved by the forlorn sight of the five "orphaned" children at their mother's funeral. He had five children himself, he allowed, and had thus been much affected. Besides, because of his sizeable family, he could use the reward money. [33]

Deputy Wiggins confidently promised fresh evidence at the inquiry, and whether he had procured it or not, Judge McElroy certainly heard from people who had not appeared before either the coroner's jury or the grand jury. One of these was D. L. Case, who said he was on the truck when it was stopped. Case positively identified Horace Wheelus as the man who had shot Ella May with "a blue steel, medium sized pistol." He was sure Wheelus was the one, he said, because the man he saw had three fingers missing from his left hand. In the courtroom, Wheelus nervously covered his left hand with his hat, but not before observant newsmen had noticed that the first three fingers were missing. Case was able to identify many other members of the mob as well, including William Borders, whom he allegedly saw shoot at men running from the truck. There were plenty of other witnesses, most of whom had been standing in the truck with Ella May, who either identified Wheelus as the man who fired the fatal shot or were able to identify other members of the mob.

As they testified, disturbing tales of earlier coverups and the intimidation of witnesses emerged, along with hints of a less than wholehearted commitment by Solicitor Carpenter. Some said that though they had offered to testify before the grand jury, they had been told there was no need to appear, and others said that they had been paid for their earlier silence. Still others alleged that potentially key witnesses had been paid to leave Gaston County altogether. Certainly, some of the men that Wiggins had hoped to locate were simply not to be found, while others suddenly had severe lapses in memory. Nevertheless, McElroy had heard more than enough—"ample evidence of concocted action for unlawful purpose" was how he described it—to order fourteen men bound over on charges of murder in the second degree. The defense, led by a grim-faced and obviously unsettled Bulwinkle, decided at the last moment to offer no evidence at this time. Bound over until January 13, besides Wheelus, were Yates Gamble, Fred Morrow, L. M. Sossoman, Jack Carver, W. M. Borders, Lowry Davis, O. H. Lunsford, Troy Jones, Theodore Sims, George Fowler, W. H. Holbrook, L. H. Thompson, and E. F. Haney, all on $2,500 bonds, except for Wheelus, whose bond was $5,000. Once again, the mill immediately bailed its loyal employees out. As for Judge McElroy, he became the new hero of the hour. "A Daniel Came to Judgement," exulted the *News and Observer*.[34]

Deputy Wiggins may have had something to do with the appearance of various surprise witnesses, but probably not as much as H. G. Gulley, the private detective who had originally been hired by the ACLU to provide investigative assistance to the defense lawyers. After the Aderholt verdict, the ILD decided to cut its losses in Gastonia, as did the Communist Party itself. As a consequence, no further funds were sent there, and, indeed, the *Daily Worker*'s editorial staff was ordered to limit the amount of space devoted to the strike's aftermath. But the ACLU decided to stay involved, partly because of its interest in a number of civil suits arising from Ella May's killing, but also largely because of their belief, on Gulley's advice, that conviction of her killers was possible. Gulley thought the local political situation had a lot to do with this. In 1928, for the first time in thirty years, Gaston County had elected a Republican sheriff, as part of the Hoover landslide, and a state of war had existed between the county and city law enforcement bodies ever since. He had got to know the sheriff well and was convinced that he was genuinely interested in getting someone indicted for the killing, if only "to aid the Republican Party in the county."[35]

The ACLU therefore decided to keep Gulley on the payroll, initially working behind the scenes with Deputy Wiggins, and also to find any evidence helpful in possible civil actions. One immediate task was to track down those prospective witnesses whom the mill had "deported" and persuade them, through bribery if necessary, to come back and testify, though the ACLU did not want to know the details. He was immediately successful. As Flowers told Roger Baldwin, he "had procured the witness Case" as well as "two or three others," who had told their stories to Judge McElroy. The sheriff's office, in fact, conceded that his work had been of great value to them and could even mean that "the conspiracy that has been formed in Gastonia and as a result of which Mrs. Wiggins was shot and killed" might yet be exposed. Gulley then continued to investigate her killing, ostensibly working as a detective for the ACLU's civil suits, but in reality operating behind the scenes for the sheriff's office. John Carpenter, the man formally responsible for preparing the case against the alleged killers, and himself probably part of the conspiracy, bitterly resented this arrangement but was powerless to change it. The situation was truly bizarre.[36]

Gulley continued to prod and poke away as the dramatic year came to an end. J. G. Flowers, having made a contract with Ella May's brother, Wesley, for half the return in any successful damage suit, duly launched one against the alleged slayers and the *Gastonia Daily Gazette*. There were a few echoes of the year, too, in the criminal courts. C. D. Saylors found himself in trouble on two counts. He was to be indicted on perjury charges for asserting before Judge Shaw that both Bulwinkle and Carpenter were members of the mob that kidnapped him. More important, he became implicated in the Aderholt murder. In a new affidavit, Robert Allen, a defendant at the mistrial who was now completely estranged from the ILD, named Saylors as someone who had fired at the murdered police chief. Carpenter announced that Saylors would be charged with conspiracy to murder—if he could be found, which was doubtful. Nevertheless, he was discovered in Charlotte early in the new year and was duly arrested and held for trial on $10,000 bond. Saylors was released after a week, however, for lack of evidence; Allen, his accuser, had himself disappeared, and that was the end of the matter. Ironically, Saylors also turned against the ILD and eventually sued the organization for money supposedly owed him.

So the residue of the Aderholt trial gradually melted away. It was still not a good idea to advertise membership in the NTWU too widely in Gaston County, as George Saul, a district organizer, found out in a costly way. He made a speech in Mount Holly in which he condemned the Aderholt verdict and attacked Judge Barnhill. He soon found himself held on charges of inciting a riot and eventually received a six-month jail sentence—the final act in the Gaston County drama. By that time, nobody was remotely interested.[37]

As the festive season drew near, Gaston County was in a forgiving mood. The *Gastonia Daily Gazette* pointed out that part of the year's Empty Stocking Fund had been used to aid former NTWU members, now destitute, in Gastonia and Bessemer City, including Ella May's sister, who "did not have a bite to eat in the house" on Christmas Day. Neither had Wes Williams, head of the NTWU in Bessemer City, nor "Old Man McDonald," another prominent striker. All of them had received a Christmas turkey and a few presents, courtesy of the newspaper. "Take this back to the union circles," crowed the editor. By this time, of course, the union had virtually abandoned the South, leaving its former supporters in desperate need.[38]

There were still the alleged killers of Ella May to be dealt with. Gulley, behind the scenes, was busily tracking down potential witnesses, and finding some, including a few of those "taken out of Gastonia on trucks shortly after the shooting." In particular, he located H. W. Branch, a former member of the Committee of One Hundred, who had declared himself willing to testify about that body's involvement not only in Ella May's death but in the climate of conspiracy throughout the year, in return for guaranteed employment. It was important that Gulley's work continue, Flowers told Roger Baldwin, because the solicitor, John Carpenter, the man responsible for prosecuting the alleged killers, was not likely to search assiduously for the people the mill had dispersed. Governor Gardner, said Flowers, also realized this. The lawyer had spoken with Gardner and believed that the governor, desperate to have credible court proceedings, was almost ready to send his attorney general, Dennis G. Brummitt, to Gaston County to direct the prosecution, regardless of the adverse political fallout.[39]

This was, in fact, what came about. It was announced on December 30 that Brummitt, at Gardner's request, would be coming to Gastonia to aid Carpenter in prosecuting the Wiggins case. Indeed, he was already there, going over the evidence gathered at the McElroy hearing. The trial itself was to begin with a new grand jury hearing on January 13. As the day approached, there was much speculation about tension between the attorney general and the solicitor, particularly because it was thought that Brummitt would seek to have the trial moved to Mecklenburg County, an alternative that Carpenter vehemently and publicly opposed. Most press opinion, however, was that Brummitt's view would prevail.[40]

And so it proved to be. The grand jury duly met under the direction of Judge J. H. Clement of Winston-Salem and again listened to eyewitnesses describe the events that led to Ella May's death. Most of them had done so at least once before, though, ominously, the state's "star witness" at the McElroy hearing, D. L. Case, could not be found and had been missing from his home for more than a week. Nevertheless, there were enough others who claimed to have seen her shot that after less than an hour's deliberation, the grand jury returned true bills against five of the fourteen men indicted, to be tried on second-degree murder charges. These were Wheelus, Fred Morrow, Lowery Davis, Troy Jones, and O. H. Lunsford, all workers at the Loray Mill. Brummitt then moved for a change of venue, arguing that opinion in Gastonia was so inflamed that a fair trial would not be possible there. Carpenter refused to join him in his motion, however, while the defense attorneys, led by Major Bulwinkle, had a field day at his expense, expressing their resentment not only at his motion but at the attorney general's very presence in the courtroom. Gaston County had been attacked unfairly, they said—"traduced" and made the victim of prejudice—and its people would not easily forget this wanton outside interference, particularly if Brummitt had gubernatorial ambitions in 1932. Judge Clement, however, ruled for the attorney general. Those accused of Ella May's murder would be tried in the same Charlotte courtroom as Beal and his associates had been, in late February. In the meantime, deputies would continue the hunt for various missing witnesses, especially Branch, who had not turned up after all, and Case.[41]

The *Gastonia Daily Gazette* was furious. It directed its anger primarily at the governor, whose actions in dispatching Brummitt to the trial it considered to be "entirely without precedent in the entire history of the state." Charlotte's mayor, George E. Wilson, was also peeved. Charlotte had been disrupted enough already by the consequences of Gastonia's labor troubles, he thought. Most opinion, however, favored Judge Clement's decision, though people doubted that it would make much difference in the end. "When the slayers of Mrs. Wiggins are acquitted," wrote Nell Battle Lewis, "as despite the most ardent efforts of the State the odds are hundred to one they will be," at least the state would have tried. Brummitt could never be held responsible "for the last word in North Carolina's recent record for the most patently partial dispensation of justice seen in this State since Reconstruction." Now all that anyone could do was wait.[42]

The last major act in Gaston County's prolonged drama began on February 24, 1930. The prosecution promised a "vigorous prosecution," and solicitor Carpenter was there bright and early, jaunty as ever, "sky blue shirt, jonquil boutonniere, handshakes and all." Nevertheless, he soon found himself frozen out of any effective part of the proceedings by Brummitt and his deputy, Judge W. D. Siler. Careless of the terminal damage he was doing to his political career, it was the attorney general who examined all the main witnesses. Case could still not be found—there was just no trace of him—and neither could Branch. However, there were plenty of others there to describe the drive back to Bessemer City, "thirty or forty cars in pursuit"; the collision when Morrow's vehicle cut the truck off; and the rain of bullets that followed. Julius "Crip" Fowler, a "one-legged mill worker," said he saw Wheelus level a pistol and fire directly at Ella May. "Oh Lord, he's shot me," she cried, as she slumped to the truck's floor. Charlie Shope asserted likewise. Witness after witness testified to the presence of all five defendants at the scene of the shooting, to the gunplay that followed the accident, and to the fact that the five not only had firearms in their possession but had also fired them at the fleeing unionists. Wheelus's neighbor, Mrs. Noah Ledford, told about how he had come to her during the McElroy investigation and asked her to give him an alibi. He wanted her to swear that he had been at home all afternoon. She refused. "I won't swear to a lie for no man and if I do go to court, I'll swear the truth that you left home between 10 and 11 o'clock in the morning and didn't come home till 7:30 or 8," she told him. Not only that, he was so drunk when he got home that he had parked his car in her garage. They were all cross-examined vigorously by Bulwinkle and the defense team, of course, and certain deficiencies of character were brought to light—in particular, the fact that Charlie Shope may have fathered Ella May's last child was made much of—but in general the case was a strong one, the cumulative evidence impressive, and Brummitt superb in his presentation.[43]

It was not, however, to be enough. The defense was based partially on an alternative theory of the shooting, contending that Ella May had been shot not from the road but from the cab of the truck itself—accidentally, of course. During the collision a gun had been discharged, and the bullet had gone through the back window, shattering it before hitting Ella May. The defense presented an impressive array of people, including G. R. Spenser, manager of the American Mills in Bessemer City, who happened to be passing the scene of the collision at the time and certainly saw no sign of the affray the prosecution witnesses had described. Indeed, said G. T. Anthony, the only guns he had seen were carried by men jumping off the truck. Still, the core of the defense was that either the defendants had not been there or they were innocent of any conspiratorial action. Wheelus, for example, swore that he was in court in Charlotte at the time of the shooting, a spectator at the preliminary hearing for the Ben Wells flogging, and there were fifteen witnesses to place him there—all Loray employees, with the exception of the court stenographer. Morrow said he was on his way to Camp Jenckes, the mill's recreation resort, along with Ed Spenser, Manville-Jenckes's employment director and a former company spy, when the truck ran into him. They heard no shots, saw no firearms, and knew nothing of Mrs. Wiggins's death until much later in the day. Lunsford admitted that he had been at the crash site, but well after Wiggins had been shot, and only to haul "a load of curiosity seekers to the wreck."

And so it continued. The defense provided ninety-six witnesses in all, most of them mill employees, and most of them obviously very well coached. Said Charles Parker of the *News and Observer*, they were "paraded like a perfectly organized army." Few in the courtroom, he said, doubted what the trial's outcome would be.[44]

Brummitt's closing address was described as "masterful" and "one of the most forceful pieces of argument ever presented to a Mecklenburg County jury." He ridiculed the collective alibis; how odd that they were "almost without variance," he thought. Ella May's morals were not on trial here, he reminded the jury, nor were her political beliefs. "No matter what she did or what she was," he said, "no one had a right to kill her," and there was overwhelming evidence that the defendants had conspired to do just that. That was the only issue to be considered, yet instead the defense had "dragged Ella May Wiggins from the grave and held her up as a vile wretched woman." "Masterful" though the address may have been, the defense was easily able to counter it by appeals to class and to prejudice. "These defendants came into court with clean hands," shouted Bulwinkle, "men who uphold the majesty of the Constitution, while this other crowd goes through the land seeking to overthrow the government, the very riff raff of civilization." Said Plummer Stewart, "the state's witnesses were too sorry to consider . . . that crowd which would destroy the government." "Everybody knows where they come from and we've got enough trouble here without importing more," asserted A. C. Jones. "I wish I could make you a patriotic speech," he continued.[45]

Communism versus Americanism—that was the issue of the Wiggins trial, as it had been throughout the year in Gastonia. The jury took less than thirty minutes to find all the defendants not guilty. Amid the general jubilation that followed, with the freed men greeting friends and family, shaking hands in an "impromptu receiving line," one of the jurors explained why. The attorney general "just didn't have witnesses that we could rely on," he said. Brummitt, for one, knew that perfectly well. After his closing argument, he had left the courtroom without waiting for the verdict. But "unlike the local authorities," wrote Fleet Williams, Brummitt could hold his head up high. He had done all he could "to secure exact justice."[46]

So "the great whitewashing trial," as the *Daily Worker* called it in one of its few comments on the proceedings, was now over. Others, too, denounced the verdict. North Carolina had been "shamed," thought the *News and Observer*. Ella May "had committed no crime. She had advocated no violence." Her only offense has been to join the union. For this alone she had been murdered, yet there "seemed no determination in Gaston County to apprehend and punish her slayers." The law there, ran the sad conclusion, was "a respecter of persons. It cannot be pictured as a blind goddess holding equally the scales of justice until the men who killed Ella May Wiggins have justice meted out to them." That was never to happen.[47]

Like the murderer of Chief Aderholt, Ella May's killer has also escaped certain detection over the years. Unsurprisingly, many have claimed knowledge of his identity. In their book, Robert and Elizabeth Williams stated that they knew who had done it, asserting that he was a Loray employee hoping to ingratiate himself with mill management. Later, overwhelmed by guilt, he confessed on his deathbed. Frank Sisk, too, claimed to have received a deathbed confession, from a mill worker named John R. Mason, who was extremely troubled by the prospect that the Almighty might judge him guilty of two murders, given that Ella May was pregnant when she died. Possibly he did shoot her; more likely, given the way the bullets were flying that afternoon, he simply thought he might have. Nevertheless, the preponderance of evidence still points toward Horace Wheelus. Many testified that they had seen him fire the shot, the Gastonia police talked openly about his action, and his frantic attempts to persuade Mrs. Ledford to give him an alibi were also indicative of his guilt. The members of the prosecution were certain of it, and the defense probably knew it as well. But in the end, it did not matter.[48]

6 THE AFTERMATH

The North Carolina Supreme Court heard arguments appealing the conviction of the seven Aderholt defendants on April 21 and 22, 1930. The defense lawyers, much boosted by the addition to their ranks of the former United States senator from Georgia, Thomas W. Hardwick, based their appeal on seventeen distinct questions of law where they contended that Judge Barnhill had erred. The prime focus, however, was on the cross-examination of Edith Miller and Barnhill's decision to permit her credibility to be attacked on account of her religious beliefs. "It is difficult to understand on what theory the political and economic beliefs of the defendant Beal, and the witness Mrs. Miller, were admitted in evidence," Hardwick contended. The state countered by pointing to the 1777 statute. "There can be no doubt," argued Carpenter, "that under existing law in North Carolina, an atheist is wholly disqualified from testifying as a witness." It was not until August that the Supreme Court announced its decision. In a thirty-one page opinion, Chief Justice W. P. Stacy dismissed the appeal, holding among other things that the cross-examination of Miller was proper. The defendants had until September 29 to put their affairs in order and return to Charlotte to give themselves up, lest their bail money be forfeited.[1]

By the time the court's decision was announced, the question of their imprisonment had become somewhat academic. Five of the defendants—Beal, Miller, Hendricks, McGinnis, and Harrison—had been in the Soviet Union for some months, while Carter and McLoughlin, though still in the United States, were in hiding and waiting to join their fellows. Though the press speculation was that at least some of them would appear at the Charlotte courthouse, there was in reality little prospect of it.[2]

The only accounts of their escape and their subsequent adventures in the USSR are contained in Fred Beal's two autobiographies, *Proletarian Journey* and the shorter and more polemical *Red Fraud: An Exposé of Stalinism*. Given the profound disillusion with which Beal came to view communism, and his bitterness at his treatment while in Russia, these books must both be read with extreme caution, yet they do provide some information as to the fate of the seven defendants, as well as Beal's justification for the rejection of his former beliefs.[3]

Beal always insisted that he had never wanted to go to the Soviet Union in the first place and that he had always planned to serve his sentence. It was Clarence Miller who was determined that they should leave, who persuaded the other members of the group to go along with him, and who made all the necessary arrangements, even though it meant deceiving the hierarchy of the CPUSA, who were opposed to their jumping bail, correctly divining that the Party would receive no more ACLU financial assistance if this occurred. Beal eventually agreed to go along, he said, only because he knew that the appeal process would take some months and he wanted to see the "workers' paradise" before the prison gates closed on him. It was just to be a holiday, he insisted. But Myra Page, a writer and Party member who would later write a novel based on the Gastonia strike and who was on the same ship as Beal, remembered things rather differently. She thought his attitude was rather that "[the] Party owed him a living" and that he was in not the slightest bit reluctant to go and claim it.[4]

Traveling under the name Jacob Katz, Beal went first to Berlin, where he met up with Miller and Hendricks. McGinnis and Harrison arrived soon after. They applied for permission to enter the USSR, which was quickly granted, and they sailed from Stettin to Leningrad on the SS *Preussen* on June 28, 1930. From his arrival, Beal insisted, he had hated the Soviet Union and was determined to return home as soon as he could. The contrast between what they had been told to expect there and the harsh reality and inequality of Soviet life was simply too much for him to stomach. When the Comintern decided that the five fugitives would stay in the USSR indefinitely, Miller and Harrison were jubilant. But Beal, Hendricks, and McGinnis had already decided that life in an American prison was preferable to life under socialism, or so Beal said.[5]

It does seem as if at least Beal and Hendricks did at one point genuinely want to return to the United States, once their appeals had been dismissed, and begin serving their sentences. Roger Baldwin thought they were coming, and he arranged passages for them both from Warsaw. The ILD, too, initially expected them to show up, or so its assistant secretary, Sam Darcy, said in August. By September, however, the ILD had changed its mind. Engdahl announced that the CPUSA certainly did not favor their surrender, and he assailed Roger Baldwin and the ACLU for being "more interested in saving the bail" than in saving the defendants "from the judicial lynching of Southern boss class justice." That was the end of the ILD, as far as Baldwin and his codirectors were concerned. They quickly announced that they would no longer provide bail for Communist Party defendants. Why Beal and Hendricks failed to turn up after promising to do so cannot be known for sure, but there seems little reason to doubt Beal's contention that despite the appeals of the men themselves and of the CPUSA—whose representative, William Weinstone, reportedly pleaded with his Soviet comrades to let them return on the grounds that the Party needed "its martyrs in this country"—the Comintern simply said no. Miller and Harrison had spoken vehemently against any of them returning, and in that situation, the Comintern was not disposed to permit the adverse political fallout such a split in the ranks of the martyrs would surely engender, especially from the Lovestoneites.[6]

However, Beal, Hendricks and, by now, McGinnis kept up the pressure to return. They began drinking, they criticized what they had seen of Soviet life, they wrote imploring letters to Roger Baldwin at the ACLU asking for his assistance in getting them out, they appealed to the Comintern to revoke its decision to keep them in the USSR, and they made plans to escape. Eventually, they were told reluctantly that they could go, provided they could find someone to pay their fare. This the ACLU was still prepared to do, in the hope of saving at least some of the forfeited bail money, and in January 1931, McGinnis and Beal left for the United States. Hendricks, who had so desperately wanted to be with them, was by this time in the hospital, being treated for the tuberculosis that would eventually kill him.[7]

When Beal secretly arrived in New York in mid-March, he was welcomed and given shelter by Roger Baldwin, who it seemed had changed his mind both about Beal's going to prison and, indeed, about the wisdom of his returning to the United States at all. Local Party members, too, urged him to return to the USSR. He therefore postponed his plans to surrender to the North Carolina authorities, deciding to wait for Hendricks before doing so. But Hendricks never came—he was still too sick to travel. Beal therefore yielded to pressure. In September he was smuggled out of New York and was soon on a ship, bound once more for the "socialist paradise."[8]

He arrived there to find Hendricks still sick and still determined to go home. Between writing *Proletarian Journey* and 1949, Beal obviously changed his mind about Hendricks, whom he eventually damned as a drunken Communist "stooge," but in 1937 he still admired his determination to leave the USSR. Beal was given a muted hero's welcome on his return, and the Soviet authorities soon sent him to Kharkov, in the Ukraine, to a position of some responsibility. A huge tractor factory had recently been opened there—a real showpiece, partly staffed by foreign Communists. He was to be in charge of propaganda and cultural relations among the foreign workers, as well as their point of contact with Soviet authorities. He lived there for two years, sharing an apartment with a teenage American named Bill Gedritis. Given the seeming absence of women in Beal's life and his obvious devotion to this young man, his private life in Kharkov, at least, may have been fulfilled.[9]

Nevertheless, he claimed that he hated his job and the lie he was living, working for a regime he was coming to despise more and more, especially as the horrors of the Ukraine famine became too obvious to ignore. Moreover, Hendricks's fate, and the way the Party accepted it, disgusted him. "Red" had finally made it home, determined to visit his ailing father, but he had been arrested in New York before setting foot in the South. He was extradited to North Carolina, where he started serving his sentence. The Party, said Beal, would do absolutely nothing for him. Because Hendricks had left the Soviet Union of his own volition and without Party consent, to draw attention to him in any way would obviously be embarrassing for his Soviet hosts, in that he had been willing to risk jail rather than stay in Moscow. Thus the American comrades, now firmly under Fosterite discipline, were perfectly willing to let him rot. Beal said that he himself became determined to leave a second time, in order to help his friend.[10]

Who knows? What is certain is that on August 7, 1933, he was given permission to go to Poland to renew his, or rather Jacob Katz's, United States passport. Instead, he and Bill made for Turkey, where Beal's young friend had arranged for some money to be waiting. They were denied entry, but they managed to reach Berlin, quite penniless. Then Beal had a stroke of luck. His lawyer from Gastonia days, Arthur Garfield Hays, happened to be in Berlin at the time, acting for the defense in the trial of those accused of burning the Reichstag. Beal went to see him, told him he planned to return to the United States, and asked for money, which Hays initially provided. This fund dried up once Hays had heard from Roger Baldwin, but Hays's sympathetic daughter, Laura, secretly provided Beal with his fare home. Bill's parents had wired him some cash, so the pair were able to sail for the States. They arrived in New York in January 1934 aboard the *Albert Ballin.*[11]

Beal said there were two tasks he wished to accomplish before giving himself up. One was to help Hendricks; the other was to tell the world the truth about the Soviet Union. There is no evidence that he did much about the first, but there is no doubt that he went about the second with zeal. He was at liberty for four more years, and during that time he moved about the northern states and Canada, denouncing Communism and the Soviet Union as vigorously as he had once defended them. He wrote articles for several magazines, including the red-baiting *American Mercury*, in which he called Soviet Russia "the greatest fraud of history," and he completed the manuscript of *Proletarian Journey*, which was serialized by the Hearst press. Solicitor Carpenter made several attempts to have him extradited but to no avail. Meanwhile, his former Communist colleagues—those who had once been his most fervent admirers—first excoriated him as a turncoat and a traitor, then tried to pretend he had never existed. Foster even expunged him from the recent historical record, rewriting the history of the Gastonia strike with Bill Dunne in the central role of strike leader.[12]

In September 1937, Beal granted a long interview to Fleet Williams of the *Raleigh News and Observer*. There he told Williams what it was like to be a fugitive from two worlds, North Carolina and the USSR. Flight to the Soviet Union had been the biggest mistake of his life, he told him, and with the exception of Clarence Miller, who had "become a real Communist bureaucrat" and did "everything Stalin said" and was rewarded appropriately, his fellow defendants felt likewise. He had spent most of his time as a fugitive in New England or Canada, he said, but had also lived briefly in New York, Detroit, and Washington. He was becoming weary of life underground, however, and was seriously thinking of giving himself up.[13]

Beal surrendered to North Carolina authorities the very next year. The circumstances of his surrender were arranged by Paul Green, a North Carolina dramatist and a professor at the University of North Carolina at Chapel Hill. Green had been out of the country during the dramatic events of 1929 but had begun a correspondence with Beal shortly after the latter's return from the Soviet Union. According to Green's account, Beal had asked him to book a hotel room in Raleigh, where he would duly present himself at an appointed hour. Green did as he was asked, keeping Governor Hoey fully informed, of course. He also requested that both Frank Graham and Jonathan Daniels, editor of the *News and Observer*, join him as witnesses to the surrender, and they agreed. When Beal arrived, there were introductions all around, and some inconsequential banter. Then the four men walked up Fayetteville Street together to the governor's mansion. Hoey, Beal's former legal foe, was waiting. He greeted him cordially before the fugitive was led away.[14]

On February 16, 1938, Beal began serving his sentence at North Carolina's Caledonia prison farm, which he compared favorably with the collective farms of his Soviet experience. By this time, support for a full pardon had grown, both within and outside of the state, especially given his outspoken anticommunism, and Beal's attorneys made such an application in June 1939. Governor Hoey refused, but he did slice seven years off his sentence. Yet Beal did not have too much longer to wait in jail. He was paroled on January 8, 1942, having served less than four years of his original term. In May 1948, in a simple procedure in Gastonia, full citizenship rights were restored to him. The only opposition came from Major Dolley, commander of the National Guard units that defended the Loray Mill. This was outweighed, however, by a warm letter of support from Judge Barnhill. In 1954, Fred Beal died in Lawrence, Massachusetts. As labor historian Irving Bernstein wrote, in the end he was "embittered and forgotten, . . . his life a tragic essay revealing the incompatibility of trade unionism and communism." He was, Bernstein went on, "a symbolic American radical, perpetually out of joint with the times." Perhaps so; but perhaps, too, he was a man simply not big enough for the job he was asked to do.[15]

With the exception of Hendricks, very little is known about the fate of the other defendants, and most of it comes via Beal. Hendricks served his prison term and then went back to working in the mills, when he could find one that would have him. Junius Scales, then an idealistic Communist, met him in 1939 at a strike in High Point, North Carolina. Hendricks, known as "Chairman of the Communist Party of the Carolinas," was in the thick of it, "bucking up the spirits and militancy of the picket line, putting starch into the weak and wavering, eliciting flashes of humor from the dead serious strikers." Scales was tremendously impressed by his example, which he says was decisive in his own decision to remain in the Party. Hendricks's health had been ruined by both his Soviet and North Carolina experiences, however, and by his excessive drinking, to which both Beal and Scales attested. He died sometime in the 1940s.[16]

McGinnis purportedly made his way back to his native South but died soon after his return. Of Harrison and Carter no trace can be found. They were both still in the Soviet Union when Beal left, both miserable and desperate to return. Harrison, in fact, had been exiled to Odessa for stealing a loaf of bread. Perhaps they both died there, though one hopes not. Victims of circumstance much more than commanders of their destiny, it would be fitting if they, too, had been eventually able to return home.[17]

Only Clarence Miller, and presumably his wife Edith, seem to have avoided the cycle of disillusion and despair, though what exactly happened to them both is a mystery. Perhaps Miller did become the archetypal Soviet bureaucrat, living high on the hog in Moscow, as Beal claimed. Others tell different stories. Sophie Melvin recalled hearing that they had been sent to work underground in Latin America, where they both disappeared. In 1932, Governor Gardner received a letter from the acting U.S. secretary of state, informing him that the British authorities in India had found Miller working underground there and were willing to extradite him if North Carolina would bear the cost. Gardner agreed, but nothing came of the matter; Miller presumably avoided capture. During the research for his massive study of the Whittaker Chambers–Alger Hiss affair, the historian Allen Weinstein believed that he interviewed Miller, who according to Weinstein was then living in retirement in California under the name Sam Kreiger, but this assertion was subsequently the subject of legal action. Miller too, then, became lost to history as a result of the Gastonia strike.[18]

What happened to the three women defendants? Here the record is clearer, at least for Buch and Melvin. For Vera Buch, the work in Gastonia was the last she ever did either for the NTWU or for the Communist Party. Her husband, Albert Weisbord, became one of the casualties of Party factional fighting. Accused of being a Lovestoneite, which he most certainly was not, he was expelled from the Party in 1930. Vera followed him into the wilderness. In 1931 they launched a new Marxist organization, the Communist League of Struggle, in order to provide a Trotskyite alternative to the Stalinist CPUSA. Predictably, they failed to secure more than a handful of adherents. The rest of Buch's life was one of political obscurity but considerable personal satisfaction. She and Albert moved to Chicago in 1935. There they involved themselves in local politics. Albert got a job with the AFL, and they worked for groups like CORE. Vera wrote some short stories that were published, and in 1952 she began again to paint—an activity that politics had left her no time for. She eventually gained a considerable regional reputation. In 1976, recognition of a sort came to them both when they were joint guests of honor at a symposium commemorating the fiftieth anniversary of the Passaic strike. The following year, Vera published her autobiography, fittingly entitled *A Radical Life*.[19]

Sophie Melvin, too, survived Gastonia to lead a long and active life, close to the Communist Party. She stayed in the South for a while, spending six months in 1930 in Greenville, South Carolina, as the sole NTWU organizer there. When the money ran out she returned to New York, married Si Gerson, and from then on combined the duties of motherhood with that of local political activism. In 1993, at the age of eighty-three, she was still going strong, now waging determined warfare on behalf of a decent health care system for all Americans.[20]

On Amy Schechter the record is nowhere near as full. Like Melvin, she stayed in the South. In March 1930, the *Charlotte Observer* carried a report of her arrest in Chattanooga, where she was charged with "lunacy." She had, it seems, been obstructing traffic in that city's main thoroughfare, diverting it round a street demonstration she was leading. No doubt the sense of fun that Sophie Melvin found so engaging had gotten the better of her. Harry Haywood reported her still in Charlotte in 1932, along with other Gastonia "stalwarts" providing the backbone of what Party activity there was there. She retained her "thick cockney accent," he said, and doubtless her high good humor.

By 1935, however, she had left the South for the coal and steel towns of western Pennsylvania and West Virginia; she contributed occasional articles for the left-wing press on the fearful living conditions she found there, the brutal suppression of any union activity, and the imminence of revolution. From then on, the trail is cold. Sophie Melvin had no idea what happened to Schechter after the 1930s, though she had heard a rumor that she had died quite young.[21]

Most of the prosecution lawyers at the Aderholt trial went on to great success. Major Bulwinkle was returned to Congress in 1930, his heroics of 1929 forming an essential component of his stump speeches. He served in Washington, with no particular distinction, until his death in 1950. It was said that Representative Vito Marcantonio, a friend of Sophie Melvin's, could always irritate him by inquiring if he had assaulted any young women that particular day, a reference to his activities with the Committee of One Hundred. Clyde Hoey served a term as governor of North Carolina, from 1937 to 1941, and then, from 1944 to his death in office, as the state's junior senator. Greg Cherry, too, had a term as governor, from 1945 to 1949. Life worked out very well for them all.[22]

Life did not similarly smile on Tom Jimison. He, too, ran for Congress, challenging Bulwinkle in the 1930 Democratic primary for the state's tenth district. He was, he said, "The People's Candidate" and would run as such. "I'll dot the district in my $50 Lizzie," he vowed, "stay where it stops, set down to dinner with the folks, drink my coffee out of a saucer, call for a gourd of water, and tell the boys to follow my boots." But "the people" resisted his folksy appeal. He was decimated by Bulwinkle in the primary, as the Major marched toward his November victory. Ironically, the Communists also fielded a candidate against Bulwinkle. It was Dewey Martin, NTWU organizer and Loray Mill striker.[23]

Shortly afterward, Jimison announced that he was giving up the law and returning to the church, having decided he could not be "useful to Christ" while retaining secular employment. Thus he closed his law office and turned his business over to his partner, Abernethy. Yet he does not seem to have followed through with his church plans. Instead he turned to journalism, writing a gossip column for the *Charlotte News*, where he became a friend of W. J. Cash. Jimison was an office character, in fact, fond of denouncing the moral hypocrisy of

Charlotte and its citizens. They were, he would proclaim, "the lowest-kneeling, loudest-praying, tightest-fisted, hardest-drinking class of Scotch Presbyterians that ever swaggered to the polls to vote dry." They would crucify Christ again, he thought, "right in front of the First Presbyterian Church if he ever dared to show up here." Later Jimison worked on the editorial staff of the *Lumberton Robesonian* and the *Richmond County Journal* (Rockingham, N.C.). He died in Spartanburg, South Carolina, in 1945, at the comparatively early age of fifty-nine, after a long period of declining health. If he had expected fame, fortune, and a chance to do good to follow in the wake of the Gastonia trial, he must have been bitterly disappointed. Rather, it seemed to unsettle what remained of his life.[24]

For Nell Battle Lewis, too, the Gastonia strike and its consequences also marked a turning point. She had fought the good fight bravely, but in the end she had felt betrayed by the Communists and used by their liberal allies. Thus began her retreat from liberalism and her return to the bosom of her mill-owning family, on whom she was increasingly dependent financially. By the mid-1930s she was admitting that "her experience in the bloody Gastonia business is the thing of all others which has done most to make me distrust so-called 'liberalism,' which so often, like mine was then, is not only ignorant and neurotic, but very dangerous." Liberals, she became fond of asserting as she mercilessly flayed those whom she had once supported so strongly, usually had severe personal problems. The Gastonia strikers, she eventually concluded, were no more than "a bunch of bums." Darden Pyron concluded that she became "virtually a caricature of the ideas and forces in Southern life that she had built her reputation attacking." His was a sad but apt judgment.[25]

The Communist Party reassessed its whole southern strategy following its involvement in the Loray strike. Though the Party maintained a presence in Charlotte throughout the 1930s, its emphasis in the South decisively shifted from working with white textile operatives in the Piedmont to organizing the black sharecroppers and ironworkers of Alabama. Meanwhile, every aspect of the Party's work in Gastonia was subjected to the most serious scrutiny—its fundamental unpreparedness, its work with African Americans, and the general instability and inconsistency of its endeavor. Of course, it was possible to blame much of this on individuals no longer within the Party's ranks:

on Weisbord and Buch, on Ellen Dawson, even on Jay Lovestone. But not everything could be explained away so easily. As Si Gerson argued in the *Daily Worker*, the Party was simply "ideologically and organizationally unprepared" to move into the South. In particular, the strike leaders had not been able to respond adequately to the militancy of the textile workers, and they had not understood its personal or spontaneous aspect. The workers were well ahead of the organizers, he ruefully concluded. The Party's central office was far too slow to respond to appeals for aid. It never gave the local organizers sufficient support when such aid might have made a difference. Only after the events of June 7 had focused national attention on Gastonia did support begin to flow at anywhere near an adequate level, and by then it was too late to affect the course of the strike, which had already been lost. There were still "tremendous possibilities" for the Party in the South, he thought, but only if the region's peculiarities were more adequately understood.[26]

Sophie Melvin made many of the same points when surveying the lessons of the Gastonia experience prior to the Party's 1930 convention. She too blamed Weisbord and Dawson for much that went wrong, but even after their removal, she pointed out, things had still not functioned properly. Work had continued to proceed in a disorganized fashion. "Organizers were sent in and withdrawn. The South became the talk at plenums, conferences and special meetings but as something obscure and mysterious rather than a field of work that demands careful guidance, best forces, planned, systematic and continuous work." Weisbord's "rolling wave" strike strategy just did not work, she said; it diffused effort needlessly and prevented the building of "solid mill committees" at the Loray Mill. The factional fighting had also been disastrous, because it had meant that "the comrades in the field," who were "clamoring for a program of work, for policies," were usually ignored. Like her husband, Melvin attacked the Party for moving southward "without any understanding of the peculiar conditions there" and, in particular, for not realizing the extent of worker militancy; the Party's leaders, she said, were hung up on Lovestoneian notions of the southern workforce as individualistic, reactionary, and apathetic. "The workers were many jumps ahead of us," she concluded. "We were overwhelmed by their response and militancy."[27]

Nevertheless, Melvin thought there was much to celebrate about the

Party's experience in Gastonia, and much on which it could build. "The outstanding achievement of the Textile Union and of the revolutionary movement as a whole is the entrance [sic] and struggle in the South," she wrote. "For the first time a revolutionary union with a program of economic, political and social equality for black workers entered the South. And through its courageous leadership in the Gastonia struggle it has rallied thousands and thousands of native American workers." And this was the view the Party came generally to adopt about the meaning of the events there: those months had provided the Party with an enormous psychological boost, as well as a learning experience, preparing it for the Scottsboro and Angelo Herndon cases, its prime southern battles of the next decade. "For however brief a moment, the Party had led American-born workers from the South," wrote Harvey Klehr. "Thus even though it was a small, unsuccessful strike, and not even the largest in the textile industry that spring, Gastonia became famous," because the Party wished it so. "Not for the last time," commented Klehr shrewdly, "was the Communist Party able to transform a failed strike into a symbolic victory." Fittingly, on April 1, 1930, the first anniversary of the Loray walkout, the Party celebrated with a grand victory banquet. It was a great occasion. Ella May's songs were sung, and Clarence Miller sent a message asserting that after Gastonia "we can proudly say we have broken through the Mason-Dixon line and laid a firm foundation for the revolutionary movement." The three hundred people who were reportedly present then took part in a "solidarity dance" under a huge portrait of Ella May. Thus was the "Gastonia myth" created.[28]

There were a few southerners, too, who refused to let the Gastonia story die, and in so doing they contributed to the making of the legend. Most important was the young Wilbur J. Cash, who was beginning to think through the themes that would eventually inform his masterwork. His February 1930 *American Mercury* article, "The War in the South," described by his latest biographer as "reflective" and "certainly more even-handed than its title suggests," was an attempt to distill general meaning from the events of 1929 and, especially, to explain what they said about the new industrial and social order. Cash's villains were the mill "barons"—hard-fisted, greedy men who had "rudely shoved" aside the planters as head of the southern social order. "Pig-headed, colossally greedy, vain and ignorant," these men were "totally incapable," unlike those they had replaced, "of the notion of noblesse oblige." They were powerful; they controlled the police, the courts, the press, and the churches, all of whom were "handmaidens of the mill owners." Against such power, Beal and his fellows had stood no chance at all.[29]

These men were also violent, as their reaction to the events of 1929 amply demonstrated. Violence had always been "the Southern response to any serious criticism or attack." "The single best weapon for putting down the 'invader' and the renegade is the Kluxery," he wrote, "the repressed sadism, the native blood-lust, the horrible mob instinct, which smoulders among the brutal and the ignorant everywhere in the South and above all, and ironically, among the mill workers themselves." The barons of Gastonia and elsewhere had callously exploited these fears in 1929 in their crusade against the "alien invaders" and those local "traitors" who supported them. They were the "real villains in southern violence," Cash would argue over the years, not the "hotheads or the rednecks" they persuaded to do their bidding."[30]

They were of course wrong, he thought, and history would prove them so, but in the short term, "the advantage in the struggle is obviously with the baron and his allied reactionaries." This above all was the lesson of Gastonia. By the time Cash wrote *The Mind of the South*, he had moderated some of the details of his argument, but the account of the Gastonia events found therein differs little in its essentials from his *American Mercury* piece of ten years before. He, too, helped greatly in perpetuating the Gastonia memory.[31]

The "Gastonia myth" became a subject of some interest for a few members of the United States Congress later in the year. Largely due to the efforts of the patrician New York Republican Hamilton Fish, the House of Representatives set up a special committee to investigate Communist activities in the United States; this group was the first of a number of precursors to the House Committee on Un-American Activities created later in the decade. The Fish Committee, as it soon came to be called, held a series of hearings throughout the year, mainly to question "friendly" witnesses, one of whom was AFL president William Green. He testified about the Communist activity in Gastonia in 1929, as did the AFL's legislative representative, Edward F. McGrady. Both were highly critical of the NTWU's efforts, while at the same time admitting that the textile workers had been "frightfully exploited." "There never has been a time the Negro in the South suffered half as much from the degradation of poverty as our white workers have been suffering," McGrady alleged.[32]

Nevertheless, the NTWU and the Communist Party had not been primarily interested in helping the workers or even in winning the strike, McGrady went on to say. "They went in to start a revolution if you please," he claimed, "and they brought in with them numbers of negroes and they put them on the platforms and patted them on the back—which, of course, created a state of mind down in that county which was hostile to the workers and hostile to everybody who had anything to do with the workers." By its insistence on the principle of racial equality, therefore, McGrady concluded bitterly, the NTWU had ensured that the strike would fail, "although fundamentally the workers were right."[33]

As for the NTWU, it maintained a presence in the South for a few more years without ever accomplishing anything remotely substantial. In 1930 organizers even made a brief return to Gaston County, attempting to influence the course of a strike that had broken out in Bessemer City at both American Mill plants, resulting from a 10 percent wage cut. Striking workers seized the NTWU men and unceremoniously ran them out of town; for good measure, they repeated the dose a few nights later. It was hardly surprising, given that type of reception, that the union sharply curtailed its southern work. In 1935, when the Red International again changed its strategy and gave up on dual unionism, the NTWU was dissolved, and its organizers were ordered to penetrate existing AFL unions.[34]

The fate of the NTWU workers in 1930 was taken to be emblematic of the fate of industrial unionism in general in Gaston County. Liston Pope, who wrote in 1942 that "the outcome of the Loray strike has been one of the chief factors preventing subsequent unionism in the county," was the first to assert what most southern labor historians have taken to be true. "It brought complete victory to the employers," Pope continued, "confirmed the public in its suspicion of unions and strikes, and, most important of all, likewise made many workers skeptical of affiliated unionism of any brand." Thus the failure of the Loray Mill strike, and the repression that followed, made future union activity in Gaston County impossible.[35]

How, then, can the events of September 1934 be explained? During the industrywide textile strike of that year, the strike flags were once again raised, the mill gates were closed, and the National Guard returned to Gaston County. As is well known, the New Deal set in motion vast changes in the structure of American labor relations. The violence of 1929 had taught southern textile manufacturers nothing, except to confirm them in their resolve to oppose any variety of union- ism in their plants. Though the work week was generally reduced from sixty to fifty-five hours, conditions otherwise worsened, as the Great Depression caused further layoffs and the cost-cutting drives con- tinued unmodified. The conservative AFL president, William Green, tried to warn the manufacturers that such conditions could not con- tinue. Speaking of the Gastonia "troubles" to the Senate Committee on Manufactures, he discounted the notion that Beal had misled the workers there with false ideology, or even that they had understood much about the differences between the NTWU and the UTW. "These southern workers know nothing about the philosophy of Communism; they do not know what it means," he said. "It is all Greek to them, but in their hour of distress, when they are rebelling against condi- tions they accept the support and the help of anyone who extends the friendly hand." But management did not hear him. Mill workers gen- erally were "ready to explode" in 1932, and even the accommodationist UTW had made some gains in the Piedmont.[36]

On June 16, 1933, Franklin D. Roosevelt signed the National Indus- trial Recovery Act into law, at the same time promising "a great cooperative movement" between business, government, and labor to ensure national recovery. The act relaxed the antitrust laws and per- mitted industry groups to control production and prices, including the power to raise wages and shorten hours. Workers were given the right to organize and bargain collectively, and union leaders loudly proclaimed, "The president wants you to join a union." Mill managers welcomed the NIRA and its executive body, the National Recovery Administration. Their trade association, the Cotton Textile Institute, quickly adopted a code that included a forty-hour week, a minimum weekly wage of twelve dollars, and an end to child labor. Across the Piedmont, eager mill hands, believing that the New Deal now gave them a guarantee of fairer treatment, flocked to join the UTW. As Hall and her colleagues commented, "To the shock of government offi- cials and businessmen alike, southern workers organized." By August

1934, UTW membership had topped 275,000. Sixteen thousand of these members were in Gaston County.[37]

Within a year, the hopes and aspirations of textile workers had been dashed, replaced by anger and despair. For all the high-mindedness of the act, its implementation in the textile industry simply produced more of the same. Management manipulated the code to their benefit whenever possible, and otherwise simply ignored it. The various mediation boards set up within the industry to ensure fairness normally ignored union protests. Wages more often than not were actually reduced, despite the twelve-dollar minimum, as managers turned to piecework, while the stretch-out was increased to such an extent that workers claimed to be doing more in eight hours than they had previously done in twelve. Finally, though Franklin Roosevelt may have wanted workers to join unions, mill management resisted the message. Intimidation was still the normal response to union activity.[38]

In June 1934, union frustration and worker anger could be contained no longer. After the textile board, oblivious to the widespread suffering that already existed in the industry, ordered another savage wage cut to meet the problems of overproduction, workers in northern Alabama mills walked off the job. Its hand forced, UTW leadership called for a general strike, to begin September 1, unless the cuts were rescinded. UTW vice president Francis Gorman had less than three weeks to organize what was to become the largest industrywide strike in U.S. history.[39]

On September 1, "flying squadrons" of tough, well-seasoned workers moved throughout the South, forcing many plants to close. They were so effective that by the end of the week more than 400,000 employees were idle, not all voluntarily, and the industry was shut down. As usual, mill executives and public officials called for military intervention, and state governors responded with alacrity. Fourteen thousand National Guardsmen were soon on duty in the Carolinas, while in Georgia, Governor Eugene Talmadge declared martial law and forced the "flying picketers" into hastily constructed detention camps. There was also violence. Seven strikers were killed in Honea Path, South Carolina, and there were scattered deaths elsewhere, including one in Gaston County.[40]

The strikers could not win, of course. Woefully underprepared, with no backing from the federal authorities, with only their anger to sustain them, and with their opponents determined to wait it out, they were bound to lose, and lose they did. Once the troops were in place, ready to protect those who wanted to return to work, the battle was over. Recognizing the inevitable, Gorman claimed victory after three weeks and called the strike off, on terms that quite obviously represented defeat. The mills reopened, and the owners took vicious revenge. Union members were systematically denied reemployment and organizers were blacklisted as textile workers learned the bitter lessons of failed endeavor. "The lesson for many was a deep distrust of government and trade unions alike," commented one historian. "Above all, the General Strike drove home the cost of challenging the established order. Better the familiar securities of job and home than air and promises, followed by exile, suffering and defeat."[41]

In Gaston County, the strike's course paralleled that of the rest of the Piedmont. When Joseph Shaplen, who had covered the 1929 events for the *New York Times*, returned to Gastonia, he found that support for unions, far from diminishing, "had grown tremendously in the past five years" and that Gaston County was expected to be the main center of the forthcoming struggle. Certainly, once the strike had begun, no county responded more enthusiastically or completely. By the end of the first day, all its mills were closed, and the intensity of worker activity, enthusiasm, and class consciousness was the clearest indication that support for unionism had not been driven from the district. Five thousand workers marched down Gastonia's main street in a huge Labor Day solidarity parade. Hardly a wheel moved in either Gastonia or the surrounding counties. The Loray Mill, the strike's symbolic center, was surrounded day and night by determined, orderly pickets.[42]

Thus the situation in Gastonia during the strike's first week was one of no work but no disorder, forcing Legette Blythe to draw a contrast with the situation of just five years earlier. Gastonia had learned a lot since the "community hysteria" of 1929. On September 12, however, three companies of the National Guard were once again stationed in Gastonia, ostensibly in response to the pleas of workers who wanted to return to work, and under their protection the mills began to reopen. Workers were keen to get back, Blythe thought, but management was much less so; managers feared that "such action might precipitate bloodshed," and they wanted no more of that. Certainly, a rumor that the Loray Mill would reopen for the night shift on September 11 brought a crowd of angry picketers to its gates, and the crowd dispersed only when it became obvious that the rumor was false.[43]

Nevertheless, the Loray Mill did reopen under the protection "of 150 National Guardsmen and scores of armed deputies," with more than six hundred pickets held back by the troops. It was the first mill in the county to do so. By September 13, one thousand operatives— almost a full complement—were back at work, something Blythe considered "most important," even "symbolic," given the events of the recent past. Most mills in Gaston County were now thought likely to follow its lead, and over the next few days they did. No violence occurred save in Belmont, where two workers, one of whom subsequently died, were stabbed in a bloody confrontation with guardsmen. The dead man's widow, who gave birth to her eighth child the day after her husband's funeral, pronounced herself proud that he had "died for organized labor."[44]

Throughout the strike, even the *Gastonia Daily Gazette* preached restraint, evoking as it did so the bitter memories of five years before. "Those who remember the tragic times we had in 1929 will not want a repetition of those days in Gaston County," warned an editorial at the strike's beginning. For the most part, the paper's coverage of the unfolding events was unremittingly low-key, while editorially it contented itself with a systematic defense of the right to work, especially after a meeting where "loyal workers of the Loray mill," with "tears streaming down" their faces, had asked for protection from the flying pickets. Toward the end of the strike, however, traces of the *Daily Gazette* of 1929 resurfaced. It was "time for law and order to re-assert itself in Gaston County," trumpeted the editor, J. W. Atkins. The law had been too often "flouted" recently by "hoodlum" pickets, who had led the textile workers astray. The troops protecting the mills and the community's loyal citizens in their right to work had been made "the target of the vilest and filthiest abuse that could be heaped on one human by another," and this must stop. The Committee of One Hundred might again be needed. "Let every community organize its Vigilantes," suggested Atkins, "who will see that law and order shall again prevail"—as they had in 1929.[45]

And so the strike was broken, in Gaston County as elsewhere, by the power of the state. Yet as Joseph Shaplen reported, until the very end the Gaston County strikers "held their lines without difficulty" for the most part, even when confronted with "formidable arrays of soldiers and deputies." The pickets would not move for the soldiers, he said. They shouted "Boy Scouts" and "Tin Soldiers" at them, just as they had done five years earlier, and made their duties as difficult as possible. Shaplen believed that no Piedmont city was more resolute in its defiance than Gastonia, and that in no county was solidarity greater than in Gaston. When the strike was called off, 90 of the county's 150 mills were still closed.[46]

A few faces from the past briefly resurfaced. Paul Crouch turned up in Charlotte, held a public meeting at which he vigorously attacked the UTW leadership for its conduct of the strike, and urged his listeners to ignore Gorman's instructions. His audience, composed mainly of striking mill workers, thereupon attempted to lynch him. He was saved only by the timely intervention of the police, who placed him in protective custody. His wife, the former Sylvia McMahon, a 1929 striker, was arrested in Gastonia for distributing Communist literature, but was given a suspended sentence. Caroline Drew showed up in Concord, where she was promptly arrested. Generally, though, the resonances with 1929 were few, except in the militancy and commitment of the workers.[47]

And, of course, in the consequences of defeat. When they tried to return to work, Gaston County strikers found themselves discriminated against, locked out, and denied their jobs. Now as in 1929, "scabs" did their work. Once more, evictions began. One of the worst offenders, allegedly, was the Loray Mill. The UTW was unable to help its members; it just did not have the power. Workers in Gaston County, as elsewhere, responded by giving up on the whole idea of unionism as a means to a better life, but it was the events of 1934 that ensured this collapse, not those of 1929.[48]

What happened to the Loray Mill? After surviving various changes of ownership and financial arrangements, it continued to dominate the town's physical aspect. The 1929 strike was scarcely over before the mill began to remake the image the events of that year had left it with. In a series of newspaper advertisements it presented itself as "Loray— the Mill with a Purpose," or "Loray, Where the Boss is the Worker's Friend," emphasizing the familial aspect of the mill's atmosphere. Management was dedicated, ran one such ad, to "fostering a spirit of co-operation, thus constituting . . . *one big family*. Each employee is made to feel that those in authority in the mill have his best interests at heart." In 1930, amid considerable publicity, the mill even sponsored an essay contest for its workers. The theme was "Why I Enjoy Working at the Loray," and there were to be three prizes—one of five dollars, one of fifteen dollars, and a grand prize of fifty dollars. The contest was judged by a panel of prominent citizens: Mayor E. B. Denny; J. P. Thomas, a local businessman; and the Reverend J. P. Craven, an uptown minister with close ties to the mill. More significantly, the mill greatly modified its employment policies after the strike, working in conjunction with the mill-village ministers. Each prospective employee was required to submit detailed references from his clergyman, his grocer, and his last employer as a condition of employment, in an endeavor to weed out troublemakers—and prospective union leaders.[49]

All the public relations exercises in the world, however, could not prevent the Great Depression's ravages. The Loray Mill's management introduced a four-day week in November 1929. Manville-Jenckes filed for bankruptcy in 1930, and conditions thereafter deteriorated steadily. By 1933 the mill was almost idle, the village run-down and semideserted, a haunt of "loose women, bootleggers, juvenile delinquents and other 'undesirables.'" There was some improvement in 1935, when the Firestone Rubber Company purchased both the mill and the village, changed the facility's name to the Firestone Mill, installed new machinery, and modernized and policed the community, while at the same time firmly resisting any further labor organization. The CIO's Textile Workers Organizing Committee found Loray far too tough a nut to crack when it tried to move in there in 1937, and it quickly retreated.[50]

The CIO returned to Gastonia in 1946 during "Operation Dixie," its postwar drive to make the South over, and once again the Firestone Mill was a symbolic target. All that year, organizers painstakingly worked at the ground level, making individual contact with workers, trying to get a local going, but they failed. The memories were too strong. Younger workers were "favorable" to the CIO, reported organizer William Neiss, but the older workers "persist in recalling the unfortunate consequences of the 1929 strike, and are fearful of a recurrence this time." Many had already conflated 1929 and 1934 in their minds. The CIO abandoned Firestone at that point but in 1951 decided to try again. This time they sought the expert advice of Liston Pope, now dean of Yale University's School of Religion, seeking "any tips you can pass along" that would help them in organizing Gaston County. Pope's response was unequivocal: leave the Firestone Mill alone, despite its obvious symbolic value. History had made this nut just too hard to crack. "It seemed to me a mistake," he told Paul Harding, the CIO's publicity director for the Carolinas, "to hit the Firestone plant first of all, unless organization in other Firestone plants around the country could be a kind of lever." It would be much better to start with "some of the surrounding mills," he thought, and the CIO took his advice. Not until 1955 did the Textile Workers Union of America mount its last assault on the Firestone Mill, and a determined effort it was. For the first time, the union was able to secure an NRLB election, yet its result simply confirmed the futility of devoting any more time to the mill. After a sustained campaign, only 509 workers voted for the union, while 1,374 voted against. The TWUA retreated to await a brighter day—which never came. The mill remained with Firestone until 1992, when it was purchased by Japanese interests, its workers still unorganized. Its continued dominant presence in the town kept memories of the events of 1929 alive for some.[51]

Other memories were also kept alive, at least for a time. Margaret Larkin and Mary Vorse, determined to maintain Ella May's memory and her music, collected her songs as best they could and took them to New York. There Larkin, herself a folk balladeer of some accomplishment, introduced them to her largely left-wing audiences, ensuring them at least some limited currency. As Richard Reuss observed, "Her articles in the *Nation* and the *New Masses*, as well as her public performances, were chiefly responsible for maintaining the fame of Ella May Wiggins as a labor balladmaker." Yet such fame was limited. Few people, save her children, recalled Ella May until the growth of the women's movement in the 1970s gained her a certain prominence, not only as a balladeer but also as a heroine of an earlier, half-forgotten struggle. In the foreword to a pamphlet commemorating the fiftieth anniversary of May's death, Vera Buch repeated her own claim that May had been killed for crossing the racial barrier. "It was for this they killed you Ella Mae [*sic*]," she said.[52]

Two years earlier, North Carolina's labor leaders had paid tribute to one they had belatedly recognized as of their own. In 1977, in a simple ceremony organized by Bill Brawley, president of the Central Labor

Council, union officials stood at her unmarked grave and spoke of Ella May's commitment and her courage. "She probably had more impact on people's lives than all the statues in this blamed state," Brawley said in explanation. Yet "how many kids in the public schools of Gaston County know who she is?" It was time, he concluded, for the labor movement in North Carolina to show a bit more of her dedication.[53]

Mary Vorse, too, tried to perpetuate Ella May's memory, by making May a central character in *Strike* (1930), her novel about the Gastonia strike. With heroes named Fer Deane and Mamie Lewes, who were based on Beal and Ella May, and a plot line drawn directly from the protest's events, *Strike* was the first of six novels that used Gastonia as their dramatic backdrop. In 1932 no fewer than four such novels were published: *To Make My Bread*, by Grace Lumpkin; *Call Home the Heart*, by Fielding Burke (a pseudonym for Olive Tilford Dargan); *Gathering Storm*, by Myra Page (a pseudonym for Dorothy Markey); and *Beyond Desire*, by Sherwood Anderson. The final "Gastonia novel," William Rollins Jr.'s *Shadow Before*, did not appear until 1934. All of these novels were written from a left-wing perspective and in accordance with the "third period" notions of proletarian literature exemplified by the editorial stance of Mike Gold in the *New Masses*. The only useful literature in a revolutionary world, Gold argued, in bidding farewell to the "pansy" poseurs of modernism and bourgeois democracy, was literature that both drew on the life experiences of the working class and helped "forge it into a revolutionary proletariat."[54]

Some, of course, were more distinctly Marxist than others. Of Myra Page's *Gathering Storm*, Sylvia Cook wrote that it was "a book so ideologically 'correct' that it was almost wholly ignored by reviewers to the right of the *New Masses*." Grace Lumpkin's *To Make My Bread*, a work whose ideological impetus was much less obvious, was nevertheless so well thought of in Party circles that it was awarded the 1932 Gorky prize, while at the same time it received a favorable review in the *New York Times*. Most literary critics, then and now, tend to agree with Cook that Dargan's *Call Home the Heart* is "by far the best of those [books] on Gastonia." While the *New Masses* considered it among "the pioneer novels in the literature of the American working class" and praised it accordingly, of all the Gastonia novels it most successfully transcends issues of ideology and class to deal with problems of a universal nature. But these six novels, though enthusiastically received by the proponents of proletarian literature, were not very widely read and were soon forgotten, especially after "third period" Communism gave way to the Popular Front and cooperation with the New Deal. Novels as dialectically obtrusive as *Strike* or *Gathering Storm* quickly became relics of another time.[55]

In the 1970s and 1980s, a few literary historians and critics looked again at these novels, not so much about the class struggle, but for what they had to say about other, more contemporary issues. Of particular interest was the fact that four of them had been written by women and that two of these, *Strike* and *Call Home the Heart*, have consequently been reissued. Sylvia Cook, Candida Lacey, and Joseph Urgo have each found powerful feminist subtexts in these works, constrained by the "masculinist" aspect of the proletarian novel but clearly present nonetheless. More recently, Suzanne Sowinska has begun to examine the way these women dealt with the race issue, particularly the question of the race/class dichotomy as it affected black and white women. Thus, memory of the events of 1929 has at least been rekindled for some through the reexamination of these forgotten works of fiction.[56]

What about Gastonia itself? How has the town remembered the violent events of 1929? Well, for much of its subsequent history, it has tried not to. As Liston Pope pointed out, the Golden Anniversary Edition of the *Gastonia Daily Gazette*, published only a year after the Loray strike, avoided any mention of the events, as did all civic promotional literature. The town's citizens, desperate to forget the strike, have traditionally been suspicious of anyone who brought the subject up, and this attitude has persisted through the years. Robert and Elizabeth Williams, joint authors of the only substantial study of the strike, *The Thirteenth Juror*, admitted that theirs was not the book they really wanted to write. They found considerable resistance to the very idea of the project; one local police officer told them firmly that the strike was dead and should be left that way. Moreover, concern for those who had spoken freely to them, along with their own situation as residents of Gaston County, caused them to pull their punches, to leave much unsaid. Both Robert Allen and Christina Baker, who grew up in poststrike Gastonia, attest to the fact that the strike was never talked about, at least in their presence. If someone inadvertently raised the topic, it was quickly dropped, and their own questions went unanswered. For more than fifty years Gastonians developed collective amnesia about the most important single event in the community's history.[57]

In 1993, however, Gastonia was finally forced to confront 1929. The Loray Mill had been sold the previous year, and it now stood almost empty as a new plant rose on the city's outskirts. What was to be the fate of the huge edifice? Should it simply be demolished, or was there another use to which it could be put? What was the point of preserving the mill, anyway? To local resident Jimmy Gray, a member of a mayoral committee to recommend action regarding the mill's future, and a descendant of George Gray, who built it, the answer to these related questions was a simple one. "There wouldn't be a Gastonia if it wasn't for the Loray Mill," he said. "That's the thing that really put us on the map." The mill and its story—including the violence and pain of 1929, that most significant of years—were an undeniable part of the town's heritage.[58]

NOTES

PREFACE

1. Pope, *Millhands and Preachers*, viii, 5–7, 49–69.

2. Ibid., 55, 62–63; Williams, *Pictorial History*, pp. 117, 125, 128–37; Vorse, "Gastonia," 701, 704.

3. McDonald, *Southern Mill Hills*, esp. 146–50.

CHAPTER ONE

1. Ford, "We Are Mill People."

2. Ibid.

3. Ibid.

4. Hall, Korstad, and Leloudis, "Cotton Mill People," 245. Unless otherwise stated, my account of the development of the Piedmont textile industry is taken from this superb article; from Hall et al., *Like a Family*; from Wright, *Old South, New South*; from Hodges, *New Deal Labor Policy*; from Flamming, *Creating the Modern South*; and from Zieger, *Organized Labor in the Twentieth-Century South*, 35–59. There is also a fine brief overview of the rise of the textile mill world in Ayers, *Promise of the New South*, 101–17.

5. Wright, *Old South, New South*, 124–32; Cash, *Mind of the South*. Cash makes frequent and derisory reference to the "phenomenally bad organization" of the mill owners (p. 343).

6. Hodges, *New Deal Labor Policy*, 26–27; Hall, Korstad, and Leloudis, "Cotton Mill People," 247; Terrill, "Southern Mill Workers," 591–92 (quoting Hall and her colleagues).

7. Hall, Korstad, and Leloudis, "Cotton Mill People," 247–50; Hall et al., *Like a Family*, 106–13.

8. Hall, Korstad, and Leloudis, "Cotton Mill People," 250–54; Hall et al., *Like a Family*, 115–80.

9. Zieger, "Textile Workers and Historians," 37–38; Newby, *Plain Folk in the New South*, 352–86, 463–92; Carlton, *Mill and Town in South Carolina*, 293–96; Flamming, *Creating the Modern South*, 164–66.

10. Wright, *Old South, New South*, 139; Hall, Korstad, and Leloudis, "Cotton Mill People," 255–59; Grigsby, "Politics of Protest," 150; Flamming, *Creating the Modern South*, 109–10.

11. Hall, Korstad, and Leloudis, "Cotton Mill People," 259–60; Hall et al., *Like a Family*, 103–5; Hodges, *New Deal Labor Policy*, 34–35; Irons, "Testing the New Deal," 22–25; Flamming, *Creating the Modern South*, 58–59, 75.

12. Hall, Korstad, and Leloudis, "Cotton Mill People," 263–65; Wright, *Old*

South, New South, 146; Irons, "Testing the New Deal," 24–26; Flamming, *Creating the Modern South*, 97–98, 102–4.

13. Wright, *Old South, New South*, 150; Flamming, *Creating the Modern South*, 112.

14. Hall, Korstad, and Leloudis, "Cotton Mill People," 265; Wright, *Old South, New South*, 147–48; Irons, "Testing the New Deal," 33–55; Benjamin U. Ratchford, "Toward Preliminary Social Analysis," 359–67.

15. Hall, Korstad, and Leloudis, "Cotton Mill People," 265–66; Irons, "Testing the New Deal," 28–33.

16. Hall, Korstad, and Leloudis, "Cotton Mill People," 266; Hall et al., *Like a Family*, 187–95; Irons, "Testing the New Deal," 33–48.

17. Hall, Korstad, and Leloudis, "Cotton Mill People," 266–69; Hall et al., *Like a Family*, 240–48; Hodges, *New Deal Labor Policy*, 12–14; Irons, "Testing the New Deal," 99–103; Flamming, *Creating the Modern South*, 185–86.

18. Wright, *Old South, New South*, 152–55; Irons, "Testing the New Deal," 100–103; Ratchford, "Toward Preliminary Social Analysis," 359–61.

19. Irons, "Testing the New Deal," 103–9; Flamming, *Creating the Modern South*, 184–85.

20. Hall et al., *Like a Family*, 211–17; Marshall, *Labor in the South*, 101–20; Tippett, *When Southern Labor Stirs*, 60–65, 117–41.

21. Pope, *Millhands and Preachers*, 215.

22. For Gastonia's development see Tullos, *Habits of Industry*, 86–87, 105–10, 149–51; Williams, *Pictorial History of Gaston County*, especially 81–84; *Gastonia, North Carolina*; Separk, *Gastonia and Gaston County*, 1–11; Ragan, *Pioneer Cotton Mills*, 1–2; Grigsby, "Politics of Protest," 143–47.

23. Williams, *Pictorial History*, 115–16; Ratchford, "Toward Preliminary Social Analysis," 359–60.

24. Pope, *Millhands and Preachers*, 213–15; Separk, *Gastonia and Gaston County*, 31–35, 67–90, 114–24.

25. Ragan, *Pioneer Cotton Mills*, vol. 1, sec. 6; Pope, *Millhands and Preachers*, 222–23.

26. Grigsby, "Politics of Protest," 150–55.

27. Pope, *Millhands and Preachers*, 222–23; Grigsby, "Politics of Protest," 152–55.

28. Porter, "Justice and Chivalry," 214–15; Pope, *Millhands and Preachers*, 224–29.

29. Pope, *Millhands and Preachers*, 229–33.

30. *Charlotte Observer*, March 6, 7, 1928; Weisbord, *Radical Life*, 204; Larkin, "Tragedy in North Carolina," 687.

31. Pope, *Millhands and Preachers*, 234.

32. *Greensboro Daily News*, August 10, 1928; Ratchford, "Toward Preliminary Social Analysis," 361.

33. Pope, "Millhands and Preachers," 236–37.

34. For more information on the American Communist Party see Buhle, Buhle, and Georgakas, *Encyclopedia of the American Left*, 146–57, 435–37; the quota-

tions are on pp. 149 and 435. See also Draper, "Gastonia Revisited," 3, and Klehr and Haynes, *American Communist Movement*, 44–47.

35. Buhle, Buhle, and Georgakas, *Encyclopedia of the American Left*, 777–79. See also Fink, *Labor Unions*, 386–87, 343–45; Cochran, *Labor and Communism*, 31–34, 43–46; and Klehr and Haynes, *American Communist Movement*, 65.

36. Draper, "Gastonia Revisited," 8–10; Fink, *Labor Unions*, 386–87.

37. Draper, "Gastonia Revisited," 9; Vorse, "Gastonia," 702; Sophie Melvin Gerson and Simon Gerson, interview by author. By 1993 Sophie Melvin also thought Beal was "probably gay," though she certainly did not suspect it at the time. Although he became vehemently anticommunist in later life, while she remained a true believer, Sophie Melvin never lost her affection for him, unlike Vera Buch, who believed him to be weak-willed and cowardly.

38. Beal, *Proletarian Journey*, 109–22.

39. Ibid., 120, 123.

40. Draper, "Gastonia Revisited," 11; Beal, *Proletarian Journey*, 123.

41. Beal, *Proletarian Journey*, 124.

42. Ibid., 126–28; *New York Times*, April 19, 1929.

43. Beal, *Proletarian Journey*, 131–32.

CHAPTER TWO

1. Beal, *Proletarian Journey*, 132.

2. *Charlotte Observer*, April 2, 1929; *Gastonia Daily Gazette*, April 3, 1929; Hendrix, "I Was in the Gastonia Strike," 169–71.

3. *Charlotte Observer*, April 3, 4, 1929; *New York Times*, April 4, 1929; Ed Spenser, interview by Robert Allen. For an interesting account of espionage in an Atlanta textile mill, see Fink, *Fulton Bag and Cotton Mills Strike of 1914–1915*. Fink's fine study tells the story of another unsuccessful strike in a southern mill, one which lasted from late spring 1914 to spring the following year.

4. *Charlotte Observer*, April 4, 1929; *Gastonia Daily Gazette*, April 3, 1929; *News and Observer*, April 4, 1929.

5. *News and Observer*, April 4, 5, 1929; *Charlotte Observer*, April 4, 1929; "Guns Flare in Gastonia," in Box 17, Paul Crouch Papers, Hoover Institution, Stanford University (hereafter cited as Crouch Papers).

6. *Gastonia Daily Gazette*, April 3, 1929.

7. *New York Times*, April 10, 1929; Blanshard, "Communism in Southern Cotton Mills," 500–501.

8. For example, see Dunne, *Gastonia*, 23–24; Tippett, *When Southern Labor Stirs*, 78, 96–98; and Hood, "Loray Mill Strike," 38. For the reaction of the strikers, see "The Textile Strikes in the South," 4, in James Myers "Field Notes," North Carolina Collection, Wilson Library, University of North Carolina, Chapel Hill; Beal, *Proletarian Journey*, 143.

9. Beal, *Proletarian Journey*, 136–37, 141–42; "Guns Flare in Gastonia," Crouch Papers; *Charlotte Observer*, April 4, 6, 1929; *News and Observer*, April 6, 1929; *Daily Worker*, April 5, 1929; "Gastonia Strike Diary," Box 122, in Mary Heaton

Vorse Papers, Walter P. Reuther Archive for Labor History and Urban Affairs, Wayne State University, Detroit, Michigan (hereafter cited as Vorse Papers).

10. *News and Observer*, April 6, 1929.

11. Tom Jimison to Forrest Bailey, April 21, 1929, in vol. 375, reel 68, ACLU Papers (microfilm), New York Public Library, New York, N.Y. (hereafter cited as ACLU Papers [microfilm]); Jimison to Gov. O. Max Gardner, April 5, 1929, Box 112, Gov. O. Max Gardner Papers, Department of Archives and History, Raleigh, N.C. (hereafter cited as Gardner Papers).

12. *Charlotte Observer*, April 6, 1929; *Daily Worker*, April 19, 1929; *Labor Defender*, May 1929; *News and Observer*, September 6, 1929; Blanshard, "Communism in Southern Cotton Mills," 500–501.

13. Hall et al., *Like a Family*, 122.

14. Hall, "Disorderly Women," 377; Grigsby, "Politics of Protest," 222–23.

15. *Charlotte Observer*, April 5, 1929.

16. *Gastonia Daily Gazette*, April 6, 1929 (reprint from the *Charlotte News*).

17. *Gastonia Daily Gazette*, April 18, 25, 1929.

18. Hall, "Disorderly Women," 356.

19. Ibid., 370–72.

20. *Charlotte Observer*, April 5, 1929; *Daily Worker*, April 11, 1929; *News and Observer*, April 8, 1929; Weisbord, *Radical Life*, 185, 195–97, 205; Grigsby, "Politics of Protest," 222–23.

21. *Charlotte Observer*, April 5, 1929; *Gastonia Daily Gazette*, April 6, 1929 (reprint from the *Charlotte News*); Hendrix, "I Was in the Gastonia Strike"; Hall et al., *Like a Family*, 226–29.

22. Garrison, *Mary Heaton Vorse*, 216–18; Weisbord, *Radical Life*, 172–74; Reeve, "Great Gastonia Textile Strike," 37–40; *News and Observer*, August 25, 1929. "Recollections of Loray," Box 4, Folder 3, Vera Buch Weisbord Papers, Chicago Historical Society, Chicago (hereafter cited as Buch Papers); *Labor Defender*, September 1929; *New York Times*, July 16, 1929.

23. Weisbord, *Radical Life*, 207–17; Beal, *Proletarian Journey*, 141–42; "Guns Flare in Gastonia," Crouch Papers; Hirson, "Ruth Schechter; Friend to Olive Schreiner," 47–71.

24. *Charlotte Observer*, April 9, 1929; *Gastonia Daily Gazette*, April 11, 1929.

25. *Charlotte Observer*, April 9, 1929; *Daily Worker*, April 11, 1929; *Gastonia Daily Gazette*, April 12, 1929; Blanshard, "Communism in Southern Cotton Mills," 500–501.

26. *Charlotte Observer*, April 9, 1929; *Daily Worker*, April 11, 1929.

27. Bailey to Jimison, April 23, 1929, vol. 375, reel 68, ACLU Papers (microfilm); *Charlotte Observer*, April 11, 13, 24, 25, 1929.

28. *Gastonia Daily Gazette*, April 12, 1929.

29. Ibid., April 9, 1929; *News and Observer*, November 7, 8, 9, 1928, April 11, 1929; Powell, *Dictionary of North Carolina Biography*, 1:267.

30. *News and Observer*, April 6, 1929.

31. Pope, *Millhands and Preachers*; "The Textile Strikes in the South," 5–6, in Myers "Field Notes."

32. Hall et al., *Like a Family*, 220; Flamming, *Creating the Modern South*, 166; Pope, *Millhands and Preachers*, 273–77; *Charlotte Observer*, April 8, 1929; *News and Observer*, April 7, 1929.

33. *News and Observer*, April 29, 1929; Pope, *Millhands and Preachers*, 280–83.

34. *News and Observer*, April 16, 17, 1929; Harriet Herring to Beulah Amidon, April 13, 1929, Box 1, Folder 10, Harriet Herring Papers, Southern Historical Collection, Wilson Library, University of North Carolina, Chapel Hill (hereafter cited as Herring Papers).

35. Weisbord, *Radical Life*, 187.

36. Vorse, "Gastonia," 700–710.

37. *News and Observer*, April 19, 1929; *Gastonia Daily Gazette*, April 18, 1929; *Charlotte Observer*, April 19, 1929; *Daily Worker*, April 19, 1929.

38. Jimison to Gardner, April 18, 1929, Box 112, Gardner Papers; Jimison to Bailey, April 26, 1929, vol. 375, reel 68, ACLU Papers (microfilm); *Gastonia Daily Gazette*, April 19, 1929; affidavits in Box 122, Vorse Papers.

39. *Gastonia Daily Gazette*, April 18, 19, 20, 22, 1929; *News and Observer*, April 29, 1929.

40. *Charlotte Observer*, April 20, 23; *News and Observer*, April 26, 29, May 1, 1929; Robert L. Lumsden to Judge N. A. Townsend, April 30, 1929, and Gardner to the Council of State, May 9, 1929, both in Box 112, Gardner Papers.

41. Pope, *Millhands and Preachers*, 255; Tippett, *When Southern Labor Stirs*, 89; Dunne, *Gastonia*, 7.

42. *News and Observer*, November 7, 1929; *Gastonia Daily Gazette*, May 22, 1929.

43. Tippett, *When Southern Labor Stirs*, 96–97; H. G. Gulley to J. G. Flowers, December 17, 1929, and Flowers to Roger Baldwin, December 20, 1929, both in vol. 375, reel 68, ACLU Papers.

44. *News and Observer*, May 5, 1929; *Charlotte Observer*, April 19, 21, 1929; Weisbord, *Radical Life*, 217.

45. *News and Observer*, April 21, 23, 24, 27, 1929; *Charlotte Observer*, April 23, 24, 1929.

46. *News and Observer*, April 23, 24, 1929; *Charlotte Observer*, April 24, 1929; Vorse, "Gastonia," 706.

47. *Charlotte Observer*, April 23, 24, 1929; Weisbord, *Radical Life*, 195–96, 203.

48. Beal, *Proletarian Journey*, 147; Weisbord, *Radical Life*, 194; *News and Observer*, May 16, 1929.

49. Weisbord, *Radical Life*, 158; Weisbord, "Gastonia 1929," 185–203; Reeve, "Gastonia," 29; Eleanor Copenhaver Anderson, interview by Mary Frederickson; Sophie Melvin Gerson and Simon Gerson, interview by Christina L. Baker; Grigsby, "Politics of Protest," 222–28.

50. Weisbord, *Radical Life*, 194; "Recollections of Loray," Box 4, Folder 3, Buch Papers.

51. R. E. Williams, "Textile Battle and its Significance," *News and Observer*, May 5, 1929.

52. Ibid.; Weisbord, *Radical Life*, 205–6.

53. Haessly, "Mill Mother's Lament," 1–4.

54. Ibid., 4–19; *Let's Stand Together.*

55. Haessly, "Mill Mother's Lament," 22–23; *Southern Textile Bulletin,* April 10, 1930.

56. Haessly, "Mill Mother's Lament," 25–30, 97; Beal, *Proletarian Journey,* 148; Weisbord, *Radical Life,* 174–75.

57. Garrison, *Mary Heaton Vorse,* 216–20; Vorse, "Gastonia," 702; Beal, *Proletarian Journey,* 156; Weisbord, *Radical Life,* 202–3; "Gastonia Strike Diary," Vera Buch to Mary Vorse, August 2, 1929, Boxes 122 and 155, Vorse Papers; "Recollections of Loray," Box 4, Folder 3, Buch Papers.

58. "Gastonia Strike Diary," Box 122, Vorse Papers.

59. Beal, *Proletarian Journey,* 148, 158–59; Weisbord, *Radical Life,* 188, 197, 217; Sophie Melvin Gerson and Simon Gerson, interview by author.

60. *Charlotte Observer,* May 3, 4, 7, 8, 9, 1929; "Gastonia Strike Diary," Box 122, Vorse Papers; *Daily Worker,* May 16, 17, 1929.

61. *New York Times,* May 1, 1929; *News and Observer,* May 10, 1929; Vorse in the *Reading (Pa.) Advocate,* May 25, 1929; Tom Tippett, bulletins for Federated Press Washington Bureau, May 2, 9, 11, 1929 in ACLU Papers, vol. 366, reel 65.

62. *New York World,* May 11, 1929; Haessly, "Mill Mother's Lament," 97–101; Reeve, "Gastonia," 26–28; Beal, *Proletarian Journey,* 148; Weisbord, *Radical Life,* 185, 205, 260.

63. *Charlotte Observer,* May 3, 4, 7, 8, 9, 1929.

64. Ibid., May 11, 1929; *Baltimore Morning Sun,* May 11, 1929; Reeve, "Gastonia," 26–28.

65. Reeve, "Gastonia," 26–28; *Daily Worker,* May 24, 1929; *New York World,* May 11, 1929; *Baltimore Morning Sun,* May 11, 1929; *Charlotte Observer,* May 14, 1929; *Greensboro Daily News,* May 11, 1929.

66. *Charlotte Observer,* May 16, 1929; Weisbord, *Radical Life,* 212–15; Sophie Melvin Gerson and Simon Gerson, interview by author. Tent colonies had been used before in southern textile strikes. The colony set up during the 1914–15 strike at the Fulton Bag and Cotton Mills in Atlanta, for example, existed for "nearly eight months before being closed down by union officials." See Fink, *Fulton Bag and Cotton Mills Strike,* 117–20.

67. Beal, *Proletarian Journey,* 153–59; *Charlotte Observer,* May 16, 19, 1929; *News and Observer,* May 21, September 18, 1929.

68. Gastonia Strike Songs, Boxes 122 and 155, Vorse Papers; Larkin, "Ella May's Songs," 382–83; Weisbord, *Radical Life,* 194–96, 260; Joyner, "Up in Old Loray," 20–24; Wiley, "Songs of the Gastonia Textile Strike of 1929," 87–98; Haessly, "Mill Mother's Lament," 73–75; ILD Press Release, July 19, 1929, in vol. 376, reel 69, ACLU Papers.

69. Dunne, *Gastonia,* 39; Tippett, *When Southern Labor Stirs,* 90; Hood, "Loray Mill Strike," 110–12; *Gastonia Daily Gazette,* May 20, 1929; *News and Observer,* May 21, 24, 26, 1929.

70. *News and Observer,* May 23, 1929.

71. *Charlotte Observer*, May 12, 1929; *News and Observer*, May 12, 1929; Weisbord, *Radical Life*, 206; "Guns Flare in Gastonia," Crouch Papers.

72. Weisbord, *Radical Life*, 217, 260–62, 288.

73. John H. Owens, "Southern Strike Vignettes," *Daily Worker*, April 19, 1929.

74. *News and Observer*, May 12, 1929; Weisbord, *Radical Life*, 206; Haywood, *Black Bolshevik*, 317–19; *Daily Worker*, October 4, 1929; Sophie Melvin Gerson and Simon Gerson, interview by author.

75. Beal, *Proletarian Journey*, 140; *Gastonia Daily Gazette*, May 17, 1929.

76. *Charlotte Observer*, June 30, 1929; Draper, "Gastonia Revisited," 20–23; "Guns Flare in Gastonia," Crouch Papers.

77. *Gastonia Daily Gazette*, May 25, June 4, 1929; *Charlotte Observer*, May 28, June 3, 5, 6, 1929.

78. Beal, *Proletarian Journey*, 159–61; Porter, "Communism Goes South."

CHAPTER THREE

1. Weisbord, *Radical Life*, 219; Vorse, "Gastonia," 708.

2. Vorse, "Gastonia," 708; Beal, *Proletarian Journey*, 162; *Daily Worker*, May 27, 29, June 8, 1929.

3. Beal, *Proletarian Journey*, 159–62; *Daily Worker*, June 3, 1929.

4. Beal, *Proletarian Journey*, 165–66; *Charlotte Observer*, June 11, 1929; Tippett, *When Southern Labor Stirs*, 100.

5. *Charlotte Observer*, July 11, 1929.

6. *News and Observer*, June 9, 12, 1929; *Charlotte Observer*, June 11, 1929; Beal, *Proletarian Journey*, 166–67; Weisbord, *Radical Life*, 221; Tippett, *When Southern Labor Stirs*, 90–100.

7. *News and Observer*, June 9, 12, 1929; *Charlotte Observer*, June 11, 1929; Beal, *Proletarian Journey*, 166–67; Weisbord, *Radical Life*, 221; Tippett, *When Southern Labor Stirs*, 90–100.

8. *Charlotte Observer*, July 11, 1929.

9. Ibid., June 8, 9, 1929; *News and Observer*, June 8, 9, 1929.

10. Beal, *Proletarian Journey*, 169–72; Weisbord, *Radical Life*, 222–23, 285.

11. *Charlotte Observer*, June 9, 10, 1929; *News and Observer*, June 9, 1929.

12. *Charlotte Observer*, June 11, 1929; *News and Observer*, June 11, 1929; Beal, *Proletarian Journey*, 172–74; Weisbord, *Radical Life*, 285.

13. *Charlotte Observer*, June 10, 1929; *News and Observer*, June 10, 1929.

14. *Gastonia Daily Gazette*, June 8, 10, 1929.

15. *Charlotte Observer*, June 9, 1929; *Daily Worker*, June 10, 11, 1929.

16. *News and Observer*, June 12, 16, 1929; Sellars, "South-Saver."

17. Margaret Dreier Robins to Nell Battle Lewis, July 23, 1929, PC 255.1, Nell Battle Lewis Papers, Department of Archives and History, Raleigh, N.C. (hereafter cited as Lewis Papers).

18. *Charlotte Observer*, June 13, 16, 26, 1929; Weisbord, *Radical Life*, 233–34, 283.

19. *Charlotte Observer*, June 11, 12, 13, 18, 1929; *News and Observer*, June 18, 19, 1929; *Gastonia Daily Gazette*, June 13, 15, 20, 1929.

20. Martin, "International Labor Defense."

21. *Charlotte Observer*, June 16, 1929; Hood, "Loray Mill Strike," 127–28; Klehr, *Heyday of American Communism*, 161; *Daily Worker*, June 12, 1929; ILD Press Release, June 13, 1929, vol. 367, reel 65, ACLU Papers; Weinstein, *Perjury*, 310–13; Klehr and Haynes, *American Communist Movement*, 56; "Guns Flare in Gastonia," Crouch Papers; "Gastonia Notes," Box 5, Folder 1, Buch Papers.

22. Jimison to Bailey, June 12, 23, 1929, vol. 375, reel 68, ACLU Papers; Weisbord, *Radical Life*, 279–87.

23. Ibid.

24. *Charlotte Observer*, June 13, 14, 19, 1929; *News and Observer*, June 13, 15, 19, 1929.

25. *Charlotte Observer*, June 19, July 30, 1929; *News and Observer*, June 19, 1929; *Daily Worker*, June 19, 1929.

26. *Charlotte Observer*, June 19, 25, 1929; *News and Observer*, June 15, 1929; Weisbord, *Radical Life*, 227.

27. *News and Observer*, July 23, 30, 1929; *Gastonia Daily Gazette*, June 21, 24, 28, 1929.

28. *Gastonia Daily Gazette*, June 27, 1929; *Charlotte Observer*, July 30, 1929; Weisbord, *Radical Life*, 228–34; Buch to Vorse, August 1, 1929, Box 155, Vorse Papers; Sophie Melvin Gerson and Simon Gerson, interview by author.

29. *New York Times*, July 28, 1929.

30. Buch to Vorse, August 1, 1929, Box 155, Vorse Papers; Beal, *Proletarian Journey*, 179–85.

31. Jimison to Bailey, June 23, 1929, vol. 375, reel 68, ACLU Papers; *News and Observer*, July 7, 1929.

32. *News and Observer*, July 7, 11, 18, 21, 1929; *Charlotte Observer*, July 18, 1929.

33. *News and Observer*, July 7, 17, 22, 1929.

34. Ibid., July 2, 5, 1929; *Daily Worker*, June 20, 22, 25, July 1, 2, 1929; *Charlotte Observer*, July 27, 29, 1929; ILD press release, July 22, 1929, Box 122, Vorse Papers.

35. ILD press releases, June–July 1929, vol. 368, reel 65, ACLU Papers; Bailey, "Gastonia Goes to Trial"; Bailey to Jimison, July 18, 1929, vol. 375, reel 68, ACLU Papers; *Charlotte Observer*, July 26, 1929; *News and Observer*, July 26, 1929. Carter was replaced by prominent Charlotte attorney Johnson McCall.

36. *Gastonia Daily Gazette*, July 26, 29, 30, 1929.

37. *News and Observer*, July 19, 1929; *Daily Worker*, July 6, 1929.

38. *Charlotte Observer*, July 29, 1929.

39. "Anonymous" to editor, July 2, 1929, *Gastonia Daily Gazette* Papers, Southern Historical Collection, Wilson Library, University of North Carolina, Chapel Hill.

40. Porter, "Justice and Chivalry," 214.

41. Harriet Herring to Beulah Amidon, August 20, 1929, Box 1, Folder 11, Herring Papers; *Gastonia Daily Gazette*, July 29, 1929; Buch to Vorse, April 1, 1929, Box 155, Vorse Papers; *Charlotte Observer*, June 28, 29, 30, 31, 1929.

42. *Charlotte Observer*, July 30, 31, 1929.

43. Ibid., July 30, 31, 1929; Porter, "Justice and Chivalry," 214.

44. *Gastonia Daily Gazette*, July 31, 1929; *News and Observer*, July 31, August 1, 1929; *Charlotte Observer*, July 31, 1929; *New York Times*, July 31, August 2, 3, 1929.

45. *News and Observer*, August 1, 11, 15, 1929; *Charlotte Observer*, August 11, 13, 14, 15, 1929; Buch to Vorse, August 1, 1929, Box 155, Vorse Papers; ILD press release, August 6, 1929, Box 122, Vorse Papers.

46. *Charlotte Observer*, August 1, 18, 1929; *News and Observer*, July 31, August 4, 8, 1929; *New York Times*, August 2, 1929; Beal, *Proletarian Journey*, 185.

47. *News and Observer*, August 9, 11, 24, 1929; *Southern Textile Bulletin* 36, no. 24 (August 15, 1929).

48. Beal, *Proletarian Journey*, 189.

CHAPTER FOUR

1. Beal, *Proletarian Journey*, 185; Weisbord, *Radical Life*, 250.

2. *Daily Worker*, June 14, July 24, August 5, 22, 1929.

3. Ibid., July 27, April 5, 22, 1929; *Charlotte Observer*, August 21, 1929; *News and Observer*, August 25, 1929; Dos Passos, "Gastonia," *Labor Defender*, August 1929.

4. Baker and Baker, "Shaking All the Corners of the Sky," 321–31; *News and Observer*, October 14, 1929.

5. *Daily Worker*, August 1, 1929; *News and Observer*, August 18, 1929.

6. *News and Observer*, August 25, 1929; *Daily Worker*, August 22, 23, 24, 1929.

7. *Daily Worker*, August 5, 16, 22, 1929; Dunne, *Gastonia*; "Justice in Gastonia," *Nation*, August 14, 1929; *New York Times*, August 15, 1929; Shaplen, "Strikers, Mills and Murder," 595–96.

8. Draper, "Gastonia Revisited," 24; Dunne, *Gastonia*, 50; *Daily Worker*, August 5, 1929.

9. *Charlotte Observer*, August 24, 1929; *News and Observer*, August 11, 18, 1929.

10. Bailey to Elizabeth Yates Webb, August 2, 1929, and membership lists of the North Carolina Committee of Liberals, vol. 376, reel 69, ACLU Papers (microfilm); Lewis Chambers to William T. Couch, April 29, 1929, Couch to Paul Blanshard, August 9, 1929, and Blanshard to Couch, August 16, 1929, all in Series 1, Folder 4, William T. Couch Papers, Southern Historical Collection, Wilson Library, University of North Carolina, Chapel Hill; Roydhouse, "'The Universal Sisterhood of Women,'" 352; Singal, *War Within*, 289.

11. Ronald J. Tamblyn to Mary Vorse, October 28, 1929, Box 155, Vorse Papers.

12. *Charlotte Observer*, August 25, 1929.

13. *Gastonia Daily Gazette*, August 22, 23, 1929; *Daily Worker*, August 20, 1929; *Southern Textile Bulletin*, August 28, 1929; *Charlotte Observer*, August 22, 23, 1929.

14. Reuss, "Roots of American Left Wing Interest in Folksong," 275; *Daily Worker*, September 20, 1929; Larkin, "Ella May's Songs," 382–83; Larkin, "Story of Ella May," 3–4; Haessly, "Mill Mother's Lament," 150–55; *Charlotte Observer*, August 26, 1929.

15. *Gastonia Daily Gazette*, August 26, 1929; "Trial of the Gastonia Strikers," Box 346, Herring Papers.

16. *Charlotte Observer*, August 27, 1929; *New York Times*, August 27, 1929; *News and Observer*, August 27, 28, 29, 1929; *Gastonia Daily Gazette*, August 27, 1929; Bailey to Hays, August 5, 1929, vol. 375, reel 68, ACLU Papers (microfilm). Complementing the defense team were R. L. Sigmon (the only Gaston County lawyer involved), Leon Josephson of the ILD, R. L. Flowers, J. D. McCall, Thaddeus Adams, and W. H. Abernethy, all prominent members of the North Carolina bar.

17. Lewis, "Tar Heel Justice," 272–73; Sophie Melvin Gerson and Simon Gerson, interview by author.

18. *Charlotte Observer*, August 30, September 5, 1929; *News and Observer*, August 29, 30, September 1, 2, 4, 5, 1929; *Gastonia Daily Gazette*, August 29, 1929; *New York Times*, August 27, 31, 1929; Mary Heaton Vorse, drafts of articles, Box 135, Vorse Papers.

19. *Charlotte Observer*, September 6, 1929; *News and Observer*, September 6, 1929; *Gastonia Daily Gazette*, September 5, 1929.

20. Ibid.; see also Beal, *Proletarian Journey*, 188–89.

21. *Daily Worker*, September 6, 7, 1929; *Charlotte Observer*, September 6, 7, 1929; *News and Observer*, September 6, 7, 8, 1929.

22. *News and Observer*, September 7, 1929.

23. Ibid., September 6, 7, 8, 9, 1929; *Charlotte Observer*, September 6, 7, 8, 1929.

24. *News and Observer*, September 9, 1929.

25. *New York Times*, August 30, September 8, 9, 1929.

26. *Gastonia Daily Gazette*, September 9, 1929; *News and Observer*, September 10, 1929; *Charlotte Observer*, September 10, 1929; *New York Times*, September 10, 1929.

27. *Southern Textile Bulletin*, September 12, 1929; *Charlotte Observer*, September 10, 1929; *News and Observer*, September 10, 1929; *Daily Worker*, September 11, 1929; *Greensboro Daily News*, September 10, 1929; *New York Times*, September 10, 1929; A. F. Parker, interview by Robert Allen.

28. *News and Observer*, September 10, 11, 1929; Lewis, "Anarchy vs. Communism," 321–22.

29. *Charlotte Observer*, September 10, 11, 1929; Lewis, "Anarchy vs. Communism," 321–22.

30. *Charlotte Observer*, September 11, 1929; *News and Observer*, September 11, 1929; *Greensboro Daily News*, September 11, 1929.

31. Ibid. See also Lewis, "Anarchy vs. Communism," 322; and statements by Ben Wells and C. M. Lell, Box 122, Vorse Papers.

32. *News and Observer*, September 11, 1929; *Daily Worker*, September 11, 12, 1929.

33. *Boston Globe*, September 4, 1929; *New York Telegram*, September 4, 1929; *Providence (R.I.) Tribune*, September 11, 1929; *New London (Conn.) Day*, September 11, 1929; *Indianapolis Times*, November 11, 1929, all from Reel 4, Harriet Herring Clipping File, North Carolina Collection, Wilson Library, University of North Carolina, Chapel Hill (hereafter cited as Herring Clipping File); *New York Times*, September 11, 1929.

34. *News and Observer*, September 11, 12, 13, 1929; *Greensboro Daily News*, September 11, 1929.

35. *Charlotte Observer*, September 11, 1929; *Gastonia Daily Gazette*, September 11, 12, 1929.

36. *Charlotte Observer*, September 13, 1929; *News and Observer*, September 13, 1929.

37. *Charlotte Observer*, September 13, 14, 1929; *Gastonia Daily Gazette*, September 13, 1929; *Daily Worker*, September 14, 1929. The charges against the eight unionists were very quickly thrown out of court. Gastonia police also arrested Caroline Drew, the WIR representative, for contravening the state's liquor laws, after they had placed a pint bottle of whiskey in her room. This ridiculous trumped-up charge was also thrown out of court (*Greensboro Daily News*, September 17, 1929).

38. H. G. Gulley to J. F. Flowers, December 17, 1929, vol. 375, reel 68, ACLU Papers (microfilm); Haessly, "Mill Mother's Lament," 150; *Charlotte Observer*, September 15, 1929; *New York Times*, September 15, 1929.

39. *Charlotte Observer*, September 15, 1929; *Daily Worker*, September 16, 1929; Lewis, "Anarchy vs. Communism," 321.

40. Ibid.

41. *News and Observer*, September 15, 16, 1929; Frank P. Graham to Lewis, September 23, 1929, Box 1, Folder 11, Frank Porter Graham Papers, Southern Historical Collection, Wilson Library, University of North Carolina, Chapel Hill (hereafter cited as Graham Papers).

42. *News and Observer*, September 22, 1929. Ella May was pregnant with her tenth child at the time of her death.

43. *Boston Transcript*, September 16, 1929; *Providence (R.I.) News*, September 16, 1929; *Bellaire (Ohio) Leader*, September 17, 1929; *Paterson (N.J.) Call*, September 17, 1929; and *Baltimore Evening Sun*, September 19, 1929, all in Herring Clipping File.

44. *Baltimore Evening Sun*, September 19, 1929, Herring Clipping File.

45. Weisbord, *Radical Life*, 260; *Let's Stand Together*.

46. *Daily Worker*, September 16, 17, 18, 1929.

47. Ibid., September 18, 1929; *Greensboro Daily News*, September 18, 1929; *News and Observer*, September 18, 1929.

48. *Greensboro Daily News*, September 14, 1929; *News and Observer*, September 18, 1929.

49. *News and Observer*, September 18, 1929; Larkin, "Story of Ella May," 3–4.

50. *Daily Worker*, September 19, 1929; *Charlotte Observer*, September 19, 20, 24, 1929.

51. *News and Observer*, September 24, 28, 1929; *Charlotte Observer*, September 28, 1929.

52. *Charlotte Observer*, September 26, 1929.

53. Ibid., September 17, 1929; *News and Observer*, September 17, 1929.

54. *Charlotte Observer*, September 24, 1929; *New York Times*, September 16, 1929.

55. *Daily Worker*, September 24, 1929.

56. *Charlotte Observer*, September 26, 1929; Beal, *Proletarian Journey*, 185; Hays to Baldwin, September 29, 1929, Bailey to Lewis, September 13, 1929, J. Frank Flowers to Bailey, September 27, 1929, Baldwin to Flowers, September 27, 1929, all in Box 375, Reel 68, ACLU Papers (microfilm); Sophie Melvin Gerson and Simon Gerson, interview by author.

57. *Charlotte Observer*, September 26, 1929; *News and Observer*, September 29, 1929.

CHAPTER FIVE

1. Pope, *Millhands and Preachers*, 295; *Charlotte Observer*, October 1, 1929; *Daily Worker*, October 1, 1929; *News and Observer*, October 1, 1929; *Gastonia Daily Gazette*, September 30, 1929.

2. Pope, *Millhands and Preachers*, 295–96.

3. *Charlotte Observer*, October 5, 6, 8, 1929; *Greensboro Daily News*, October 5, 1929; *Daily Worker*, October 5, 1929. The *Charlotte Observer* ran the trial transcript daily, and I have chosen to refer to these reports rather than to the official trial transcript, which I have in my possession.

4. *Charlotte Observer*, October 7, 8, 1929; *News and Observer*, October 8, 1929; *Greensboro Daily News*, October 8, 1929.

5. *Charlotte Observer*, October 8, 1929; *New York Times*, October 19, 1929.

6. *Charlotte Observer*, October 8, 13, 1929; *Greensboro Daily News*, October 13, 1929; *News and Observer*, October 13, 1929; *Southern Textile Bulletin*, October 10, 1929; *Daily Worker*, October 8, 1929.

7. *News and Observer*, May 21, 1929.

8. *Charlotte Observer*, October 10, 11, 1929; *News and Observer*, October 11, 1929.

9. *Charlotte Observer*, October 19, 1929; *New York Times*, October 11, 1929.

10. *Charlotte Observer*, October 11, 1929; Pope, *Millhands and Preachers*, 296.

11. *Charlotte Observer*, October 15, 1929; *News and Observer*, October 15, 1929; *Daily Worker*, October 15, 1929; Pope, *Millhands and Preachers*, 300–301.

12. *Charlotte Observer*, October 15, 1929; *News and Observer*, October 15, 16, 1929.

13. *Charlotte Observer*, October 19, 1929.

14. Ibid., October 16, 1929; *News and Observer*, October 16, 1929; *Greensboro Daily News*, October 16, 1929; Pope, *Millhands and Preachers*, 298–99.

15. Beal, *Proletarian Journey*, 195–96; Pope, *Millhands and Preachers*, 298–99.

16. Pope, *Millhands and Preachers*, 299; Weisbord, *Radical Life*, 283–86; *Daily Worker*, October 19, 1929.

17. *Charlotte Observer*, October 18, 1929; *Greensboro Daily News*, October 18, 1929.

18. *Charlotte Observer*, October 18, 19, 1929; *Greensboro Daily News*, October 18, 1929; *News and Observer*, October 19, 1929; Pope, *Millhands and Preachers*, 302–4.

19. *News and Observer*, October 19, 21, 1929; *New York Times*, October 21, 1929; *Charlotte Observer*, October 22, 1929; *Gastonia Daily Gazette*, October 22, 1929.

20. *New York Times*, October 20, 1929.

21. Cash, *Mind of the South*, 355; Williams and Williams, *Thirteenth Juror*; Robert L. Williams and Elizabeth Williams, interview by Christina L. Baker (hereafter cited as Williams interview); Frank Sisk and Ellen Sisk, interview by Christina L. Baker (hereafter cited as Sisk interview); Christina L. Baker, interview by author; Mareda Cobb and Carrie Sigmon, interview by Jacquelyn Hall and Patty Dilley, *Charlotte News*, July 14, 1935.

22. *New York Times*, October 28, 1929; *Labor Defender*, October 1929, November 1929.

23. *Charlotte Observer*, October 18, 1929; *New York Times*, October 16, 1929; *New York World Telegram*, October 17, 1929, vol. 369, reel 66, ACLU Papers (microfilm); *New York Times*, October 22, 1929.

24. *News and Observer*, November 10, 1929.

25. Ibid., October 22, November 1, 1929.

26. *Charlotte Observer*, November 4, 1929. J. Louis Engdahl to Jimison, September 22, 1929; Thaddeus Adams to John Randolph Neal, September 10, 1929; J. D. McCall to Bailey, October 23, 1929; Adams to ILD, October 26, 1929; Flowers to Bailey, September 27, 1929, all in vol. 375, reel 68, ACLU Papers (microfilm).

27. *Charlotte Observer*, November 9, 10, 1929.

28. *Daily Worker*, November 25, December 2, 11, 16, 1929, January 16, 1930; *Charlotte Observer*, November 12, 1929; *Greensboro Daily News*, February 11, 1930.

29. *News and Observer*, October 18, 19, 20, 1929.

30. Ibid., October 24, 25, 26, 1929; *Charlotte Observer*, October 24, 25, 26, 1929.

31. *News and Observer*, October 25, 27, 18, November 1, 1929; *Daily Worker*, October 28, 1929; Nelson, "North Carolina Justice," 314–16.

32. Gardner to Senator Lee Overman, September 28, 1929, and Gardner to Colonel Wade Harris, October 5, 1929, Box 112, Gardner Papers; *News and Observer*, October 26, 29, 1929; *New York Times*, November 6, 1929.

33. *News and Observer*, November 5, 1929.

34. Ibid., November 5, 6, 7, 8, 9, 1929.

35. *Daily Worker*, June 10, 1930; Flowers to Baldwin, October 31, 1929, vol. 375, reel 68, ACLU Papers (microfilm).

36. Flowers to Baldwin, November 2, 6, 8, 9, 1929, vol. 375, reel 68, ACLU Papers (microfilm).

37. *Charlotte Observer*, November 15, 16, 29, December 10, 12, 1929, January 8, 15, February 20, April 1, 1930; *News and Observer*, April 23, 1920.

38. *Gastonia Daily Gazette*, December 27, 1929; *Daily Worker*, June 10, 20, 1930.

39. Flowers to Baldwin, December 7, 14, 20, 1929; H. G. Gulley to Flowers, December 9, 17, 1929, all in vol. 375, reel 68, ACLU Papers (microfilm).

40. *Gastonia Daily Gazette*, December 30, 1929; *News and Observer*, December 29, 31, 1929, January 11, 12, 1930.

41. *News and Observer*, January 14, 15, 16, 17, 1930.

42. *Gastonia Daily Gazette*, January 19, 1930; *News and Observer*, January 17, 19, 20, 1930.

43. *News and Observer*, February 25, 26, 27, March 4, 1930.

44. Ibid., March 5, 6, 7, 1930.

45. Ibid., March 7, 1930; *Greensboro Daily News*, March 7, 1930; *Charlotte Observer*, March 7, 1930.

46. *Charlotte Observer*, March 7, 1930; *New York Times*, February 23, March 7, 1930.

47. *Daily Worker*, March 8, 1930; *News and Observer*, March 8, 1930.

48. Williams and Williams, *Thirteenth Juror*, 152–53; Sisk interview; Fay Sams, interview by author. Both Sams's husband and her father-in-law were members of the Gastonia police force in 1929.

CHAPTER SIX

1. *Charlotte Observer*, April 5, 1930; *News and Observer*, April 22, 23, August 21, 1930.

2. *News and Observer*, September 20, 1930; Beal, *Proletarian Journey*, 242.

3. Beal, *Proletarian Journey*; Beal, *Red Fraud*.

4. Beal, *Proletarian Journey*, 214–16; Baker, "In Generous Spirit," 220–21; Donohue, *Politics of the American Civil Liberties Union*, 136–37.

5. Beal, *Proletarian Journey*, 251–70.

6. *New York Times*, August 22, 23, September 20, 22, October 11, 1930; Beal, *Proletarian Journey*, 244–65.

7. Beal, *Proletarian Journey*, 251–70.

8. Ibid., 271–75.

9. Ibid., 275–82; Beal, *Red Fraud*, 60.

10. *Greensboro Daily News*, June 17, 1932; *News and Observer*, July 7, 1932; Beal, *Proletarian Journey*, 291–306, 329–38.

11. Hays, *City Lawyer*, 190, 376–80; Beal, *Proletarian Journey*, 339–42.

12. *Durham Morning Herald*, September 6, 1937; *News and Observer*, July 9,

1935, September 15, 1937; Klehr, *Heyday of American Communism*, 420; Beal, *Proletarian Journey*, 343–45.

13. *News and Observer*, September 23, 1937.

14. Paul Green, interview by Jacquelyn Hall.

15. *Durham Sun*, February 15, 1938; *Greensboro Daily News*, June 8, 10, 1939; Beal, *Red Fraud*, 74–85; Bernstein, *Lean Years*, 28. Unlike other ex-Communists —such as Paul Crouch—Fred Beal never became a right-wing apologist or FBI informer. Though he was certainly fiercely anti-Communist as a result of his Soviet experiences, he never lost his faith in the union movement. This, at least, Hendricks and Beal continued to share. Junius Scales, interview by author.

16. Scales and Nickson, *Cause at Heart*, 71–74, 242.

17. *News and Observer*, September 23, 1937; Beal, *Proletarian Journey*, 348–49.

18. Beal, *Proletarian Journey*, 349–50; Weinstein, *Perjury*, 100–103; Williams and Williams, *Thirteenth Juror*, 211; Acting Secretary of State to Gardner, April 16, 1932, Box 112, Gardner Papers; Sophie Melvin Gerson and Simon Gerson, interview by author.

19. Weisbord, *Radical Life*, 290–320.

20. Sophie Melvin Gerson and Simon Gerson, interview by author.

21. *Charlotte Observer*, March 8, 1930; Haywood, *Black Bolshevik*, 377; Sophie Melvin Gerson and Simon Gerson, interview by author; Schechter, "Fascism in Pennsylvania," 713–14; Schechter, "75,000 Captive Miners," 10–13; Schechter, "Coming: 'A Damn Big Strike,'" 13–15; Baruch Hirson to author, October 17, 1993.

22. *Charlotte Observer*, June 8, November 5, 6, 1930, September 1, 1940, May 13, 1954; *Durham Morning Herald*, June 29, 1957; *News and Observer*, May 13, 1954; Powell, *Dictionary of North Carolina Biography*, 1:267; Sophie Melvin Gerson and Simon Gerson, interview by author.

23. *Charlotte Observer*, December 31, 1929, June 8, 1930; *News and Observer*, January 16, 1930; *Greensboro Daily News*, July 29, 1930.

24. *Charlotte Observer*, March 6, 1932; *News and Observer*, September 11, 1945; Clayton, *W. J. Cash*, 90–91.

25. Sellars, "South-Saver," 6–9, 49–60.

26. Kelley, *Hammer and Hoe*, 13–33; Draper, "Gastonia Revisited," 26–27; Si Gerson, "Our Work in the South"; *Daily Worker*, June 10, 1930.

27. Melvin, "Trade Union Work—Task of Party Convention," *Daily Worker*, July 20, 1930.

28. Ibid.; Klehr, *Heyday of American Communism*, 31; *Daily Worker*, April 1, 2, 1930; Grigsby, "Politics of Protest," 195. In fact, the Party never made any significant impact in the South. Throughout the 1930s the region remained "a vast wasteland" (Klehr and Haynes, *American Communist Movement*, 74).

29. Cash, "War in the South," 163–69; Clayton, *W. J. Cash*, 90–91.

30. Clayton, *W. J. Cash*, 90–91; Cash, "War in the South," 165–66.

31. Clayton, *W. J. Cash*, 90–91; Cash, "War in the South," 167.

32. House of Representatives, *Investigation of Communist Propaganda*, 60,

70, 126–27. For more information about the Fish Committee, see Latham, *Communist Controversy in Washington*, 29–31.

33. House of Representatives, *Investigation of Communist Propaganda*, 60, 70, 126–27.

34. *News and Observer*, August 19, 24, 1930; Pope, *Millhands and Preachers*, 313; Fink, *Labor Unions*, 386–87.

35. Pope, *Millhands and Preachers*, 313.

36. Ibid., 315; Hall, Korstad, and Leloudis, "Cotton Mill People," 275–76; Draper, "Gastonia Revisited," 28–29.

37. Hall, Korstad, and Leloudis, "Cotton Mill People," 276–77; Leuchtenburg, *Franklin D. Roosevelt and the New Deal*, 55–58, 63–70; Hodges, *New Deal Labor Policy*; *Charlotte Observer*, September 7, 1934.

38. Hall, Korstad, and Leloudis, "Cotton Mill People," 277–80; Hall et al., *Like a Family*, 325–29.

39. Hodges, *New Deal Labor Policy*, 96–103; Hall et al., *Like a Family*, 329–32.

40. Hodges, *New Deal Labor Policy*, 104–18.

41. Ibid., 104–18; Hall, Korstad, and Leloudis, "Cotton Mill People," 284. See also Irons, "Testing the New Deal."

42. *Charlotte Observer*, September 4, 5, 1934; *New York Times*, September 2, 6, 1934; Irons, "Testing the New Deal," 440–41.

43. *Charlotte Observer*, September 9, 12, 1934.

44. Ibid., September 13, 14, 19, 23, 1934; *New York Times*, September 13, 1934.

45. *Gastonia Daily Gazette*, August 31, September 4, 10, 14, 19, 1934.

46. *New York Times*, September 17, 18, 22, 1934.

47. *Charlotte Observer*, September 15, 18, 28, 1934; *New York Times*, September 22, 1934.

48. *Charlotte Observer*, September 25, 26, 27, 1934; Draper, "Gastonia Revisited," 26.

49. *Gastonia Daily Gazette*, September 28, October 5, 12, 1929; Pope, *Millhands and Preachers*, 307–8; *Greensboro Daily News*, March 2, 1930.

50. Ragan, *Pioneer Cotton Mills*, vol. 1, sec. 6; Pope, *Millhands and Preachers*, 309–11.

51. Weekly report of E. C. Nicolson, July 7, 1946; weekly report of William Neiss, July 20, 1946; weekly reports of J. Prestwood Jr., August 17, September 1, 1946, in Box 76, Operation Dixie Papers, William R. Perkins Library, Duke University, Durham, N.C. (hereafter cited as Operation Dixie Papers); Paul Harding to Liston Pope, March 28, 1951, Lucy Randolph Mason to Pope, April 18, 1951, and Pope to Harding, April 23, 1951, all in Box 268, Operation Dixie Papers; Earle, Knudson, and Shriver, *Spindles and Spires*, 185–91; *Gastonia Daily Gazette*, June 21, 1993.

52. Reuss, "Roots of American Left Wing Interest in Folksong," 275; Haessly, "Mill Mother's Lament," 150–55; *Let's Stand Together*.

53. *Charlotte Observer*, November 25, 1977.

54. Rabinowitz, *Labor and Desire*, 22–23; Urgo, "Proletarian Literature and Feminism," 64–84.

55. Reilly, "Images of Gastonia," 498–517; Cook, *From Tobacco Road to Route 66*, 98, 118; Urgo, "Proletarian Literature and Feminism," 71, 77; Lois McDonald, interview by Marion Roydhouse.

56. Cook, *From Tobacco Road to Route 66*, 85–124; Urgo, *Proletarian Literature*, 64–84; Lacey, "Engendering Conflict"; Rabinowitz, *Labor and Desire*; Sowinska, "Writing across the Color Line."

57. Pope, *Millhands and Preachers*, 321; Williams and Williams, *Thirteenth Juror*; Williams interview; author's conversations with Professors Christina Baker and Robert Allen.

58. *Gastonia Daily Gazette*, June 21, 1993.

BIBLIOGRAPHY

BRIEF ESSAY ON SOURCES

The first point I should make is that in some important respects the manuscript material available to me was not as extensive as I had anticipated. In particular, the International Labor Defense Papers, now available on microfilm, and so rich in material pertaining to the great trials of the 1930s in which the ILD was involved—the Scottsboro Boys, for example, and Angelo Herndon—proved to contain almost nothing of value for my study. Similarly, the records of the North Carolina adjutant-general's department are silent on the National Guard's activities in Gastonia. Furthermore, the records of the Loray Mill were destroyed in 1935. Fortunately, both the American Civil Liberties Union Papers and the Mary Heaton Vorse Papers contained voluminous ILD material, including correspondence, broadsheets and pamphlets, and copies of the *Labor Defender*. Relevant copies of the *Labor Defender* were also available in the Nell Battle Lewis Papers, the George S. Mitchell Papers, and the Theodore Draper Papers.

The ACLU collection was the most important single manuscript source; in addition to the material described above, it contained a wealth of correspondence with the strike leadership, with the general public, and with the lawyers involved in the various trials during the year. There were also eyewitness accounts of the events of 1929. The Vorse Papers, too, contained much useful material, including the diary she kept during her weeks in Gastonia, drafts of the newspaper and magazine articles she wrote while on assignment there, transcripts of the strikers' songs, and a considerable amount of personal correspondence relating to the strike. The Harriet Herring Papers were of value principally because of the long, astute letters she wrote describing the trials of those accused of conspiring to kill Chief Aderholt. Both the Vera Buch Weisbord and the Paul Crouch Papers contained a few items of interest, from the perspective of the strike's leadership. The Nell Battle Lewis, William Terry Couch, and Frank Porter Graham Papers shed some light on the travail of North Carolina's liberal community during the long year.

It is difficult to find anyone now who can remember the strike. I was fortunate, therefore, in being able to interview two women whose recollections of 1929 were exceedingly clear. One was Fay Sams, whose husband and father-in-law were both on the Gastonia police force in 1929, and who shared with me her recollections of the events of June 7 and September 14. The other was Sophie Melvin Gerson, the only survivor of the sixteen put on trial in Charlotte in August that year. Her recollections of the trial, her comrades, and the people she came to work with have been an invaluable source for this book; so have those of her husband, Si Gerson, who was also in Gastonia for part of 1929, having replaced George Pershing as the representative of the Young Communist League. Both Robert Allen and Christina Baker generously made available transcripts or tapes of interviews they had conducted earlier with surviving strike participants or observers; they also shared with me their recollections of growing up in Gastonia. There was little relevant material in the Southern Oral History Collection at the University of North Carolina at Chapel Hill.

Obviously, I have made extensive use of newspapers. I read every issue of the *Raleigh News and Observer*, the *Charlotte Observer*, the *Gastonia Daily Gazette*, the *Greensboro Daily News*, the *Daily Worker*, and the *Southern Textile Bulletin* for the strike year, and I supplemented these with other, more selective checking. I also made extensive use of the Harriet Herring Clipping File, held in the North Carolina Collection, Wilson Library, University of North Carolina at Chapel Hill. Thus, I exposed myself to a range of press opinion—from the hysterical stridency of the *Daily Worker*, to the equally hysterical and equally strident *Gastonia Daily Gazette*, to the balance of the *Raleigh News and Observer*. I also used the liberal and leftist newsmagazines *Nation*, *New Republic*, and *New Masses*, reading every issue for the strike period.

As far as secondary reading is concerned, the bibliography gives an adequate indication of its extent. I relied heavily on the autobiographies of the two strike leaders, Fred Beal's *Proletarian Journey* and Vera Buch Weisbord's *Radical Life*. These accounts have to be used with some caution, given the biases of the authors, their mutual personal and ideological antagonisms, and the fact that both found themselves outside the Communist Party relatively soon after leaving Gastonia. Nevertheless, taken together, both books were indispensable in helping me come to grips with the details of the strike. I also made some use of William Dunne's polemical yet well-written *Gastonia, Citadel of the Class Struggle in the South*, while Irving Bernstein's section on Gastonia in *The Lean Years* was invaluable. As far as the background to the strike is concerned, my debt to Jacquelyn Dowd Hall and her coauthors, both in "Cotton Mill People" and the superb *Like a Family*, is obvious from the frequency of the references to them. In general, I have followed their interpretation of the rise of cotton mill culture, though I have supplemented it by reference to James Hodges's excellent *New Deal Labor Policy*; Douglas Flamming's magisterial *Creating the Modern South*; Gavin Wright's overview of the South's post–Civil War economic history, *Old South, New South*; and Janet Irons's impressive dissertation, "Testing the New Deal," which, hopefully, will soon be published. On the development of Gastonia itself and the Loray mill, I, like all previous scholars, have drawn frequently from Liston Pope's 1942 study, *Millhands and Preachers*.

Few biographies were of much use to me. Two notable exceptions were Dee Garrison's *Mary Heaton Vorse*, which deals extensively with her 1929 Southern sojourn, and Jo Lynn Haessly's unpublished M.A. thesis, "Mill Mother's Lament." This was the main source for the details of Ella May Wiggins's life, though I also used some biographical material from Ellen Grigsby's solid Ph.D. thesis, "The Politics of Protest." Incidentally, Garrison has written an excellent overview of the strike in her introduction to Mary Heaton Vorse's recently republished Gastonia novel, *Strike*.

MANUSCRIPTS

Atlanta, Georgia
  Robert Woodruff Library, Emory University
    Theodore Draper Papers

Chapel Hill, North Carolina
  North Carolina Collection, Wilson Library, University of North Carolina
    Harriet Herring Clipping File
    James Myers "Field Notes"
  Southern Historical Collection, Wilson Library, University of North Carolina
    William Terry Couch Papers
    Gastonia Gazette Papers
    Frank Porter Graham Papers
    Harriet Herring Papers

Chicago, Illinois
  Chicago Historical Society
    Vera Buch Weisbord Papers

Detroit, Michigan
  Walter P. Reuther Archive for Labor History and Urban Affairs
    Mary Heaton Vorse Papers

Durham, North Carolina
  Special Collections Room, Perkins Library, Duke University
    George S. Mitchell Papers
    Operation Dixie Papers

New York, New York
  New York Public Library
    American Civil Liberties Union Papers (microfilm)

Princeton, New Jersey
  Firestone Library, Princeton University
    American Civil Liberties Union Papers

Raleigh, North Carolina
  Department of Archives and History
    Governor O. Max Gardner Papers
    Nell Battle Lewis Papers

Stanford, California
  Hoover Institution, Stanford University
    Paul Crouch Papers

NEWSPAPERS

Baltimore Morning Sun
Charlotte News

Charlotte Observer
Daily Worker
Durham Morning Herald (Durham, North Carolina)
Gastonia Daily Gazette
Greensboro Daily News
Labor Defender
News and Observer (Raleigh, North Carolina)
New York Times
New York World
Southern Textile Bulletin

INTERVIEWS

Anderson, Eleanor Copenhaver. Interview by Mary Frederickson. November 5, 1974. In Southern Oral History Collection, Wilson Library, University of North Carolina at Chapel Hill.

Baker, Christina L. Interview by author. July 4, 1993.

Cobb, Mareda, and Carrie Sigmon. Interview by Jacquelyn Hall and Patty Dilley. June 16, 18, 1979. In Southern Oral History Collection, Wilson Library, University of North Carolina at Chapel Hill.

Gerson, Sophie Melvin, and Simon Gerson. Interview by author. World Fellowship Center, Conway, N.H., July 8, 1993.

———. Interview by Christina L. Baker. New York, N.Y. June 15, 1987. Tape in Baker's possession.

Green, Paul. Interview by Jacquelyn Hall. May 30, 1975. In Southern Oral History Collection, Wilson Library, University of North Carolina at Chapel Hill.

McDonald, Lois. Interview by Marion Roydhouse. June 24, 1975. In Southern Oral History Collection, Wilson Library, University of North Carolina at Chapel Hill.

Parker, A. F. Interview by Robert Allen. December 22, 1971. Tape in Allen's possession.

Sams, Fay. Interview by author. Gastonia, N.C. September 14, 1993.

Scales, Junius Irving. Interview by author. Orlando, Fla. November 11, 1993.

Sisk, Frank, and Ellen Sisk. Interview by Christina L. Baker. May 5, 1987. Tape in Baker's possession.

Spenser, Ed. Interview by Robert Allen. December 23, 1971. Tape in Allen's possession.

Williams, Robert, and Elizabeth Williams. Interview by Christina L. Baker. March 21, 1987. Tape in Baker's possession.

BOOKS, PAMPHLETS, ARTICLES, AND UNPUBLISHED WORKS

Ayers, Edward L. *The Promise of the New South: Life after Reconstruction.* New York: Oxford University Press, 1992.

Bailey, Forrest. "Gastonia Goes to Trial." *New Republic*, August 14, 1929. Clipping in ACLU Papers, vol. 368, reel 65.

Baker, Christina L. "In Generous Spirit: The Life of Myra Page." Ph.D. diss., Graduate School of the Union Institute, 1991.

Baker, Christina, and William J. Baker. "Shaking all the Corners of the Sky: The Global Response to the Gastonia Strike of 1929." *Canadian Review of American Studies* 21, no. 3 (Winter 1990): 321–31.

Beal, Fred E. *Proletarian Journey: New England, Gastonia, Moscow*. New York: Hillman Curl, 1937.

———. *The Red Fraud: An Exposé of Stalinism*. New York: Tempo Publishers, 1949.

Bernstein, Irving. *The Lean Years: A History of the American Worker, 1920–1933*. Boston: Houghton Mifflin, 1960.

Blanshard, Paul. "Communism in Southern Cotton Mills." *Nation*, April 24, 1929, pp. 500–501.

Buhle, Mari Jo, Paul Buhle, and Dan Georgakas, eds. *Encyclopedia of the American Left*. New York: Garland, 1990.

Carlton, David L. *Mill and Town in South Carolina, 1880–1920*. Baton Rouge: Louisiana State University Press, 1982.

Cash, Wilbur J. *The Mind of the South*. New York: Knopf, 1941.

———. "The War in the South." *American Mercury* 19, no. 74 (February 1930): 163–69.

Clayton, Bruce L. *W. J. Cash: A Life*. Baton Rouge: Louisiana State University Press, 1991.

Cochran, Bert. *Labor and Communism: The Conflict That Shaped American Unions*. Princeton: Princeton University Press, 1977.

Cook, Sylvia Jenkins. *From Tobacco Road to Route 66: The Southern Poor Whites in Fiction*. Chapel Hill: University of North Carolina Press, 1976.

Donohue, William. *The Politics of the American Civil Liberties Union*. New Brunswick: Transaction Books, 1985.

Dos Passos, John. "Gastonia." *Labor Defender*, August 1929, p. 8.

Draper, Theodore. "Gastonia Revisited." *Social Research* 38, no. 1 (Spring 1971): 3–29.

Dunne, William F. *Gastonia, Citadel of the Class Struggle in the New South*. New York: Workers Library Publishers, 1929.

Earle, John R., Dean D. Knudson, and Donald W. Shriver Jr. *Spindles and Spires: A Restudy of Religion and Social Change in Gastonia*. Atlanta: John Knox Press, 1976.

Fink, Gary M. *The Fulton Bag and Cotton Mills Strike of 1914–1915: Espionage Labor Conflict and New South Industrial Relations*. Ithaca: ILR Press, 1993.

———, ed. *Labor Unions: The Greenwood Encyclopedia of Labor Institutions*. Westport, Conn.: Greenwood Press, 1977.

Flamming, Douglas. *Creating the Modern South: Millhands and Managers in Dalton, Georgia, 1884–1984*. Chapel Hill: University of North Carolina Press, 1992.

Ford, Ella. "We Are Mill People." In *Writing Red: An Anthology of American Women Writers 1930–1940*, edited by Charlotte Nekola and Paula Rabinowitz (New York: Feminist Press, 1987): 264–69. Originally published in *New Masses* 5 (August 30, 1929): 3–5.

Garrison, Dee. *Mary Heaton Vorse: The Life of an American Insurgent.* Philadelphia: Temple University Press, 1989.

Gastonia, North Carolina, The Combed Yarn Cotton Manufacturing Center of America. Gastonia: Chamber of Commerce, 1938.

Gerson, Si. "Our Work in the South." *Daily Worker*, June 10, 1930.

Grigsby, Ellen. "The Politics of Protest: Theoretical, Historical, and Literary Perspectives on Labor Conflict in Gaston County, North Carolina." Ph.D. diss., University of North Carolina at Chapel Hill, 1986.

Haessly, Jo Lynne. "Mill Mother's Lament: Ella May, Working Women's Militancy, and the 1929 Gaston County Strikes." M.A. thesis, University of North Carolina at Chapel Hill, 1987.

Hall, Jacquelyn Dowd. "Disorderly Women: Gender and Labor Militancy in the Appalachian South." *Journal of American History* 72, no. 2 (September 1986): 354–82.

Hall, Jacquelyn Dowd, Robert Korstad, and James Leloudis. "Cotton Mill People: Work, Community, and Protest in the Textile South, 1880–1940." *American Historical Review* 91, No. 2 (April 1986): 245–86.

Hall, Jacquelyn Dowd, James Leloudis, Robert Korstad, Mary Murphy, Lu Ann Jones, and Christopher B. Daly. *Like a Family: The Making of a Southern Cotton Mill World.* Chapel Hill: University of North Carolina Press, 1987.

Hays, Arthur Garfield. *City Lawyer: The Autobiography of a Law Practice.* New York: Simon and Schuster, 1942.

Haywood, Harry. *Black Bolshevik: Autobiography of an African American Communist.* Chicago: Liberator Press, 1978.

Hendrix, Bertha. "I Was in the Gastonia Strike." In *Working Lives: The Southern Exposure History of Labor in the South*, edited by Marc S. Miller (New York: Pantheon, 1980): 169–72.

Hirson, Baruch. "Ruth Schechter: Friend to Olive Schreiner." *Searchlight South Africa* 9 (August 1992): 47–91.

Hodges, James A. *New Deal Labor Policy and the Southern Textile Industry, 1933–1941.* Knoxville: University of Tennessee Press, 1986.

Hood, Robin. "The Loray Mill Strike." M.A. thesis, University of North Carolina, 1932.

Irons, Janet C. "Testing the New Deal: The General Textile Strike of 1934." Ph.D. diss., Duke University, 1988.

Joyner, Charles. "'Up in Old Loray': Folkways of Violence in the Gastonia Strike." *North Carolina Folklore* 12, no. 2 (December 1964): 20–24.

"Justice in Gastonia." *Nation* 129, no. 3345 (August 14, 1929).

Kelley, Robin. *Hammer and Hoe: Alabama Communists during the Great Depression.* Chapel Hill: University of North Carolina Press, 1990.

Klehr, Harvey. *The Heyday of American Communism: The Depression Decade.* New York: Basic Books, 1984.

Klehr, Harvey, and John Earl Haynes. *The American Communist Movement: Storming Heaven Itself.* New York: Twayne, 1992.

Lacey, Candida Ann. "Engendering Conflict: American Women and the Making of a Proletarian Fiction, with Particular Reference to the Period 1929–1935." Ph.D. diss., University of Sussex, 1985.

Larkin, Margaret. "Ella May's Songs." *Nation*, October 9, 1929, pp. 382–83.

———. "The Story of Ella May." *New Masses*, November 1929, pp. 3–5.

———. "Tragedy in North Carolina." *North American Review*, November 1929, pp. 686–90.

Latham, Earl W. *The Communist Controversy in Washington: From the New Deal to McCarthy.* Cambridge: Harvard University Press, 1966.

Let's Stand Together: The Story of Ella Mae [sic] *Wiggins.* Charlotte: Metrolina Chapter, National Organization for Women, 1979.

Leuchtenburg, William E. *Franklin D. Roosevelt and the New Deal, 1933–1940.* New York: Harper and Row, 1963.

Lewis, Nell Battle. "Anarchy vs. Communism in North Carolina." *Nation*, September 25, 1929, pp. 321–22.

———. "Tar Heel Justice." *Nation*, September 11, 1929, pp. 272–73.

McDonald, Lois. *Southern Mill Hills: A Study of Social and Economic Forces in Certain Textile Mill Villages.* New York: Alex L. Hillman, 1928.

Marshall, F. R. *Labor in the South.* Cambridge: Harvard University Press, 1967.

Martin, Charles H. "The International Labor Defense." In *Encyclopedia of the American Left*, edited by Mari Jo Buhle, Paul Buhle, and Dan Georgakas (New York: Garland, 1990): 366–67.

Melvin, Sophie. "Trade Union Work—Task of Party Convention." *Daily Worker*, July 20, 1930.

Miller, Marc S., ed. *Working Lives: The* Southern Exposure *History of Labor in the South.* New York: Pantheon, 1980.

Nekola, Charlotte, and Paula Rabinowitz, eds. *Writing Red: An Anthology of American Women Writers, 1930–1940.* New York: Feminist Press, 1987.

Nelson, Frederic. "North Carolina Justice." *New Republic* 60, no. 779 (November 6, 1929): 314–16.

Newby, I. A. *Plain Folk in the New South: Social Change and Cultural Persistence, 1880–1915.* Baton Rouge: Louisiana State University Press, 1989.

Owens, John H. "Southern Strike Vignettes." *Daily Worker*, April 19, 1929.

Pope, Liston. *Millhands and Preachers: A Study of Gastonia.* New Haven: Yale University Press, 1942.

Porter, Paul. "Communism Goes South: Gastonia Makes Mill Owners See Red." *New Leader*, June 16, 1929. Clipping in ACLU Papers, vol. 366, reel 65.

———. "Justice and Chivalry in North Carolina." *Nation*, August 28, 1929.

Powell, William S., ed. *Dictionary of North Carolina Biography.* Vol. 1, *A-C.* Chapel Hill: University of North Carolina Press, 1979.

Rabinowitz, Paula. *Labor and Desire: Women's Revolutionary Fiction in Depression America*. Chapel Hill: University of North Carolina Press, 1991.

Ragan, Robert A. *The Pioneer Cotton Mills of Gaston County, N.C.: The First Thirty*. Charlotte: Robert A. Ragan, 1973.

Ratchford, Benjamin U. "Toward Preliminary Social Analysis: II Economic Aspects of the Gastonia Situation." *Social Forces* 8, no. 3 (March 1930): 359–67.

Reeve, Carl. "The Great Gastonia Textile Strike." *Political Affairs* 63, no. 3 (March 1984): 37–40.

———. "Gastonia: The Strike, the Frameup, the Heritage." *Political Affairs* 63, no. 4 (April 1984): 23–31.

Reilly, John M. "Images of Gastonia: A Revolutionary Chapter in American Social Fiction." *Georgia Review* 28, no. 3 (Fall 1974): 498–517.

Reuss, Richard A. "The Roots of American Left Wing Interest in Folksong." *Labor History* 12, no. 2 (Spring 1971): 258–79.

Roydhouse, Marion W. "'The Universal Sisterhood of Women': Women and Labor Reform in North Carolina, 1900–1932." Ph.D. diss., Duke University, 1980.

Scales, Junius, and Richard Nickson. *Cause at Heart: A Former Communist Remembers*. Athens: University of Georgia Press, 1987.

Schechter, Amy. "Coming: 'A Damn Big Strike.' A First Hand Report from the Men in Steel." *New Masses* 15 (April 16, 1935).

———. "Fascism in Pennsylvania." *Nation* 140, no. 3650 (June 14, 1935).

———. "75,000 Captive Miners. First Hand Report from the Pennsylvania Coal Fields." *New Masses* 14 (February 26, 1935).

Sellars, Linda William. "South-Saver: Nell Battle Lewis in the 1920s." M.A. thesis, University of North Carolina at Chapel Hill, 1985.

Separk, Joseph H. *Gastonia and Gaston County, North Carolina: Past Present and Future*. Kingsport, Tenn.: Kingsport Press, 1936.

Shaplen, Joseph. "Strikers, Mills and Murder." *Survey* 42, no. 12 (September 15, 1929).

Singal, Daniel J. *The War Within: From Victorian to Modernist Thought in the South, 1919–1935*. Chapel Hill: University of North Carolina Press, 1982.

Sowinska, Suzanne. "Writing across the Color Line: White Women Writers and the 'Negro Question' in the Gastonia Novels." Unpublished paper in Sowinska's possession, March 1993.

Terrill, Thomas. "Southern Mill Workers." *Reviews in American History* 16, no. 4 (December 1988): 591–92.

Tippett, Tom. *When Southern Labor Stirs*. New York: Jonathan Cape, 1931.

Tullos, Allan. *Habits of Industry: White Culture and the Transformation of the Carolina Piedmont*. Chapel Hill: University of North Carolina Press, 1989.

U.S. House of Representatives. *Investigation of Communist Propaganda: Hearings before a Special Committee to Investigate Communist Activities in the United States*. Pursuant to House Resolution 220. 71st Cong., 2d sess. Part 1, vol. 1. Washington, GPO, 1930.

Urgo, Joseph R. "Proletarian Literature and Feminism: The Gastonia Novels and Feminist Protest." *Minnesota Review*, n.s. 24 (Spring 1985): 64–83.

Vorse, Mary Heaton. "Gastonia—Looking Behind the Murder Trial." *Harper's*, November 1929, pp. 700–710.

———. *Strike*. With an introduction by Dee Garrison. Urbana: University of Illinois Press, 1991.

Weinstein, Allen. *Perjury: The Hiss-Chambers Case*. New York: Knopf, 1978.

Weisbord, Vera Buch. *A Radical Life*. Bloomington: Indiana University Press, 1977.

———. "Gastonia 1929—Strike at the Loray Mill." Ed. Dan McCurry and Carolyn Ashbough. *Southern Exposure* 1, nos. 3–4 (1974): 185–203.

Wiley, Stephen R. "Songs of the Gastonia Textile Strike of 1929: Models of and for Southern Militancy." *North Carolina Folklore Journal* 30, no. 2 (Fall/ Winter 1982): 87–98.

Williams, Robert L. *A Pictorial History of Gaston County*. Virginia Beach, Va.: Donning Company, 1981.

Williams, Robert L., and Elizabeth Wise Williams. *The Thirteenth Juror: The Story of the 1929 Loray Strike*. Kings Mountain, N.C.: Herald House Publishers, 1983.

Wright, Gavin. *Old South, New South: Revolutions in the Southern Economy since the Civil War*. New York: Basic Books, 1986.

Zieger, Robert H., ed. *Organized Labor in the Twentieth-Century South*. Knoxville: University of Tennessee Press, 1991.

INDEX